US FOREIGN POLICY AND THE HORN OF AFRICA

US Foreign Policy and Conflict in the Islamic World

Series Editors:
Tom Lansford
The University of Southern Mississippi-Gulf Coast, USA
Jack Kalpakian
Al Akhawayn University, Morocco

The proliferation of an anti-US ideology among radicalized Islamic groups has emerged as one of the most significant security concerns for the United States and contemporary global relations in the wake of the end of the Cold War. The terrorist attacks of September 11, 2001 demonstrated the danger posed by Islamic extremists to US domestic and foreign interests. Through a wealth of case studies this new series examines the role that US foreign policy has played in exacerbating or ameliorating hostilities among and within Muslim nations as a means of exploring the rise in tension between some Islamic groups and the West. The series provides an interdisciplinary framework of analysis which, transcending traditional, narrow modes of inquiry, permits a comprehensive examination of US foreign policy in the context of the Islamic world.

Other titles in the series

US-Pakistan Relationship
Soviet Invasion of Afghanistan
A.Z. Hilali
ISBN 0 7546 4220 8

Eurasia in Balance
The US and the Regional Power Shift
Ariel Cohen
ISBN 0 7546 4449 9

Uneasy Neighbors
India, Pakistan and US Foreign Policy
Kanishkan Sathasivam
ISBN 0 7546 3762 X

US Foreign Policy and the Persian Gulf
Safeguarding American Interests through Selective Multilateralism
Robert J. Pauly, Jr
ISBN 0 7546 3533 3

US Foreign Policy and the Horn of Africa

PETER WOODWARD
University of Reading, UK

ASHGATE

Published by
Ashgate Publishing Limited
Gower House
Croft Road
Aldershot
Hampshire GU11 3HR
England

Ashgate Publishing Company
Suite 420
101 Cherry Street
Burlington, VT 05401-4405
USA

Ashgate website: http://www.ashgate.com

British Library Cataloguing in Publication Data
Woodward, Peter, 1944–
    US foreign policy and the Horn of Africa. – (US foreign
    policy and conflict in the Islamic world)
    1. Islam 2. United States – Foreign relations – Africa,
    Northeast 3. Africa, Northeast – Foreign relations – United
    States 4. United States – Foreign relations – 1989–
    I. Title
    327.7'3063

Library of Congress Cataloging-in-Publication Data
Woodward, Peter, 1944–
    US foreign policy and the Horn of Africa / by Peter Woodward.
        p. cm. -- (US foreign policy and conflict in the Islamic world)
    Includes index.
    ISBN 0-7546-3580-5
    1. United States--Foreign relations--Sudan. 2. United States--Foreign relations--
Somalia. 3. United States--Foreign relations--Africa, Northeast. 4. Sudan--Foreign
relations--United States. 5. Somalia--Foreign relations--United States. 6. Africa,
Northeast--Foreign relations--United States. 7. Islam and politics--Africa,
Northeast. 8. United States--Foreign relations--1989– 9. Africa, Northeast--Foreign
relations--1974– 10. Eritrean-Ethiopian War, 1998– I. Title. II. Series: US foreign
policy and conflict in the Islamic world series

    E183.8.S73W66 2005
    327.73063--dc22

2005023190

ISBN 0 7546 3580 5

Printed and bound in Great Britain by Antony Rowe Ltd, Chippenham, Wiltshire.

Contents

Acknowledgements		*vii*
Map		*ix*
Introduction		*xi*
1	US Foreign Policy Making and the Horn of Africa	1
2	The US and the Horn in the Cold War	17
3	Facing Sudan's Islamist Regime	37
4	Intervention in Somalia	59
5	New Friends for the US? Ethiopia, Eritrea and Djibouti	77
6	Confronting Sudan	93
7	Peacemaking in Sudan	113
8	Somalia's Long Shadow	135
Conclusion		*153*
Bibliography		*163*
Index		*167*

Acknowledgements

My thanks are due to Tom Lansford and Jack Kalpakian for offering me the opportunity to write the book as one of a series 'on the impact of US foreign policy on interstate and intrastate conflict in Muslim nations', concerned in this case primarily with Somalia and Sudan. In the end it turned out to be as much concerned with their impact on the US as vice versa. I had not thought of writing a book on US foreign policy, but when the suggestion arrived I realized that I had had occasional involvement with various people in the US government and American organizations through the years and that it would make an interesting subject. Thanks are due too to the British Academy for funding research trips to the US in 2003 and to the Horn and East Africa in 2004. I am most grateful to all those people who gave me interviews on my travels, as well as to friends and colleagues in Europe who have been of assistance. I would thank particularly Jemera Rone and Awad al-Sid al-Karsani for their help with interviews in Washington and Khartoum respectively. Millard Burr and Bob Collins were very helpful, especially with regard to the Washington labyrinth and those who inhabit it. Special thanks to Millard Burr, David Shinn and Kjetil Tronvoll for reading some of the chapters. I alone am of course responsible for the outcome and hope that the views expressed to me have not become distorted.

Peter Woodward
Reading, 2005

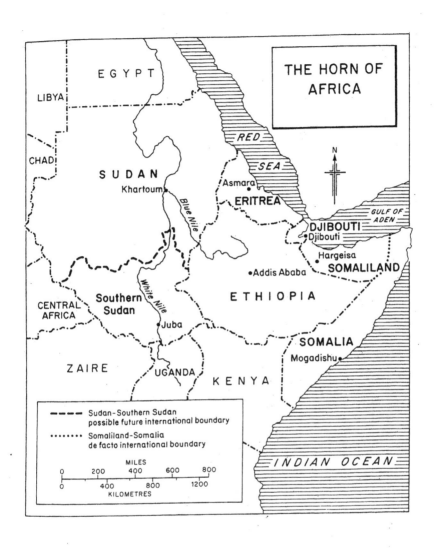

THE HORN OF
AFRICA

EGYPT

LIBYA

CHAD

SUDAN

Khartoum•

RED

SEA

Asmara•

ERITREA

GULF OF
ADEN

DJIBOUTI
•Djibouti

Hargeisa
•

SOMALILAND

•Addis Ababa

ETHIOPIA

Southern
Sudan

White Nile

Blue Nile

CENTRAL
AFRICA

•Juba

ZAIRE

UGANDA

KENYA

SOMALIA
Mogadishu•

N

- - - Sudan–Southern Sudan
       possible future international boundary
· · · · · · Somaliland–Somalia
       de facto international boundary

MILES
0   200   400   600   800
0   400   800   1200
KILOMETRES

INDIAN OCEAN

Introduction

The first concern of this book is with US foreign policy in the wake of the Cold War. Ever since the collapse of the Soviet Union there has been an outpouring of literature about the kind of policies that the US should pursue ranging from re-examination of the meaning of 'isolationism' on the one hand to 'interventionism' and even a possible 'new imperialism' on the other. Both these extremes have been discussed from theoretical and ideological perspectives of a 'global' character. Beside them, however, lie the questions of US national interests and their identification and implementation: what really matters to the US and what can actually be achieved? These latter questions open up a host of empirical questions that are relevant for and impact upon the theoretical issues. What branches and agencies of government are involved in foreign policy making? What pressures are influencing policy, especially from non-government lobbying groups in Washington or the country at large? What policies emerge from the decision making process and how are they implemented? What have been the outcomes of the policies pursued and how have they shaped the subsequent development of policy?

This book endeavors to review US policy with regard primarily to the Horn of Africa. The concept of the Horn is not indigenous but has grown over the years. It came into common currency after World War II and related mainly to Somalia and Ethiopia, for this tip of the Horn seemed to have particular problems of identity that pitted Somalia against its neighbors especially after its independence in 1960. In time the Horn was seen to include Ethiopia particularly as domestic conflict spread in that country including wars of secession and liberation in the north and coups or attempted coups at the centre. In time these developments also fed into the Somalia-Ethiopia dispute, notably in the major war between the two countries in 1978-1979. However conflict did not appear to be contained in those two countries alone, but was increasingly perceived to include Sudan as well, especially through its connection to opposition movements in Ethiopia; while the latter in turn responded by its involvement in Sudanese opposition. Thus interconnected conflict expanded the concept of the Horn and by the 1980s books on the region increasingly discussed affairs ranging from Sudan on the one side to Somalia on the other. Complex conflict was also regarded as increasingly central to the region's social and economic predicament. While there were environmental factors contributing to repeated food shortages and even famines across the region, there was also growing realisation that the political problems, especially conflicts of various kinds, were a continuous factor.

In origin many of the conflicts appeared to be national or sub-national issues, but an emerging concern after the Cold War was the extent to which there might also be an Islamic dimension. At a time when Islam was being discussed increasingly in the US it appeared that there might be connections between the conflicts of the Horn and the region's Islamic dimensions. The population of Somalia was overwhelmingly Muslim; the majority of the population of Sudan were Muslims; and Muslims comprised approximately half of the population of Ethiopia: was there then a Muslim dimension? This debate grew as the issue of Islamism developed from the end of the Cold War and was intensified by the attacks on the US mainland on 11 September 2001 (9/11). Islamism was perceived as a new ideological development within the Muslim world concerned with the attainment of political power for the implementation of the ideologues' perceptions of a Muslim community, both in regard to existing states and also the wider Muslim world. The analysis in the US of the links between Islamism and the Horn is thus a central concern of this book.

While issues pertaining to Islam are at the centre of the book there are also other relevant themes running through it. One is the relationship between the US and international organizations, notably the UN. These were to arise across the region in response to humanitarian issues in particular, but were not to be confined to them: by 2004 the US was even invoking the term genocide to describe certain developments in the region with implications for the UN and the whole of the international community. Another broad question for the US was its involvement in conflict resolution, an area of growing concern both in theory and practice as the Cold War seemed in danger of being superseded by an increasing number of national and regional conflicts, not least in Africa. It was the combination of humanitarian and conflict issues that contributed much to the rising concern of many different voices in the US calling for action of various kinds. Through the 1990s these voices were increasingly joined by numerous Christian groups whose concerns were also with Islamism and the apparently growing threat that it mounted for the US: perhaps even a manifestation of that new concern with the clash of civilizations.

The book begins with a survey of US foreign policy making, especially with regard to Africa. This is important since there were to be questions asked, especially after 9/11 when it was realized that the growth of Islamism in the Horn was relevant to the emergence of al-Qaeda to challenge the US first in Africa and the Middle East and then on the American mainland itself. The questions asked then included who knew what when, and how was information evaluated and used? Various individuals and agencies came forward to offer their views on the system in general. However most of America's involvement in the Horn had been during the Cold War and this had shaped both perceptions of the Horn in Washington and also developments in the region itself. From the perspective of the US, policy during the Cold War was largely about its rivalry with the Soviet Union in the Horn as a whole, and that is the subject of chapter two. After the Cold War there was no comparable overarching framework for policy and it became a matter far more of assessing individual countries. This proved particularly difficult in Sudan as Islamists seized power in 1989 and then embarked on a radical agenda that was enveloped in a deliberate ambiguity that served to confuse policy making in Washington and the West in general. While that chapter, chapter three, reflects the problem of deciding and implementing policy, chapter four examines the apparently much more decisive action that the US took in Somalia. But while a humanitarian intervention appeared so straight forward there, it turned out to be fraught with unexpected problems and the outcome for the US was to have significance well beyond Somalia. Throughout the twists and turns on Sudan and Somalia, relations with Ethiopia appeared to be solidifying and it was becoming central to US policy in the Horn, as considered in chapter five. Chapters six and seven return to Sudan to examine first the efforts to confront Sudan's Islamist movement; and then when the regime there proved unexpectedly durable and capable of adjusting its own foreign policy in an endeavour to ensure its survival the US turned instead to efforts at conflict resolution. The final substantial chapter is concerned with the US and Somalia and the way that the US remained aloof from conflict resolution there while seeking to manage any possible Islamist threat from the country after 9/11. The conclusion comes back to the questions the Horn has raised for the US ranging from the processes of decision making in Washington itself, especially during the period of the growth of Islamism in the 1990s, to the direct actions it could take on the ground in the region.

Chapter 1

US Foreign Policy Making and the Horn of Africa

The United States' foreign policy making towards the Horn of Africa combines a number of elements. The Horn itself has been a source of concern for decades and developed its specialists with their own expertise and experience. Interest originally lay predominantly in Ethiopia, and to some extent 'the Horn of Africa' has grown around it. Early interest as the US became involved after World War II usually referred to Ethiopia and Somalia, which became linked in an antagonistic relationship over borders as the old colonial powers, Italy and Britain, departed from the scene. Certainly until the early 1980s, it was unusual to include Sudan in the Horn, but it became increasingly connected in a realisation of common problems resulting from the famine that raged across the eastern Sahel (the southern fringe of the Sahara desert), into northern Ethiopia, and also affected Somalia. At that stage people spoke more frequently of 'the Greater Horn', sometimes including parts at least of East Africa. This book will simply refer to 'the Horn' as comprising Ethiopia, Djibouti, Somalia (including what is now known as Somaliland), Sudan and since 1993 Eritrea. While Somalia and Sudan are the focus of most attention here, having caused particular dilemmas for US policy makers, it is very appropriate to refer to 'the Horn' since, though separated from each other geographically by Ethiopia, the latter has been very significant for its two major Muslim neighbours and the ways that the US has conducted its policy towards them.

The policy itself has developed not only since the end of the Cold War, the main concern of this book, but essentially since the end of World War II. In doing so it has involved different concerns at different times, and with it received attention from different agencies of the US government. Given the generally low levels of interest in, and knowledge of, Africa, questions about who gets involved in decision making, when and why may be crucial to understanding the policies pursued and their outcomes.

Policy Makers

It is common to speak of the Cold War as contributing to the growth of presidential involvement in the determination of US foreign policy. Yet the question here is whether any president should ever have an interest in developments in the Horn? The most obvious answer, in relation to the Cold War at least, is when there have been geo-strategic reasons for so doing. Though in Africa, the Horn is not always of Africa: its history is as much linked to Arabia as to Africa, including the influence of Islam. Thus the broad context for Middle East policy, including the Arab-Israeli dispute, may be as relevant for understanding US policy towards Ethiopia in particular as that country's role in Africa. Indeed Emperor Haile Selassie was an important ally of both Israel and US, as well as first chairman of the Organization of African Unity (OAU), and the question of Israel and the Horn was to recur. Furthermore from the standpoint of great powers, for many years the Horn has been as much as a strategic concern with regard to the Red Sea shipping lanes, especially the potential southern pinch point of the Bab al-Mandeb Straits, as it has been a concern in relation to the rest of Africa. In this regard the Horn has offered opportunities for base facilities not only for the Red Sea and the Arabian Sea, but also with potential use for the Gulf which was off limits for great power bases during much of the Cold War and in effect until the Gulf War of 1990-1991. After the Cold War it was to appear less significant in terms of security, but rose again as the dangers of Islamism were perceived. Thus in 1998 President Clinton was to authorise the missile attack on a factory in Khartoum North, Sudan; while his successor George W. Bush was to include in his response to the attack on the US on 11 September 2001 (9/11) the deployment of American troops to Djibouti.

Thus from time to time the Horn appeared on the agenda in the White House mainly for geo-strategic reasons, and also occasionally at times of the greatest humanitarian need. This was to be the case for President Bush in 1992 when the Somali famine received wide media attention and led to his decision to deploy American troops for humanitarian intervention. In addition, some presidents are more interested in foreign policy than others, being temperamentally and perhaps politically more attuned to global issues. For example, as will be seen, George Bush was regarded as a foreign policy president and his pursuit of the holy grail of a New World Order also contributed to his commitment of forces to Somalia, when a more domestically focused president might have kept away. However Bush's action was the exception that proves the rule. Years before, Kennedy had seen clearly the moral case for involvement in development in Africa, though it was to be through new initiatives such as the Peace Corps rather than American forces that he had in mind. However, once involved in Vietnam the moral sheen was largely taken off much American involvement in far flung parts of the world and it gave way once more to the predominance of the Cold War, which had only a limited impact on Africa compared to some other regions.

In addition, in US government circles it was often thought that Africa should be essentially a responsibility of the former European colonial powers, though in reality it was France that took this most seriously, partly accounting for the absence of American involvement in West Africa in particular. In any case, the end of the Cold War appeared likely to weaken presidential leadership in foreign affairs. Successive presidents had been unifying figures in the struggle with the USSR, but deprived of that rival superpower, the role of the president was less clear. President Clinton was originally reluctant to become involved significantly in any field of foreign policy, 'Foreign Policy was to be minimized and, if at all possible, kept on the back burner' (Halberstam, 2002, p.168). Nevertheless no American president is able to avoid the issues of the Middle East, including after the Cold War the rise of Islamism, and Clinton duly became involved (Gerges, 1999). Moreover, he did eventually recognise the need to give Africa some of his attention, remarking 'When I became President, it seemed to me that our country didn't really have a policy towards Africa' (*Africa Confidential*, 22 September 1995). He even went as far as visiting the continent while in office, which was very unusual for any president; and later supported the Africa Growth and Opportunity Act. Al Gore also made four visits to Africa during his time as Clinton's Vice-President. Clinton's successor, George W. Bush, was not expected to show much interest having had little international experience before taking office, but the attack on America on 9/11 was a wake up call. Middle East insecurity brought more attention on Africa's existing and potential contribution to US oil supplies; while Africa's domestic decay held out possible security problems such as providing bolt holes for terrorists, especially when al-Qaeda's connections there were examined.

With presidential input on Africa, let alone the Horn, usually limited, expectations are more likely to be that the State Department will play a leading part in policy making. The State Department is after all the institution that is supposed to 'know' about 'abroad'. Unlike the presidency it is expected to have continuous knowledge drawing on its staff in post abroad, and filtered through its own bureaucracy in Foggy Bottom. Yet there are problems. First, the department will be influenced in its priorities by the Secretary of State, appointed by the President. During the presidency of George Bush, Secretary of State James Baker showed little interest in Africa; and nor did Warren Christopher, Clinton's first Secretary of State. However later in the 1990s Madeleine Albright was to be particularly important in focusing attention on the continent which she visited every year that she held the office; and on Africa, as on many things, she held forthright views. She was, for instance, to be very involved personally in US encouragement to Ethiopia, Eritrea and Uganda in their efforts in 1996-1998 to destabilize the Islamist regime in Sudan. Second, the 'knowledge' in the State Department is not always as full or accurate as it might be. It may be that relations with the US and/or conditions in certain countries deteriorate to a point at which the department's staff cannot remain at their posts and can only watch events from a distance – perhaps from a neighbouring country. As will be seen, for much of the post-Cold War era the US had no official representation in Somalia, and none in Sudan from 1996-2001. Or, third, it may be that for certain information the State Department is relying on another agency, or even a foreign government. Furthermore, though the staff at the department have considerable expertise, professionally many may prefer postings to what are perceived as more important or less demanding areas of the world than Africa; or if their careers do develop an African specialism they may prefer places not regarded as hardship posts, especially the likes of capital cities such as Khartoum in Sudan and Mogadishu in Somalia with ferocious climates and few facilities.[1] Ambassadorships in these two countries have not been keenly sought and often went to officials who were nearing the end of their careers. And when they have been posted to those cities, they will probably have more experience of Africa generally than of the Muslim world to which the majority in both countries adhere, for the State Department regards both Sudan and Somalia as parts of its Africa operations.[2] But whatever the background, the continuity and professional concern of State Department officials can lead to charges of over-concern for the host country – sometimes known as 'clientitis' or 'going native' – being levelled against them.

At the top of the State Department's Africa personnel stands the Assistant Secretary of State for African Affairs, who heads the Bureau of African Affairs, which was created in 1958 as European de-colonization accelerated in sub-Saharan Africa. This is a political appointment, which has sometimes gone to State Department professionals and sometimes to people from outside, such as academia or business. But whoever is appointed may cut little ice, since Africa is generally low in the pecking order in Washington being regarded as marginal to US interests. Times change though and occasionally an Assistant Secretary of Sate for Africa will come to prominence and appear to have a significant role. One such was Chester Crocker and his wide identification with the policy known as 'constructive engagement' with regard to South Africa, its relations with its neighbours, and efforts to end apartheid in the 1980s. However, by the early 1990s, where this book really starts, Crocker had been succeeded by a career diplomat, Herman 'Hank' Cohen (Cohen, 1999). Other sections in the State Department with some interest in Africa include the Bureau of International Organization Affairs, which includes seeking support of the many African states in the United Nations, and those dealing with human rights, refugees and humanitarian affairs (Schraeder, 1994). Another of significance for this book is the US Commission on International Religious Freedom, which was established in 1998.

Reference above to State Department links to other agencies includes necessarily the Central Intelligence Agency (CIA). The agency is generally represented by one or more officials operating in country under embassy cover, but usually quite easily identifiable. These agents will create their own intelligence webs and report back to their bosses in Washington as well as liasing with other embassy staff. In the Cold War, it was the CIA more than the State Department that focused on the activities of the USSR and radical regimes in Africa, and gave less weight to the domestic origins of many of the continent's problems and conflicts. The agency has also worked closely with European counterparts, and even the security services of 'friends' in the continent, including Zaire, Morocco and apartheid South Africa (Schraeder, 1994). Over the years questions have been raised about the CIA, including the quality of its information, with concern that it has come to rely too much on technical devices of one form or another – from bugging to aerial surveillance – perhaps at the expense of human intelligence ('humint'). Yet the latter can also be problematic. If the US is for some reason unrepresented for periods in particular countries, as has been the case in Somalia and Sudan, then human intelligence may be weak. In contrast, when there are agents on the ground they may be able to obtain more information, but still give rise to questions about evaluating the quality of material which locals may be all too happy to impart, perhaps sometimes for personal reasons. For the CIA, as for the US government generally, Africa may not have high priority, but due to such factors as the weakness of the state and the increasingly international character of crime, there are reasons for concern, including the activities of those regarded by Washington as terrorists. However if and when the activities of African terrorists or criminals extend to America itself, they become the concern of the Federal Bureau of Investigation (FBI), which has not always worked closely with the CIA.

The Department of Defense may also have its own interests in foreign policy issues. In general its perspectives are likely to be similar to those of the CIA but the means are different, involving support to friendly African militaries including weapons and training. In a continent in which military coups and military regimes have been so common, especially in the Cold War, US military support could be an important prop for regimes, as the Horn illustrates clearly. Contrary to some expectations, the military were not always warmongers. It has been argued that after the Vietnam War the military became more cautious, not only in the commitment of regular troops, but even special forces that might have seemed the obvious choice for the kind of unconventional action that African countries appeared at times to call for (Halberstan, 2002; Shultz, *The Weekly Standard*, 26 January 2004). Sometimes it was the politicians who were keener for action than the military: President Reagan, in particular, several times rejected the caution of his senior military advisers to send US forces into various trouble spots in the Third World (Schraeder, 1992, p.39). The foreign policy team put together by President George W. Bush also pushed military power in foreign policy, especially after 9/11. Secretary of Defense Donald Rumsveld was particularly hawkish and military spending rose rapidly in support of a policy of developing and maintaining US military superiority over any other potential power in the world, for the indefinite future. In addition there were threats of pre-emptive action whenever and wherever the US deemed necessary, whatever the views of other countries. In contrast it was the former senior military figure in Bush's cabinet in the first term, Secretary of State Colin Powell, who was seen generally as the most cautious on military intervention. However in the major use of US forces discussed here, that of Somalia in 1992-1993, there was little disagreement between the political and military leaderships about the suitability of deploying them.

Other agencies involved in Africa include the Agency for International Development (USAID). In the years after independence swept across Africa in the late 1950s and early 1960s the symbol of clasped hands of friendship became ubiquitous across the continent, whether on the doors of 4-wheel drive vehicles bearing experts, or sacks of humanitarian food relief when development was failing. In later years USAID was sometimes a target for cuts, especially by the right, and humanitarian crises could be useful in defending the agency in Washington. While it was concerned primarily with development issues, it could not fail to be aware of the scale of humanitarian crises and of the extent to which they were man-made, especially in the Horn. Such humanitarian crises were primarily the responsibility of the Office of Foreign Disaster Assistance which is a special section within USAID. In such circumstances attitudes in USAID could become politicized and feed into the policy process. With the right political connections and links to the NGOs it could be a very powerful voice, perhaps, in times of humanitarian crises, as big as any other government department or agency.

In Sudan in the 1990s, USAID was to be very active in areas under the control of the Sudan Peoples Liberation Army (SPLA) and it also maintained a small local staff in the capital, Khartoum, at a time when there was no US diplomatic representation actually in the country. In addition, the 1990s emphasis on US economic interests globally, together with growing concern for the security of oil supplies from the Middle East, had departments such as Commerce and the Treasury giving more consideration to Africa's potential. Indeed it was a boast of the Clinton years that by the start of his second term most US government agencies had active programmes and staff on Africa-related activities.

The various departments and agencies of the executive branch also conduct their own brands of bureaucratic politics (Halperin, 1974). It is natural for each agency to have its own views on what its role should be, sometimes leading to conflicting policy proposals, as for instance between political (State Department) and military (Defense Department) moves in particular countries. A further dimension of bureaucratic politics is provided by the actions of departments and agencies to maximise their own resources, sometimes at the expense of each other, or if not that much in conflict, perhaps leading to envy at the success of one rather than another and a consequent lack of cooperation. There was a general perception in the 1990s that with the threat of the USSR removed there was an emphasis on saving money in the Treasury and increasing America's international trade that helped the Commerce Department. In contrast the State Department and USAID saw budget cuts that restricted their activities, and for the latter in particular its significant role in relief in the Sudan situation, with its growing political importance as well, was a useful resource in the bureaucratic struggles in the capital. Also in the 1990s as peacekeeping rose on the post-Cold War agenda in response particularly to the situations in Somalia and the Balkans it led to new strains over responsibilities and resources between Defense and the State Department (Hersman, 2000, pp.39-40). Overall the likelihood of such bureaucratic rivalries has grown since the end of the Cold War and after 9/11. The former made foreign policy making more complex than it had been in the days of two rival superpowers bringing more claims for involvement from many different departments and agencies. The latter meant that in searching for explanations of failure there was more intense rivalry and mutual criticism.

It was in part to coordinate these various parts of the executive that the National Security Council (NSC) was created in 1947. It includes the President, Vice-President, Secretary of State, Joint Chiefs of Staff as well as the President's Special Assistant for National Security Affairs. Traditionally the NSC has been an advisory rather than an executive body, and in reality its actual work depends largely on the president of the day, and Africa has rarely been high on the agenda of the NSC. However, it was notable that President Clinton's National Security Adviser, Anthony Lake, did become engaged in the Horn in particular when war broke out between Ethiopia and Eritrea in 1998. For Africa the route to the NSC generally came through various departments and committees leading to the Deputies Committee. It was chaired by the Deputy National Security Advisor and included the deputies of the departments and agencies, where a decision could be taken to make a recommendation to the NSC. The eventual outcome of the process could be the NSC issuing a Presidential Decision Directive (PDD) (Cohen, 2000, p.4). At these various levels there was plenty of room for bureaucratic infighting, not only between the departments and agencies, but sometimes involving NSC staff as well. Disagreements about the content of intelligence as well as about its significance for policy were to proliferate with regard to the Horn, and after 9/11 were to lead to many recriminations when it was realised how central the region had been to the development of al-Qaeda in the 1990s.

Congress also plays its part in the foreign policy process though most of its members are well aware that foreign affairs, let alone Africa, are of little concern to the majority of their constituents. Both the House of Representatives and the Senate have Africa sub-committees of their foreign relations committees, and these sub-committees have tended to grow in influence within Congress, though little reported outside (Hersman, 2000, p.14). Some members have real concern for the continent and its problems which they take very much to heart, though others may tend to see it as the first step towards what are perceived to be more important positions. However Congress can be important in its granting of appropriations that generally entail economic and military aid. The ending of the Cold War, and with it the lessening of the immediate concern of the president for foreign policy, led to attempts by the Congress to be more assertive. This included the attempts by Republicans led by Newt Gingrich in the mid-1990s to take a lead on defense matters. Though the Clinton administration was able to resist some of those moves, Congress was at the forefront of cuts in expenditure on foreign aid, including aid to the poorest continent, Africa. Congress can also pass legislation that may, on occasion, be of significance for Africa in areas such as sanctions. At the same time the uncertainty about the aims and directions of foreign policy meant that members of Congress felt freer to express themselves, and this included humanitarian and human rights issues that were particularly prevalent in Africa. Both Somalia in the early 1990s and Sudan later were of considerable concern in Congress and did much to push successive administrations.

All branches of the government in Washington may at times feel the pressure of interest groups, which became particularly influential in the uncertainty over foreign policy after the Cold War. Interest groups were now in a far stronger position to seek not only to influence policy, but even to try to set the agenda, sometimes emerging as rivals of one another. Understandably there are expectations that the large African-American community would make its views felt, but in practice this has been intermittent and mixed, with limited organization or coordination. At times African-Americans have shown concern, as with the interest displayed at the time of Alex Haley's book *Roots* in the 1980s, but those who have followed in his footsteps back to the continent have often found it an ambiguous and disturbing experience. Amongst African-Americans the later rise of the Nation of Islam, headed by Louis Farrekhan, brought a new concern of particular relevance for this book; though both the movement and the interest later waned. Another significant collection of interest groups has arisen on the Christian right. Often evangelical in character, and increasingly active across the Third World, 'The new activists seek to redress the previous marginalization of religious freedom by giving it unique status in the policy process' (Hehir, 2001, p.37). Some even perceive an intensifying rivalry between the Christian and Muslim worlds, with parts of the Horn as being on the front line. From the 1990s their interest in the southern Sudan in particular was to grow dramatically and it had a major impact on US policy. More continuing concerns have been shown by humanitarian groups, as Africa has thrown up one crisis after another. Public attention was caught particularly by the Live Aid concerts in New York and London in 1984, when Western pop and famine in the Horn combined to generate international awareness and concern. Though less in the limelight thereafter, especially as elements of famine fatigue set in, the concern has not gone away, as the activities of organizations such as Oxfam and Save the Children Fund have shown; while former President Jimmy Carter has sustained his involvement in Africa and the Third World generally. Alongside humanitarian relief has come awareness that Africa's disasters have been, in part at least, man made and related to various forms of political, social and economic repression. Groups such as Amnesty International and Human Rights Watch have been particularly active in drawing attention to all aspects of human rights abuses, not least in Africa; and overall it appears that the influence of NGOs of all kinds in the policy making process has grown since the end of the Cold War (Hersman, 2000, p.49).

The activities of all of the above are also reflected in, and influenced by, the media. In early years that meant largely the print media, but the cost of keeping reporters in Africa when weighed against the limited interest of the American public in any foreign policy issues, let alone those of Africa, has led to a decrease in staff on the ground. Instead of print, it has been Africa's visual images, especially of its victims of famine and conflict that have made it to the TV screens of American homes. At times the impact has been powerful, especially the famines in the Horn of the 1980s and early 1990s, but 'famine fatigue' can in time affect editors and viewers. NGOs will often provide opportunities for the media, in the hope of raising concern and resources. At the same time politicians may also seek out media attention by a connection to causes deemed worthy by their publics. In recent years the NGOs and the media have played a growing part in influencing policy towards Africa, as the three presidencies most discussed here – those of George Bush, Bill Clinton and George W. Bush – will all illustrate.

The process of American foreign policy making towards Africa is thus as complex as it is in any other area of the world. The various branches of government, as well as the interest groups and the media, all have their parts to play. Sometimes their involvement appears confrontational and those occasions are likely to be the relations picked up by the media. But much is also cooperative in ways described as the 'informal universe' so vital to making government function (Hersman, 2000, p. 4). However, in the everyday processes of foreign policy in Washington, issues concerning Africa are generally low on the agenda especially in the upper echelons of power. On occasions though it has grown in importance and the Horn, together with southern Africa, has had moments in the spotlight of American attention. Indeed the end of the Cold War has tended to highlight that possibility. Instead of the clarity of purpose in confronting an external enemy, the lack of a unifying threat tended to promote issue-based foreign policy. One major issue of particular relevance here is that of when and where to embark on military intervention, with Somalia emerging as an important test case. A major global threat in the post Cold War era had to await the attacks of 9/11, though exactly who and where the enemy was appeared much less clear than the past challenge of the Soviet Union. One fact that was clear however was that the organization behind it, al-Qaeda, as well as other radical Islamist groups, had had some connection with Sudan at least, and been active across the Horn; and thus the region had particular resonance for the making of US foreign policy in the post Cold War period.

Interests

The various contributors to US foreign policy making are one general dimension of this book, but another is the interests the country has had in the Horn in the context of regional and global policies. Some interests at least are longstanding with strategic interests always a prominent consideration. In this respect the Horn is the south-western flank of the Red Sea, which gives it particular importance in regional strategic thinking. The Red Sea has long been a vital artery for international trade, that was why the Suez Canal was cut in the late nineteenth century and though it initially benefited European powers primarily, with the later growth of its reliance on Middle Eastern oil, America was no less concerned. The periods in which the canal was closed – at the Suez crisis of 1956 and the Six Day war of 1967 – as well as the growth of super tankers using the Cape route showed that the canal was not critical for US supplies, but it still remained an important international waterway. As such it mattered not only to the US but close allies in the region, and the US had to steer a path between them. Israel was obviously concerned with Eilat on the Red Sea, an important port for its trade with the east, and in consequence concerned to prevent the Red Sea becoming an 'Arab lake' and this drew it into close relations with Ethiopia – the other non-Muslim country on the Red Sea (Peters, 1992). But at the same time the US knew too of the importance of the Red Sea for the trade of its staunchest major Arab ally, Saudi Arabia, and its sometime ally Egypt. It was a difficult equation that different administrations handled in different ways. The Horn was also close to the source of much Middle Eastern oil in the Gulf, and thus the question of protecting that source by possible military facilities and even bases in the region arose from time to time. The northern Ethiopian region of Eritrea, with its important communications base at Kagnew as well as the Dahlek islands offshore, was particularly useful for many years.

In comparison with the Horn's strategic significance, other issues seemed comparatively minor, but still far from irrelevant. There were economic possibilities to be considered. The most obvious direct possibilities lay in opportunities for mineral exploitation, especially of oil and gas. For years hopes were to be unfulfilled, but in time Sudan and its northern neighbour Egypt were to show significant potential. Egypt, a close ally of the US from the 1970s, also had total reliance for economic survival on the Nile waters that flowed down from Ethiopia in particular; and the US and American-based agencies, notably the World Bank, were increasingly drawn into water issues (Waterbury, 2002). Also linked to that question was the agricultural potential of Sudan in particular that was to make the country widely touted, in the 1970s at least, as the future breadbasket of the Middle East.

However, it was not the abundance of food but the lack of it that arose repeatedly in the Horn and gave rise to international humanitarian concerns, especially in the US with its vast reserves. Food shortages and even famines were recurrent across the region, and in consequence US grain stores were contributing to one or other part of the Horn for years on end. But that created further issues, for food shortages were not just the result of drought but of man made conflicts as well. The most obvious response was that of wanting to participate in peace efforts, as the US was to do on a number of occasions; but humanitarian crises also raised the issue of direct intervention and that too was to be attempted at one point, in Somalia, and at least considered at others.

If strategic, economic and humanitarian issues were to be the most continuing concerns for the US, there were also the changing circumstances in the region itself that fed back into policy making.

An early post-World War II consideration for the US was that of rising nationalism that affected the Horn and many other parts of the Third World, as much of Africa, the Middle East, Asia and Latin America were becoming known collectively. In general the US seemed sympathetic. Until 1945 the Third World was not a major issue for American foreign policy makers, both because of the strength of isolationism after World War I, and the dominance of European empires in Africa, Asia and the Middle East; however after 1945 nationalism was once more on the march and a powerful force in international politics. The US could identify with Third World nationalism having itself fought a revolutionary war to throw off British imperial rule, and that strain of thought was encouraged by such domestic developments as the African-American civil rights movement.

At the same time America's European allies were in decline. The war had proved immensely damaging and draining for them, and even the will for empire was receding especially where the Left in Europe was on the march, as in Britain the largest imperial power that had cast off India, 'the jewel in the crown', in 1946. For its part the US was more than ready to encourage these allies to concentrate on European security and integration and allow their empires to give way to a whole new wave of independent states that was to transform the map of the world. This was to be particularly relevant to developments in the Middle East and Africa, and the Horn stood at the junction of the two regions. The US was to have a different view to that of Britain with regard to the latter's role in Ethiopia, Sudan and Egypt in the years after 1945.

However, the rapid decline of European empires was accompanied by the rise of the Cold War that opened up new dangers for America in the Third World. Rather than seeking to follow the model of America as the 'first new nation' (Lipsett, 1964), some nationalist movements showed sympathy for the Soviet Union, a sympathy which the latter had tried to encourage ever since Stalin founded the Comintern in the inter-war years. In places where nationalism was to take the form of armed insurgency, as in Vietnam from the 1950s, support from the USSR was likely to be through the supply of military material. Violent nationalism could be contagious and threaten US interests. In Southern Africa the US had for years allowed arms to its fascistic NATO partner Portugal to be used against the Marxist guerrillas of Angola and Mozambique in their wars of liberation from one of the most repressive colonial rulers on the continent; in return for which the US maintained its use of facilities in the strategically important Azores. In other situations where colonialism had bowed out with less violence, as in the majority of British and French territories, it might be economic aid that was sought from the USSR, as in Ghana and Guinea in West Africa. The Soviet Union appeared to show newly independent states an alternative economic model which would free them from the constraints of economic neo-colonialism, and one that had brought with it rapid industrialization – the hallmark of modernity in the 1950s and 1960s. Guns and butter from the Eastern Bloc were both potential threats to US interests. The Soviet experience was to have an impact on domestic developments in the Horn with Sudan, Somalia and Ethiopia, in that chronological order, all endeavouring to embrace at least parts of its political and economic model.

Meanwhile the Cold War also impinged directly on the Middle Eastern side of the Horn. For decades the Middle East appeared the most unstable area of superpower confrontation, and one that seemed to pose the greatest real threat of nuclear confrontation: a situation that made the Cuban missile crisis somewhat unexpected in terms of the impact of the Cold War on the Third World. It was proximity to the Middle East more than a desire to export ideology that made both superpowers increasing willing to support friendly regimes in the Horn, and their involvement contributed to the making of increasingly repressive regimes and violent opposition.

The end of the Cold War appeared to herald a less threatening international environment for the US It was not only the USSR that collapsed, but also some Marxist regimes in the Third World, including the Ethiopian regime in the Horn; while those that survived found themselves in isolated situations, namely Cuba and North Korea. It was not only the regimes that went, but the ideology of Marxism-Leninism and the centralized economic models they had sought to construct. Moreover the US now no longer had to consider its rival superpower as it contemplated action in the Third World. A classic case was that of the Middle East where first the liberation of Kuwait and then immediately following it the kick starting of the Israeli-Palestinian peace process could be undertaken with the agreement of Russia rather than the rivalry of old.

The world thus appeared more open for US contemplation of its own choices in foreign policy, and the seemingly boundless opportunities ranged from retreat into isolationism to a new quasi imperial role: the making of a New World Order as President George Bush once called it. Defining that order was more difficult, but some ingredients were clear: liberal economies in an increasingly globalized world; a crusade for liberal democracy; and potential intervention, by whatever means, when and where it was deemed necessary (Cox, 1995).

There were however different views about those ingredients. The agenda of global trade and liberal economies over the following decade raised its own set of problems. It involved the move out of the US of large numbers of manufacturing jobs many to areas of the Third World with far lower labour costs; and thanks to

NAFTA, that might mean no more than crossing the Mexican border. It was to lead to elements of protectionism for such basic products as agriculture and steel, at the same time as continuing to talk the free trade doctrine. From another angle rampant corporate growth across the world was to produce a backlash from the Greens and the anti-globalization movement generally. The Horn appeared unimportant in such economic discussions, but as US concern grew for sources of oil in Africa it was to rise on the agenda, especially the possibility of significant new fields in Sudan, as well as the region's proximity to emerging opportunities first in Egypt and later in Libya.

Support for democratization and the general agenda known as 'good governance' was intended to build a political consensus across the world, as if Fukayama's 'end of history' had finally come true (Fukayama, 1992). But the outcome was mixed. In the former Soviet Union the move away from communism produced a rough and ready picture of democracy in which elections were less than free and fair, while corruption thrived and with it organized crime. Arguably it made the region a bigger nuclear threat in reality – through decay and possible leakage to other parts of the world – than it had been in the Cold War. In Latin America democratization seemed to have stronger roots, but economic problems still threatened to de-stabilize what had been achieved politically. In the Middle East and Asia there were less dramatic political changes with old ways largely continued; while in Africa weak authoritarianism generally gave way to weak democratization (Berman, 2004). The Horn was to prove a part of the African challenge, especially the US encouragement of former guerrilla forces in Ethiopia and Eritrea to create open political systems once they had assumed power at the end of the Cold War.

As for potential intervention, though the Gulf War of 1990-1991 suggested the ease of such action in the Third World, it did not clarify the criteria for deciding when and where to act. In the event some cases proved more difficult than others – notably Somalia which will be discussed here – and contributed to the general view that humanitarian intervention, rather than intervention to defend more directly discernible American interests, was not worth American lives. Instead humanitarian concerns, especially after the international inaction in the face of the Rwanda genocide of 1994, should be a matter for international bodies such as the UN or regional bodies such as the US-backed Africa Crisis Response Initiative (ACRI) of 1995, which trained selected African forces; though African intervention in the Democratic Republic of Congo (DRC) was hardly to be a good advertisement. At the same time the US continued to be a major source of relief aid as in Sudan and Ethiopia; and intermittently involved in efforts at conflict resolution. In view of the effective disappearance of the New World Order announced by President George Bush it was hardly surprising that the National Security Adviser for his son President George W. Bush, Condoleeza Rice, should proclaim a doctrine of neo-realism based on hard headed concern for American interests tightly defined, when the Republicans again took office in 2001.

However US foreign policy was not to be just about how America viewed the world, but how the world reacted to the single remaining superpower to emerge from the 40 year contest of the Cold War (Crockatt, 2003). Even before the attack of 9/11 it was clear that there were a number of threats to the US, and that most of them were in the Third World. The events of 9/11 were to be answered by George W. Bush with the 'war on terror': but terrorism was already a phenomenon in the international environment, used by politically motivated groups and various states. It had been used against the US overseas for decades: the difference was that 9/11 took place on American soil. The US had been trying to combat terrorism before that event, and had been seeking to gather intelligence about the groups involved. It had also recognized that terrorism might be state sponsored and had created its own official list of states alleged to be involved in such activities, against which various forms of action had already been taken: Cuba, Iran, Iraq, Libya, North Korea, Syria and in the Horn, Sudan. Sudan was the only one in the list where the terrorism was essentially Islamist in character for there, as in some other parts of the Muslim world, Islamism – the mobilization of Islam for the gaining of power and the enactment of a self-proclaimed Islamic agenda – had largely replaced 'secularist' ideologies such as nationalism, communism, socialism and Ba'athism. The growth of Islamist terrorism had been recognized as being in part a manifestation of anti-Americanism, and questions were being raised about why this sentiment should be so apparent? Was it simply envy at America's success, especially as triumphalists proclaimed victory in the Cold War? Or was it that with the end of the Cold War the US was no longer the paymaster that it had been for radical Islamist groups that it had helped in the past such as the *mujahadin* in Afghanistan (Sardar and Davies, 2002)? Whatever the reasons, threats from Islamism seemed greatest in the Middle East, especially following the Iranian revolution of 1979, but there was a danger of it spreading across Muslim Africa, possibly beginning with Sudan's efforts in the Horn and East Africa in the 1990s.

In Africa anti-Americanism might be less ideological for the people as a whole, and toned down by governments in need of Western aid. But though less virulent than Islamism, criticism of the US still existed. Cuts in aid after the end of the Cold War contributed to a sense of betrayal and cynicism on the continent with regard to America's motives in the previous 30 or so years. Yet after 9/11 there was instant US concern to counter terrorism and possible links between Africa and al-Qaeda, with a focus on the Horn given its past involvement and large Muslim population. The limited successes of democratization and economic liberalization in the continent contributed to the weakness of many states and/or criminalization (Bayart, 1999), and after 9/11 in particular to the fear in America that such weak or failed states were potential harbourers of terrorist groups like al-Qaeda. Wittingly or not they could provide territory, including remote areas where training could be carried out and arms dumps established. Well-funded groups could take opportunities to go into business themselves in host countries, sometimes boosting the local economy, or at least the private interests of regime members. The latter might then have little interest or capability to limit whatever international activities terrorist groups might be undertaking: indeed as sovereign governments they could provide cover through relaxed controls on financial systems, or even assistance with passports and other international facilities. In the Horn, both the collapsed state of Somalia and the 'rogue' state of Sudan were to give rise to such concerns (Takeyh and Gvosdev, 2002).

It was too, in the Third World, that the dangers of Weapons of Mass Destruction (WMDs) were felt. For decades it had been in the interests of both superpowers to limit nuclear proliferation, which had also become a goal of the UN, as well as outlawing the development of chemical and biological weapons. However after the Cold War, Russia, amongst others, was feared as an essentially commercial source, for leakage of materials for the construction of WMDs by rogue states in the Third World, perhaps via its own decaying military and burgeoning mafia. President George W. Bush's depiction of the powers in the 'axis of evil' – Iraq, Iran and North Korea – had less to do with any axis between those three, than a belief that they were involved in trying to develop WMDs. Yet it was not only those three states, but others still on the US terrorism list that might be engaged in the production of WMD and, in the Horn, Sudan was to find itself a suspect.

While the above points relate to specific threats to the US and ways to address them, there remains also the bigger question raised after the Cold War by Samuel Huntington: the Clash of Civilizations (Huntington, 1996). This is not the place to rehearse the arguments of Huntington and his critics, but there is a need to recognize that thinking about security is not simply tactical, but brings in more strategic questions – including US relations with the Muslim world generally. A part of that question is not just threat and confrontation, but also US needs. Much has been made of America's reliance on oil from the Muslim world. Oil may be the most obvious resource the US has sought there, but it is far from the only one; and there is also the question of markets and investment opportunities for US companies.

The danger of isolationism, or a foreign policy based largely on protecting narrowly focussed 'national interests', such as anti-terrorism or the need for oil, is not the sum total of US foreign policy. The broader wish continues: to promote liberal democracy around the world; spread capitalism, with US companies maintaining a strong competitive position; to deter aggression – especially from WMDs that might threaten the US directly; and to maintain America's role as the dominant superpower, the position in which she had emerged at the end of the Cold War, even should rivals arise from Europe or Asia. The attainment of such objectives also raises the question of how they should be achieved. Should the US act largely unilaterally, or with ad hoc 'coalitions of the willing', or should it seek for multilateral approaches through international organizations? Should it proceed unilaterally with its vast military capability allowing it to choose force as its main means of policy attainment, or proceed primarily within the framework of international law? All these questions and more have arisen as the US has addressed the region of the Horn, not only after the Cold War but since it came seriously into US foreign policy sights after World War II.

Notes

[1] A large and expensive US embassy compound in Mogadishu had just been completed when Siad Barre lost power in 1991. Following the US military intervention and withdrawal the compound was comprehensively trashed.

[2] In contrast the British Foreign Office has included Sudan in the Middle East and usually headed the embassy with Arabists. (In the US State Department, North Africa only is the responsibility of the Bureau of Near Eastern and South Asian Affairs.)

References

Berman, B., Eyoh, D. and Kymlicka, W. (eds) (2004), *Ethnicity and Democracy in Africa*, Ohio, James Currey.

Crockatt, R. (2003), *America Embattled: September 11, anti-Americanism and the global order*, London, Routledge.

Cox, M. (1995), *United States' Foreign Policy after the Cold War: Superpower without a mission?*, London, Pinter for RIIA.

Fukayama, F. (1992), *The end of history and the last man*, London, Hamish Hamilton.

Gerges, F. (1999), *America and Political Islam*, Cambridge, Cambridge University Press.

Haas, R. (1999), *Intervention: The use of American Military force in the post-Cold War world*, Washington, Brookings.

Halberstam, D. (2002), *War in a Time of Peace: Bush, Clinton and the Generals*, Bloomsbury, 2002.

Halperin, M. (1974), *Bureaucratic Politics and Foreign Policy*, Washington, Brookings.

Hehir, B. (2001), 'Religious Freedom and US Foreign Policy', in Abrams, E. (ed.), *The Influence of Faith: Religious Groups and US Foreign Policy*, Lanham MD, Rowman and Littlefield.

Hersman, R. (2000), *How Congress and the President Really Make Foreign Policy*, Washington, Brookings.

Huntington, S. (1996), *The clash of civilizations and the remaking of world order*, New York, Simon and Scuster.

Lipsett, S. (1964), *The First New Nation*, London, Heinemann.

Lynn-Jones, S. and Miller, S. (1992), *American Strategy in a Changing World*, Cambridge MS, MIT Press.

Peters, J. (1992), *Israel and Africa*, London, Tauris.

Sardar, Z. and Davies, M.W. (2002), *Why do people hate America?*, Cambridge, Iconbooks.

Schraeder, P. (1992), *Intervention in the 1980s: US Foreign Policy in the Third World*, Boulder, Rienner.

Schraeder, P. (1994), *US Foreign Policy Towards Africa: Incrementalism, Crisis and Change*, Cambridge, Cambridge University Press.

Takeyh, R. and Gvosdev, N. (2002), 'Do Terrorist Networks Need a Home?', *The Washington Quarterly*, Summer.

Waterbury, J. (2002), *The Nile Basin: National determinants of collective action*, New Haven, Yale University Press.

Chapter 2

The US and the Horn in the Cold War

The Horn of Africa, as it was to emerge after 1945, hardly formed a region as far as the US, or many others inside or outside it were concerned. The significance of Ethiopia as an independent state had become more recognized, especially after the Emperor Haile Selassie's dramatic but forlorn appeal to the League of Nations as Italian forces ravaged his country ten years previously: the rest of the region however was little more than relatively unimportant territories under European control. The Horn stood on the fringe of two regions as far as the State Department was concerned, the Middle East and Africa, and was scarcely top priority for either. In the circumstances it was understandable that it was within the context of the countries of the Horn rather than a wider regional view that US policy was to evolve in the Cold War.

Ethiopia

US policy in the Horn in the aftermath of World War II was centred on Ethiopia. The rest of the Horn appeared firmly under European control, with Britain the most powerful country, especially since in the war it had driven Italy out of Ethiopia, which Mussolini had invaded in 1935. Britain remained dominant in Sudan where it had been since 1898, ruling nominally in a condominium government with Egypt, but in practice controlling Africa's largest state territorially. Britain was also entrusted by the UN with the administration of Italy's former colonial territory of Eritrea on Sudan's eastern border. On the eastern side of the Ethiopian highland lay the Somali peoples. Some were in Ethiopia itself, but Britain also held the territory of Somaliland in the north facing the Arabian Sea; while Italy was allowed back after the war by the UN to administer its former colony of Somalia, the long strip of territory running south flanked by the Indian Ocean on the east, and the Somali-populated territories of Ethiopia and northern Kenya to the east and south. The final element of European control was provided by the French in the tiny enclave around the strategic port of Djibouti on the Arabian Sea.

Ethiopia however had resisted imperial conquest, and with Liberia was the only part of Africa that had not been under European control. In Ethiopia's case this had been achieved by the famous victory over the Italians by the Emperor Menelik at Adowa in 1896. Italy had sought to reverse that humiliating experience by the invasion of 1935, but after Britain's victory in 1941 the Emperor Haile Selassie had no wish to be tied to his restorers. He saw his kingdom as an ancient independent country and propagated its history as running from the union of the Solomon and the Queen of Sheba deep in the mists of antiquity. In reality Ethiopia had had a long and varied history that included a legacy of suspicion if not antagonism with the Christian kingdom's Muslim neighbours in modern day Sudan and Somalia. Ethiopia's own deep-rooted Coptic church had historic links with the Copts of Egypt; but while the latter had been conquered by the Muslim Arabs and become a minority in their own country, Ethiopia had resisted the spread of Islam, most notably in defeating the invasion led by Imam Ahmed Gran in the sixteenth century.

The real takeoff into modern Ethiopia had occurred in the nineteenth century. During the reign of the Emperor Menelik, from 1889-1911, the highland kingdom had begun to transform itself into an African empire, mainly by the acquisition of land to the south and east of the highland fortress with its new capital at Addis Ababa. In doing so it was consciously rivalling European imperial expansion in Africa, as well as similar dreams in Egypt, and included the defeat of the Italians in 1896. The areas acquired included about a quarter of the Somali peoples in the Haud and Ogaden regions, as well as many Oromo the largest community in the enlarged imperial kingdom. Incorporation into the expanding Ethiopian empire involved a degree of exploitation, particularly when the newly acquired lands were handed out to former soldiers in Menelik's army. But there was also assimilation into the evolving society for those who managed to rise in the imperial framework. Importantly for this book, the territorial acquisition of the late nineteenth century expansion raised the number of Muslims in the kingdom as a whole, while entrenching their position under the rule of a Coptic Christian ruler and church. Ethiopia not only looked down on Muslim neighbours, it now incorporated nearly as many Muslims as there were Christians in the kingdom.

Following Menelik's death there was a troubled succession that resulted in the emergence of Ras Tefari as the real power behind the throne, and his final accession to it in 1930 as the Emperor Haile Selassie. Haile Selassie followed Menelik in his foreign, as well as his domestic, policy and in the former was determined to play off one outside power against another. He had little innate sympathy for any of them having felt abandoned by the international community at the time of Italy's invasion in 1935, and though it was British-led forces that had restored him to the throne he felt no particular obligation as a result. He further believed that the British empire was waning, and, more directly, that it might attach the Eritrean lowlands to Sudan and seek to unite the Somalis: both possibilities that ran counter to the Emperor's expansionist ambitions. The obvious answer was to look towards America as a new partner in his plans.

For its part the US was prepared to become involved in Ethiopia. From as early as 1942 the US first used Asmara, capital of Eritrea then under British control, on an ad hoc basis; and in the following year it signed a lend-lease agreement with Ethiopia. For the US the use of the communications facility outside Asmara, which became known as Kagnew, was a vital part of its global radio system and highly valued by the military, so much so that maintaining it became top priority with regard to US policy in the region. The initial US presence in Eritrea had been in conjunction with the British administration that had replaced the Italians, but after the war Britain did not intend to remain there. Instead it saw three real possibilities for Eritrea: the return of Italy under UN trusteeship arrangements (as happened in Italian Somalia); full independence; or some form of incorporation into Ethiopia. Haile Selassie was naturally keen on the latter, not least because it would give Ethiopia – the world's largest landlocked state – access to the sea through the ports of Massawa and Assab. To assist in this he swiftly showed his support for America, including sending a contingent of troops to Korea from where the name Kagnew was taken for the vital communications base. In return the US showed sympathy for Ethiopia's wish to enter into a federation with Eritrea, and it used its influence in the UN for agreement to the arrangements by which that was achieved in 1952. Nor was there a significant protest by the US when Ethiopia steadily eroded the federal arrangements over the subsequent decade and finally incorporated the former Italian colony firmly into the rule of the Emperor. Ethiopia was then a direct beneficiary of access to the sea, and consequently more attractive to friends in the international community as well. Ethiopia figured in the calculations of US Secretary of State John Foster Dulles who conceived of a 'southern tier' from Ethiopia across the Middle East to be a part of the containment of the Soviet Union as the Cold War deepened. In 1952 a technical agreement programme was signed between the two countries; and the following year there was an assistance pact in exchange for use of facilities at Kagnew and the port of Massawa.

Ethiopia's importance was further enhanced following the coup in Egypt in July 1952 which brought Gamal Abdel Nasser and his fellow Free Officers to power. Nasser sought to rebuild Egypt's leadership of the Middle East, and after being denied by the West first weapons and then support for the Aswan Dam, he turned to Eastern Europe, acquiring arms from Czechoslovakia and aid from the Soviet Union. By 1955 this new alliance spelled the end of the US-backed arrangements for the 'northern tier' which through the Baghdad Pact would have linked Turkey, Iraq and Pakistan, and possibly Syria, Lebanon and Jordan as well, in the containment of the Soviet Union. Instead by the link to Egypt the Soviet Union was connected to the southeast corner of the Mediterranean. Then in 1956 came the Suez crisis, in which the US opposed the collusion of Britain, France and Israel and forced them to cut short their attempt not only to re-take the Suez Canal, but topple Nasser as well. Nasser emerged from it as a vastly enhanced figure in much of the Middle East, and a leader of a pan-Arab movement seeking radical change across the region with the backing of the Soviet Union. In time this was to have repercussions for the Red Sea, where from 1962 Egypt became embroiled in a civil war in Yemen (sometimes known as Egypt's Vietnam), and where there were fears in various quarters, including America, of it becoming an 'Arab lake'. By the early 1960s there were links between the growing revolt of the Eritrean Liberation Front (ELF) in Eritrea against what was perceived as Ethiopia's assimilation, and the rising tide of Arab nationalism.

While US and Ethiopian interests were becoming closer on the question of the Red Sea, on the Indian Ocean the Emperor had another concern that was less obvious to the Americans. The rise of Somali nationalism and the moves towards the independence and unification of British and Italian Somali territories posed a potential threat, since it was clear that the further unification with Somalis in

Ethiopia, Kenya and Djibouti could become an aim. Haile Selassie wanted more American support, and to underline the point he shocked the US by flirting with the USSR in 1959, a tactic he had also used shortly after World War II. Certainly the tactic worked and US military aid was soon raised.

However, the problem of Somalia did not go away. Ethiopia's Ogaden region had had only the most exiguous administration and following Somalia's independence in 1960 there were guerrilla activities with Somali encouragement, and then clashes along the border between regular troops of the two countries. The US had to keep them both in check. Haile Selassie seemed to want to fulfil Menelik's ambition of sweeping down to the coast and forcibly embracing all Somalis in the empire; while Somalia needed an aid package to check it becoming too close to the Soviet Union, but the package came on the condition of not pursuing an armed resolution of the border dispute between the two countries.

The US also had to reckon with changes within Ethiopia itself. As well as military aid, America was involved in various modernization efforts, including the development of the national airline and the growth of the country's university in Addis Ababa. Such developments contributed to social strains that were much cited when in 1960 there was a serious coup attempt against the Emperor by the Imperial Bodyguard, in which even Haile Selassie's son, Asfer Wassen, seemed briefly to be implicated. The US was to back both the Emperor and modernization, though how far they were compatible remained open to doubt, especially as guerrilla warfare developed in the 1960s in Eritrea in the north as well. But its generosity declined when the high costs of the Vietnam War forced cutbacks in military commitments elsewhere; while the Kagnew communications base proved outdated with the development of satellite communications and the opening of Diego Garcia in the Pacific in 1967 as a major US base covering the oil producing states of the Gulf.

By the 1970s the tensions in Ethiopia were appearing again. While the ageing emperor still ruled in an archaic and autocratic manner, opposition was rising. In 1973 there were signs of unrest in the army at all ranks which led in the following months to the emergence of what became known as the Dergue (Committee), initially comprising 108 military of different ranks and units. Spurred on by news of serious famine in Wollo and Tigre provinces, that the government had sought to ignore until revealed by foreign journalists, students took up the cry of revolution, and were supported by striking workers. The government, out of touch and losing control, tried to offer some concessions, but they were too little too late. However, as often in revolutions, the revolutionaries fell out. In the army, policy differences in the Dergue produced killings that resulted in the emergence of the ruthless Major (later Lieutenant-Colonel) Mengistu Haile Mariam. In 1974 the Dergue first arrested and then murdered Haile Selassie. The Dergue knew more what it was against than what it was seeking to achieve, and here the students and other intellectuals, many of them schooled in Marxist-Leninist ideology (some from studies overseas), provided an answer. Yet they too were divided notably between the Ethiopian People's Revolutionary Party (EPRP) and the All Ethiopia Socialist Movement (MEISON). In the beginning of the Red Terror in 1977 MEISON encouraged the Dergue to crush the EPRP, but having done so the

Dergue then turned on MEISON as well. By the end of the year the Dergue was firmly in charge; and Mengistu Haile Mariam was firmly in charge of the Dergue. In the following years he was to take Ethiopia more clearly down a Marxist path than any of the other 'Afro-Marxist' regimes.

The question for the US was how far and how long it could continue to stand by its greatest ally in Africa? While some of its significance had passed when Kagnew became outdated, Ethiopia was still strategically important and the dominant state in the Horn. In the early stages of the revolution there was not great concern in Washington (Korn, 1986). The lack of reform in Ethiopia had long been recognized and the first leaders to emerge from the Dergue seemed as if they might be moderate and indeed an improvement: in particular it was hoped that the popular General Aman Andom might make peace with the Eritreans fighting in the north. Thus the American response was to work with the moderates in the Dergue in the hope of influencing future change in a pro-Western manner. However as events became more violent and Mengistu emerged doubts set in about whether the regime should be supported, or if it was not whether an opening would be presented to the Soviet Union. On balance Washington continued to give support, including military aircraft in 1976, though the Red Terror was causing rising concern. This grew with the election of President Jimmy Carter, who was to give a new priority to human rights issues in US foreign policy. In 1977 Ethiopia was publicly criticised for its human rights record, military aid was cut, and the Kagnew base closed. Mengistu responded by expelling most American officials and military personnel from the country and 35 years of America's closest involvement with a major African country of strategic significance for the Red Sea, and with it the Middle East, was ended.

Yet throughout that long association the Muslim dimension of Ethiopia had not been significant. In population terms Ethiopia was estimated to have more Muslims than its neighbours in the Horn, but that had not emerged as a major factor for which the US needed to take account, even though Ethiopia had a history of conflict with its Muslim neighbours from Somalia and Sudan. The first challenge to which the US had had to respond in regard to Ethiopia had come from abroad in the form of Arab nationalism inspired by Nasser, which served to tighten the relationship between the two countries. The second challenge had come from various pressures for change in Ethiopia. In the north in Eritrea the ELF did have roots in the Muslim lowlands but it was replaced as the main guerrilla opposition by the Eritrean Peoples Liberation Front (EPLF), whose leaders came from the Christian highlands and were Marxist-Leninists. While the challenge to the Emperor's rule in central Ethiopia came not from the Muslim community but from a variety of urban social groups and the army and the movements progressed from reform to Marxist revolution from above.

Having broken with the US, Ethiopia then continued its path building Afro-Marxism at home, and cementing a close relationship with the Soviet Union abroad. In fact as Soviet ambition in the Third World had intensified in the late 1970s it had been making moves to extend its influence from Somalia, where it was then ensconced, into Ethiopia as well. It was intended to contribute to a *pax Sovietica* at the southern end of the Red Sea that would embrace Yemen as well. In

1977 Fidel Castro himself travelled to the region to try to cement relations, but Somalia's implacable opposition to an agreement with Ethiopia prevented him from achieving any success. The Soviet Union was being forced to choose between the two states, and Ethiopia appeared increasingly attractive. It offered the ports of Massawa and Assab in Eritrea; and Mengistu seemed a more disciplined and determined ally than Somalia's ruler Siad Barre. The Soviet Union's decision was finally made for it when, against its warnings, Barre launched Somali troops into Ethiopia in July 1977. The USSR airlifted immediate military aid to Ethiopia, and 25,000 Cuban troops joined the Ethiopian forces in repulsing the invading army. In addition to its commitment to Ethiopia, in 1981 the Soviet Union, Libya and Yemen signed the Aden Treaty that appeared to cement the Soviet position on the southern Red Sea directly threatening US strategic interests.

However by the mid 1980s Gorbachev had attained power in the Soviet Union, and combined reform at home with a reduction in Soviet involvement in the Third World. In Ethiopia this involved a reduction in the high level of arms to Mengistu's regime, and its encouragement to move to negotiation with the Eritrean and Tigrean guerrillas in the north. As the Soviet Union itself collapsed at the end of the decade, it pulled out of Ethiopia. Briefly Mengistu turned to Israel, another old strategic friend of Ethiopia, obtaining weapons in exchange for the last of the Falasha (the 'Black Jews' of Ethiopia), but it was a forlorn hope and Mengistu's regime finally collapsed in 1991. As it collapsed, the US moved in to try to maintain a modicum of order. Both the regime and the guerrilla forces advancing towards Addis Ababa were amenable to mediation. Mengistu fled to his refuge in Zimbabwe, leaving others to pay the price; the TPLF took Addis Ababa, but with support from other regions as well; and Eritrea was offered self-determination within two years. The US congratulated itself on having helped to head off a bloodbath of the kind already experienced in Somalia.

Somalia

Throughout its time in Ethiopia the US was aware that the greatest external challenge in Haile Selassie's eyes was not from the Soviet Union so much as Somalia. Unlike Ethiopia, Somalia was not an historic state, but rather a people: in one classic anthropological study 'a pastoral democracy' (Lewis, 1999). The Somali pastoralists of the coastal plains had been divided up by imperial intervention. In 1902 Italy, France and Britain signed a Tripartite Convention that saw Somalis divided between France in Djibouti, British Somaliland and northern Kenya, and Italian Somaliland; while inland Menelik's territorial claim over other Somali areas was also accepted.

However, colonial boundaries were of limited significance to the Somali pastoralists who followed their established migratory routes largely irrespective of borders. Somalis claimed a common ancestor in Samaale, but also had a complex system of clans and sub-clans. Among the pastoralists the major clan families are the Darod, the Dir, the Hawiye and the Isaaq, while in the more fertile south are the agriculturalists of the Digil and the Rahanwayn. 'Pastoral clan organization is an unstable, fragile system, characterized at all levels by shifting allegiances. Power and politics are exercised through temporary coalitions and ephemeral alliances of lineages' (Samatar, 1991, p. 13). At the same time there was a form of institutionalism through *heer* that formed a kind of social contract between families and clans. A mixture of local and Islamic law, *heer*, is agreed at ad hoc assemblies of men known as *shirs*. These are very open, as might be expected among people who are culturally very egalitarian and individualistic. While most Somalis are pastoral, there have long been city states on the coast like Berbera, Djibouti and Zeila in the north, and Baraawe, Merka and Mogadishu to the south. Trade went through the ports, especially to the highlands of Ethiopia.

The Somalis are a Muslim people. The penetration of the area inhabited by the Somalis began in the early years of the religion reflecting proximity to Arabia and the regular links between the two sides of the Arab Sea. Indeed Arabs and even Persians were significant in the coastal city-states such as Mogadishu and Zeila. In the rural areas however Islam spread slowly at first, but made great strides from the eleventh to the thirteenth centuries especially as a result of the work of Sheikh Daarood Jabarta and Sheikh Isahaaq (Laitin and Samatar, 1987, pp. 10-11). This reflects in part the significance of holy figures who were to spread Sufism, a mystical form of Islam comprising distinct communities of believers whose own pathways to Allah were led by their saintly figures. The three largest Sufi orders or *tariqas* (paths) were the Qaadariya, the Ahmadiya and the Saalihiya, but there were also other smaller groups. Often belief in a particular *tariqa* was linked to clan and sub-clan membership. Both mysticism and rural society limited the role of *sharia* (Islamic law). The mysticism of Sufism gave a different understanding of Islam to that of *sharia*, which is more commonly associated with the application of law as the centre of the religion. The predominantly rural Somali society was rarely an appropriate environment. It is not that Sufism contradicts the *sharia*: rather 'the sectors of the Shariah which elaborate a corpus of private and public law based upon the concept of citizenship are not applicable, save with major limitations, to a stateless clan-based society'. While insofar as there has been a role, 'The scope of the application of the Shariah, although supported by strong religious sanctions, is limited by the power of the clan leaders' (Lewis, 1998, pp.24-5).

In more modern times the great Somali national hero, Sayed Mohammed Abdille Hasan, was an Islamic scholar who took his inspiration from the Mahdi in Sudan, and was critical of Sufism with its veneration of saintly figures from the past. Mohammed Hasan was capable of inspiring a considerable cross-clan following. An Ogadeeni by origin, from the 1890s he led resistance to Ethiopia, Italy and Britain (the latter dubbed him the 'Mad Mullah'), that lasted for over two decades until his death in 1920. His vision of Somali unity became an inspiration for later Somali nationalists and symbolized their ability to join together against foreign invaders. However he did less to achieve a unification of Somalia's Muslim communities that remained largely wedded to the traditions of Sufism and to their clans.

Colonialism may have divided the Somali peoples, but after World War II they showed the same kind of nationalism led by the intelligentsia as other territories, though with the added dimension of wishing to unite all the Somali peoples in one state. Independence in 1960 was accompanied by the unification of the Italian and British territories; though in the latter there was widespread concern about possible subordination to the larger territory to the south. With a liberal democratic constitution (a common part of British de-colonizing arrangements) and a dominant party in the Somali Youth League (SYL) the country looked tolerably stable. However by the end of the decade the rivalry of clan and sub-clan groups was becoming very evident: in the 1969 elections there were over 1,000 candidates, and 63 political parties.

For the US the main issue with regard to Somalia was the latter's irredentist claim to the Somali populated areas of Ethiopia. At independence the Somali flag had five stars on it, three of which were to represent Somalis in Ethiopia, Djibouti and Kenya. Ethiopia's administration in the Ogaden had always been exiguous and it was easy enough for the Somali government of Abdirashid Shermarke to support Somali guerrillas in the region that in time grew into an open revolt. Tension rose as Ethiopia fought back and then went on to cross border attacks bringing the danger not only of full scale war between the two countries, but a possible attempt by Haile Selassie to fulfil an old dream of extending his country's control right down to the sea incorporating the newly independent Somalia in doing so.

The US remained convinced throughout that its main commitment was to Ethiopia, and it continued to supply arms, though never as many as Ethiopia wished. The US made it clear that it disapproved of Somali irredentism and agreed with the founding fathers of the Organization of African Unity (OAU) in their Charter's commitment to the maintenance of Africa's existing borders. But America also feared a major Ethiopian incursion into Somalia, or the latter's falling under Soviet domination especially when it began supplying arms in 1963. Thus the US gave support to the Somali police force, and encouraged both countries to negotiate on their border dispute rather than becoming embroiled in continuing conflict. Fortunately for the US the task was made easier after 1967 when Shermarke was replaced as prime minister by Mohammed Egal, a more pro-Western figure who was more conciliatory over the Ogaden.

Egal however was not to last, for in 1969 a coup d'etat brought Mohammed Siad Barre to power. Siad Barre, who had started in the police under Italian rule, was by then the most senior military officer and, 'spoke a language of national unity that transcended kinship' (Laitin and Samatar, 1987, p.79). His intervention seemed an understandable response to growing clan tensions, especially following the murder of Shermarke, but it was also noted that the Somali military had been armed by the Soviet Union for some years. Certainly in the years that followed Siad Barre was to seek to take Somalia in the direction of 'scientific socialism', while claiming initially that this was quite compatible with Islam in Somalia (Laitin and Samatar, 1987, pp. 109-110). Naturally he had Soviet support in this and in 1974 signed a Soviet-Somali Treaty of Friendship and Cooperation. Barre went on to create a one-party state with the establishment of the Somali Revolutionary Socialist Party two years later. Social mobilization was also undertaken with various efforts to encourage development beyond pastoralism; and linked to these was the nationalization of the upper levels of the economy. Barre also sought to move against public manifestations of clan in social and political life. However, increasingly his regime was being perceived in just such clan terms, including his reliance on his own clan, the Mareehan, that of his mother, the Ogadeeni, and the connected Dulbahante, known collectively as 'MOD'. The involvement of the Ogadeeni was especially significant since the Ethiopian revolution seemed to give opportunities for renewed action against the old enemy. Revolutions are always potentially threatening, but also in periods of domestic turmoil such as Ethiopia was experiencing they appear vulnerable. Barre, with his forces built up by the Soviet Union, and under pressure domestically to act saw an apparently irresistible opportunity and launched his forces on 17 July 1977.

Another factor that led Barre to act was the changing policy of the US after the break with the old client, Ethiopia, and with a new president in Jimmy Carter. Carter himself became involved in the discussions about the Horn. While his security advisor Brzezinski saw the Horn largely in terms of global security and rivalry with the Soviet Union from Afghanistan to Africa as the 'arc of crisis' in the emerging Second Cold War, Carter himself was thinking more of the principle that countries breaking with the Soviet Union, as Somalia appeared willing to do fearing the growing Soviet-Ethiopian connection, should be welcomed into the American camp. Regionally Carter was also encouraged by America's Arab friends, most notably Saudi Arabia, which had long tried to woo Somalia from the Soviet camp, including encouraging it to join the Arab League in 1974 and rewarding it with increased aid from the Saud's oil-enriched coffers. Carter had agreed US military assistance to Somalia only two days before Barre launched his troops across the border into Ethiopia.

This naked aggression in clear defiance of international law and the strictures of the OAU was a considerable embarrassment to the new administration in Washington, and it joined the Soviet Union in condemning it. However the USSR not only condemned it, the 1974 Treaty with Somalia was torn up and Soviet personnel departed swiftly. The failure of Soviet attempts to mediate between the socialist states of Ethiopia and Somalia led to the decision to put its full weight behind the new friends in Addis Ababa. Somali forces had at first swept across the Ogaden lowlands before being eventually halted as they approached the fastness of the highlands. With a large airlift of equipment from Eastern Europe, and 25,000 Cuban troops to stiffen the army, the Ethiopians were able to hold the Somalis off and then drive them back to the border. Indeed the danger then was of an Ethiopian advance into Somalia, but both superpowers exerted pressure to prevent that. In any case for Somalia the damage was largely done without Ethiopian forces needing a counter invasion. But the war had meant the crystallization of the superpower positions in the Horn of Africa, including Sudan as will be seen.

The defeat suffered by Somalia in the 1977-1978 war was shattering. Not only had it failed to take the Ogaden, the largest point of the star on the national flag outside Somalia's rule, it had also led to a crisis of national identity. Growing unrest was everywhere apparent over the following years. Almost immediately after the war a coup attempt, mainly by Maraheen officers, was crushed, and then other clan and sub-clan armed groups proliferated. Ethiopia itself encouraged the

Somali Salvation Democratic Front though its guerrilla efforts were not very successful. However in the north, in former British Somaliland, the Isaaq based Somali National Movement (SNM) proved more effective, with backing from Ethiopia and South Yemen (PDRY). The situation for Barre was becoming so pressing that in 1988 he did the apparently unthinkable by making a pact with Mengistu. The main part of the agreement was that Ethiopia would stop supporting Barre's enemies, while Somalia would cease encouraging guerrillas in the Ogaden, releasing more Ethiopian troops for the war in the north that was going badly for the government. It was likened at the time to the Hitler-Stalin pact of 1939. Shortly after it the SNM launched a pre-emptive attack in the north that was countered by Barre's forces with great ferocity. Conflict however continued, apparently with Ethiopian support in spite of the 1988 agreement. In 1989 Ogadeeni opposition spread, since the agreement of the previous year had apparently been Barre's abandonment of the region's cause. Also in and around the capital Mogadishu opposition was mounting especially from the Hawiye-based United Somali Congress (USC).

For the US its new ally, to which it had turned after years of working closely with Ethiopia, had become a quagmire in the 1980s. After the war of 1977-1978 the US did supply 'defensive' arms to Somalia, but on nothing like the scale that the Soviet Union had done formerly. However the new ally's importance appeared to increase with the Iranian revolution and the commitment of Soviet troops to Afghanistan. Indeed some analysts in the US were suggesting that the Soviet Union's own oil reserves could run out and lead it to turn to a more aggressive policy in the Middle East, with the new friendship with Ethiopia helping in a strategy of encircling Arab oil. Carter responded by stating that the US would if necessary intervene militarily in the Gulf if international oil supplies were threatened, a statement that became known as the Carter Doctrine. Access facilities for US forces were negotiated with Kenya and Oman as well as Somalia that would act as rear support bases for the Rapid Deployment Force (RDF) being developed. Though Carter's successor Ronald Reagan was to be more concerned with southern Africa than the Horn, the development of the access facilities went ahead, and joint exercises took place in 1983 under operation Bright Star.

While America's concerns with Somalia were largely strategic, the provision of 'defensive' weapons was a small part of its approach. Much more importance was attached to development aid with USAID in particular seeing Somalia as something of a test case. Barre had been building a socialist state, but now he was to be encouraged via aid conditionality to dismantle it and instead build a more free market economy in close association with the IMF and the World Bank. There was very substantial economic aid, though that itself caused problems in a country that had difficulty in absorbing and using it effectively. Moreover by 1988 the tension of the Second Cold War was falling, and the Somali forces' destruction in the north was giving rise to growing international criticism. In Congress especially voices were being raised about the level of human rights abuse accompanied by pressure to disengage. Democratic Congressmen especially were voicing their growing concerns, which were also being picked up in the media leading to growing pressure on the administration to re-evaluate its priorities in

Somalia. However in 1988 the US avoided direct criticism of Barre's repression because of the importance of the military facilities at Berbera and it was not until 1990 that aid was finally stopped (Cohen, 2000, p.222). One year later the new and expensive embassy complex in Mogadishu was hastily evacuated as Barre's regime finally fell.

Throughout the American engagement with Somalia from 1977, the question of Islam did not emerge very publicly, but was always simmering just below the surface. During the parliamentary period it had been central to inconclusive debates about the adoption of a script for the oral Somali language, and whether it should be in Arabic or the Latin alphabet. In the 1970s Barre was perceived as becoming more hostile to the religious authorities as he sought to build a socialist state. But while he pushed for scientific socialism, he claimed he was not anti-Islamic and often stressed that both socialism and religion had common intentions in terms of attaining social justice. However he also made it clear that he would not tolerate any interference in politics by religious leaders. When in 1975 he chose a Latin script rather than Arabic for the Somali language and introduced more secular laws he hastily executed in public 10 influential Muslim clerics who criticised his policies, an action that caused considerable shock to Somali society. At the same time the Arab states, including Saudi Arabia, consistently sought to woo him rather than denouncing his rule. Though when opposition mounted in the 1980s it was essentially clan and sub-clan based, rather than seeking to utilise Muslim solidarity against an increasingly tyrannical movement, there were also signs of Islamic revival. Koranic study circles began to proliferate, especially among students and intellectuals; while more women took to appearing in public in forms of Islamic dress. Various small groups came and went from time to time, but there was nothing that appeared to pose an Islamist challenge to Barre's regime until it was in its final stages. In 1990 an Islamic Call organisation finally appeared, and it was clear that there was a growing domestic and foreign interest in the potential for an Islamist movement in Somalia at the same time as the state was collapsing.

Sudan

While the US was largely dealing with a state-centred polity in Ethiopia and the politics of statelessness in Somalia, Sudan was a complex mix of both tendencies. The largest country territorially in Africa, its political history has reflected its half way house between Africa and the Middle East, with the most salient link being provided by the Nile: the White Nile from east and central Africa fed from Lake Victoria and the Blue Nile from the Ethiopian highlands, meeting to form the main Nile at what is now Khartoum, the capital of Sudan. Along the main Nile there has been a history of state formation from ancient times. The upper Nile was linked from the outset with the emergence of pharaonic civilization, and as that declined Kushite civilization succeeded it based in northern Sudan. Subsequently there was a series of Coptic Christian states on the main Nile until the coming of the Arabs and Islam from Egypt and across the Red Sea from Arabia. For the most part the

Arabs came slowly and without major conflict intermarrying with the indigenous population to produce a people who appeared to be of mixed descent, though with a broad cultural homogeneity through adherence to Islam and the spread of Arabic language and culture. Many of the Muslims were adherents of the Sufi orders that spread across northern Sudan and linked the various ethnic or tribal groups.

The Arab and Islamic influences were disseminated from the Nile to other areas of what became Sudan, but many other identities remained strong. In the north the three main highland areas preserved strong local identities: the people of Darfur in the far west, influenced as much by West Africa as the Nile; the Nuba of the Nuba Mountains of central Sudan; and in the east the Beja of the Red Sea Hills. Even greater separation was maintained by the vast swamps of the White Nile known as the *sudd*, which were virtually impenetrable until the nineteenth century. Here the Arab and Muslim influences had made little headway, and instead the various local communities – ranging from the hierarchical Azande of the forests of Western Equatoria to the Dinka and Nuer pastoralists of the swampy plains of the upper Nile – had more in common with the peoples of east and central Africa than the lands to the north.

The modern Sudan's borders are the product of imperially imposed borders incorporating this heterogeneous population. And just as nineteenth century Ethiopia had been an indigenous state with imperial ambitions, so too was the Egypt in the same era. It was the dynasty established by Mohammed Ali's seizure of power in Egypt following Napoleon's failure at the start of the century that led to the invasion and acquisition of northern Sudan in 1821. Mohammed Ali's army went initially in search of gold and slaves and stayed to establish a colonial-style state, nominally a part of the Ottoman Empire thus giving rise to what is commonly known as the Turco-Egyptian period. By the middle of the century the remote southern Sudan was being penetrated as well, now for such luxuries as ivory as well as slaves. It was a mixture of Egyptians, European traders and northern Sudanese adventurers who developed the slave trade in the south, and the conflict and destruction they brought left a bitter legacy.

Resistance to Turco-Egyptian encroachment was not only in the south, but in the north was to take the form of the revolt of Mohammed Ahmed al-Mahdi, seen as one of the great movements of the Muslim world in the modern era, and which led to the defeat of Egyptian forces and the death of the British general Charles Gordon at Khartoum in 1885, before the establishment of an independent state based on Omdurman, across the river. The Mahdi died shortly after his famous victory, but his successor the Khalifa Abdullahi was to rule until 1898, during which time he both tried unsuccessfully to invade Egypt to the north, and fought with Ethiopia in the east. The Mahdiyya, as the period of independence from 1885-1898 has become known, has been widely seen as the first attempt to establish an Islamic state in Sudan, and it was to prove an inspiration to more than one political movement in later years. The Khalifa was eventually defeated by an Anglo-Egyptian force, followed by the establishment of condominium rule that was in reality only a fig leaf for British control. Britain's motives were largely about protecting the Suez canal, which had caused it to occupy Egypt in 1882, as well as the Red Sea and keeping out its European rivals in the region, as illustrated by the Fashoda crisis with France in 1898.

Britain's rule in Sudan was marked by its efforts to manage the country's heterogeneity, which increasingly became polarised into north and south. In the north it proved necessary to accommodate the Islamic groups, which eventually saw the domination of the Mahdists, around Mohammed Ahmed al-Mahdi's descendents, and their main rivals the Khatmiyya, led by the Mirghani family. After World War II they provided core support for the main political parties, the Umma Party and Unionist Party respectively. As Britain and Egypt became increasing rivals in the post-war Middle East, so the parties effectively linked up with them: the Umma with Britain and the Unionists with Egypt. It was this rivalry between the codomini backed up by the competing northern Sudanese parties that hurried Sudan along the path to independence in 1956: a bi-product of essentially Middle Eastern politics. However southern Sudan had largely lain outside these developments. Deliberately kept in semi-isolation from the north by Britain from 1930, there had been loose talk of attaching it to East Africa, but nothing was done before it became clear that incorporating the south was part of the price of maintaining significant northern Sudanese political support for Britain. But it was done with little consultation with southerners who became ever more marginalized and aggrieved as independence approached. There were violent incidents in the region in 1955, though they served only to accelerate Britain's departure, leaving the south to its fate, but ensuring that Sudan as a whole would be independent in spite of the ambitions of the new radical regime under Gamal Abdel Nasser in Egypt.

It was at about this point that the US showed some slight interest in Sudan. Clearly the situation in the Middle East was causing concern with both Britain and Egypt under Farouk weakening. Having washed its hands of Palestine, Britain was in trouble in Egypt where it had a major military base on the Suez Canal. Anti-British feeling had helped to undermine the monarchy contributing to the Free Officers' coup of July 1952 that ended the dynasty Mohammed Ali had established. The US could see the problem and was not unhappy with the coup, though within three years it was to fall out significantly with Nasser and the Free Officers. But before that happened, the US also took the view that Egypt might be placated by Britain pulling out of Sudan, even if that heightened resentment in the south (Woodward, 1979).

However, US involvement at that time was a minor matter: more important developments were to take place once Sudan had attained independence. In domestic affairs post-independence Sudanese politics were to be dominated by the rivalries of the northern Sudanese parties leading to weak coalition governments; while promises of possible federation made to southerners were forgotten. In foreign affairs the major question remained that of relations with Egypt, which itself meddled constantly in Sudan's party politics. The US had opposed the British, French and Israeli collusion to invade Egypt in 1956 but subsequently grew concerned as the rise of Nasser's Egypt and pan-Arabism across the Middle East provided the opportunity for the Soviet Union to become involved by providing military and economic aid to a growing number of client states. By

1958 the Eisenhower doctrine had evolved by which American aid was available to states resisting links to the USSR. Whether to accept US aid had by then become the major issue of Sudanese politics with the Umma Party broadly in favour, while the Unionists continued to look towards Egypt and the doctrine of non-alignment being preached by Nasser. The US aid package was eventually accepted in July 1958, but only narrowly, and the divisions surrounding it contributed later that year to the first of what was to become a series of military coups in the country.

The new government of General Abboud seemed something of a compromise. Abboud did go on to improve relations with Egypt, most notably by a new Nile Waters Agreement linked to the building of the High Dam at Aswan and the creation of Lake Nasser which flooded much of Nubia including the far north of Sudan. But Abboud also had links to the Umma Party and was basically pro-Western and certainly not one of the eager young radicals who sought power in so much of the Middle East at that time. Thus the US felt comfortable in continuing its aid package mainly for transport infrastructure, agriculture and education. There was though growing disquiet at the development of civil war in the south from 1962 with guerrilla forces known as Anya-Nya emerging and the government seeking to crush the revolt. The war also triggered popular disturbances in Khartoum in 1964 that became known as the October Revolution and forced Abboud and his colleagues to retire from office. A year later Sudan returned to its old multi-party democracy, but the restored civilian leadership only intensified the war in the south.

Relations between the US and Sudan were however broken over the Six Day War of 1967. Though Sudan had little direct involvement in the most devastating of the Arab-Israeli wars, it sympathised with Nasser's plight and showed solidarity by breaking diplomatic relations with the US based on the Egyptian allegations of American aid to Israel in the conflict. Sudan went on to host the Khartoum summit at which the famous 'three noes' were agreed: no peace treaty with Israel; no negotiations with Israel; and no recognition of the state of Israel. But after its moment of fame Sudan returned to its own usual problems of competing northern parties and civil war in the south; few were surprised at the coup of 1969 that brought Jaafar Nimeiri to power. Nimeiri's coup brought a new direction: encouraged by the well organized Sudan Communist Party Nimeiri embarked on a socialist programme at home that saw sweeping nationalization. Of more concern to the West he also turned for assistance to the Soviet Union and soon military and economic aid was arriving. With Egypt still in the Soviet camp, the addition of Sudan to the ranks of its clients seemed a significant strategic gain.

However the course of Sudanese politics rarely runs smooth and two years later there was a major clash within the new regime. Nimeiri and some of his army colleagues were more Arab nationalists in Nasserite and Baathist moulds than communists and by 1971 the tensions were so great that the communists backed a coup against him. It failed when troops loyal to Nimeiri staged a counter coup during the course of which there was a good deal of blood letting. After the dust had settled it was clear that much had changed, including moves towards peace in the south at Addis Ababa in 1972 and a desire to re-open relations with the US The latter was willing to respond, though relations remained cool following the assassination of the new ambassador and his deputy by the Palestinian Black September group at a reception in the Saudi Arabian embassy in Khartoum in 1973. A recovery was made over the following years, and advances included oil prospecting rights for the American company Chevron that were finally to confirm the country's potential as an oil producer.

By the end of the 1970s developments had occurred relating to three of Sudan's eight neighbours that made Nimeiri's regime of particular importance to the US One was the Camp David agreement of 1979. This caused Nimeiri a great dilemma, for although he was close to Sadat and sympathized with the reasons for Egypt's signing, he was aware of the hostile Arab sentiment generally. In the end he took the chance of siding with Egypt along with only two other Arab states. The second factor underlining Nimeiri's importance was the installation of the Soviet Union as the major backer of Mengistu's regime in Ethiopia. Sudan took on a new strategic importance, together with Somalia on the opposite side of the USSR's new client. Third Libya was developing its designs on Chad, and via Chad on west and equatorial Africa generally. In the next few years Sudan was to become a major recipient of American aid in a world order that ran first Israel, second, Egypt, and third Sudan. It included military aid which, initially at least, bolstered Nimeiri within the armed forces; and it allowed covert US operations involving the US in Chad (with help from France and Egypt as well) and in Ethiopia (including operation Moses to 'rescue' Falasha – 'Black Jews' from Ethiopia) (Burr and Collins, 1999). Overall US support for Sudan was quite successful until about 1983, with Libya and Ethiopia contained, and Egypt's backdoor on the upper Nile kept shut. But into the 1980s there were to be setbacks as far as the US was concerned. In 1977 Nimeiri had achieved National Reconciliation with some of his northern critics who had been in opposition since he had seized power in 1969. The Umma Party leader, Sadiq al-Mahdi, was one and another was Hasan al-Turabi, leader of the growing Muslim Brotherhood. The latter was soon to become very influential and supported Nimeri's decision in 1983 to introduce *sharia*, which was vigorously applied in an attempt to cow an increasingly disaffected population. Popular feeling was itself fuelled by the failure of the bread basket strategy to expand Sudanese agriculture, largely based on Arab oil money, which had offered so much in the 1970s, and been replaced by the reality in the early 1980s of widespread famine in central Sudan, due not only to drought but also government inaction.

Disaffection was at its height amongst southern Sudanese who had seen the return of mainstream Muslim politicians from 1978, and amongst whose regional government in the south Nimeiri was deliberately creating trouble. It was widely believed that he was destroying the regional government in order to ensure his control of the new oil resources expected to come on tap and the new waters made available through the building with Egypt of the Jonglei Canal to circumvent the *sudd*. In 1983 civil war broke out again in the south, amidst rising discontent in the north. The US was generally horrified at this turn of events: *sharia* was regarded as a retrograde step; the famine pointed to the indifference and ineptitude of its ally (USAID stepped in to try to organize the numerous NGOs that flooded into the country); and civil war was a self-inflicted disaster, especially when attacks soon halted work on Chevron's new oil field, and the canal being built at Jonglei. America's Vice-President George Bush actually visited Sudan and was made aware of popular feeling shortly before Nimeiri was overthrown in 1985 (while in Cairo on his way back from Washington): some felt that it was more than a coincidence.

Following the overthrow of Nimeiri, Sudan returned to its familiar pattern of politics. There was an interim government for one year which was an uneasy alliance of senior military figures, who had readily ditched Nimeiri in his bloodless overthrow, and the leaders of the popular *intifada* (uprising) known as the National Alliance for National Salvation, during which little was achieved. It was followed by elections (except in the war affected areas of the south), and then a return to the old coalition governments, this time under the leadership of Sadiq al-Mahdi. As well as leading a series of unstable governments, Sadiq himself seemed congenitally indecisive. He had inherited *sharia* from Nimeiri, and though critical of its form he felt unable to repudiate it and return the country to more secular ways, even though it was a crucial aspect of peace. He did meet the southern leader, John Garang, but there was little sign of agreement and instead the war intensified with Sadiq arming local militias known as *murahaleen* in western Sudan, who were encouraged to raid into the south, raping and pillaging at will. In response the Sudan Peoples Liberation Army (SPLA) took the war to the north briefly seizing northern towns on the Ethiopian border. The war was central to the famine of 1988-1989 that was largely man made and led in turn to the establishment of an umbrella UN relief agency, Operation Lifeline Sudan (OLS). It was the first time that a UN programme delivered relief to both sides in a civil war; and it was to become the largest operation of its kind in the world and ran for many years. Meanwhile Sudan's economy continued to flounder with a major debt burden as a result of the bursting of the bubble of 1970s failed international investment.

US policy was in something of a dilemma (Anderson, 1999). Sudan's strategic significance in relation to the Soviet Union – meaning essentially Ethiopia – was in decline once Gorbachev had come to power in 1985 and begun the end of the Cold War. However there was still Libya, which Reagan's administration had demonized and bombed in 1986, after which the Libyan shooting of an American in Khartoum led to the rapid withdrawal of most US personnel from Sudan. Sadiq al-Mahdi had a particular connection to Libya that had supported his attempted coup ten years previously, though it was also an ambiguous relationship. Sadiq still talked of non-alignment and his relationship with Libya continued to concern America, while he in turn criticized the US for having supported Nimeiri for so long. In addition Sudan had returned to democracy which the US generally applauded, ever more loudly as the Cold War receded; while for all Sadiq's shortcomings there seemed no real alternative to his leadership and that of the Umma Party. In short there seemed little that the US could do, apart from voicing its continued frustration with both sides, though the famine of 1988-1989 heightened awareness and America's support for food aid via the establishment of OLS (Burr and Collins, 1995; Anderson, 1999).

Amidst Sadiq al-Mahdi's travails another movement had been growing that now saw that its moment was approaching. The Muslim Brotherhood in Sudan had started after World War II partly as an offshoot of the then powerful movement in Egypt, and partly in response to the growth of the sectarian-backed parties in Sudan and also the Sudan Communist Party, for many years the *bete noir* of the Brotherhood. It attracted a minority of students in particular, often those outside the mainstream of established party politics and hostile to the perceived secularism of the Communists. The Brotherhood first came to prominence after the return from London and Paris of the dynamic and ambitious Hasan al-Turabi. At the start of the October Revolution of 1964 that brought down Abboud Turabi was a leading figure. The following year he and four others from the Brotherhood were elected to parliament as the Islamic Charter Front where they soon raised a voice beyond their small number calling for an Islamic constitution. Nimeiri's coup of 1969 drove the Muslim Brothers into opposition and often exile, but they maintained their struggle until National Reconciliation in 1977. Turabi was then elevated into ministerial office becoming attorney general, a position he used to press for an Islamic constitution, and Nimeiri's decision to introduce *sharia* in 1983 was seen as a victory for the Brotherhood. Relations between Nimeiri and the Brotherhood deteriorated in the months before the former's downfall, but that only facilitated the Brotherhood's position as the country returned to democratic rule. It now emerged as the National Islamic Front (NIF or *jebha*- front- as it is often known) winning 51 seats in the elections of 1986. Under Sadiq al-Mahdi's rule the NIF was the third largest party behind the Umma and the Unionists and joined his coalitions, though out of power early in 1989 over possible compromises on *sharia* arising from efforts to make peace with the SPLA in the south.

Alongside this entry into political life, the Muslim Brotherhood/NIF had also been carrying out a programme of entryism since 1977 (El-Affendi, 1991). The student body had always been a good recruiting ground: attracted by ideology that had seen Arab nationalism and socialism fail, while Islamism had never yet had an opportunity to wield power. Always critical of whatever government was in power students could provide the foot soldiers of the movement. Another important point of growth was via Sudan's financial system. Islamism was a growing cause regionally and there was Arab money available especially with the oil price hikes of the 1970s. Islamic banking swept across the region, with Sudan seeing the founding in 1978 of the Faisal Islamic Bank, backed by Mohammed bin-Faisal, son of King Faisal of Saudi Arabia, and several other banks following. The Islamic banks were given important concessions that enhanced their competitiveness, and they in turn sought to build up the small business sector in the process creating a new body of supporters. With the support of the banks, members of the Brotherhood also made considerable advances in the press, from where they criticised and lampooned successive rulers (Simone, 1994). Another more covert area of activity was through the planting of sympathizers in various arms of the state, where they were often 'sleepers' waiting their moment to act. These included the army, long politicized and with various factions; and with indecisive and unstable parliamentary politics, as well as worsening war in the south, there was considerable speculation about a coup, though to what possible end was far from clear. From late 1988 there seemed a growing chance that Sadiq al-Mahdi would finally be pushed to renounce *sharia* for the sake of peace in the south. The NIF was now out of government and openly critical of such a move when on 30 June 1989 its sympathizers in the army struck and seized power in the name of the National Salvation Revolution.

Conclusion

US engagement with the Horn appeared to have gone full circle. The Cold War had largely brought it into the region, and with its ending interest appeared to be on the decline. In the course of the Cold War America and the USSR effectively played a game of checkers from Egypt in the north to Somalia in the south in which both had been aligned with Egypt, Sudan, Ethiopia and Somalia at different times: a unique record in international politics. Yet though the Cold War was over, there were continuing interests. The Horn continued to be strategically significant. While US troops were stationed in the Gulf, the Horn could be an important staging post; and there was still the need to keep the Red Sea open. The region was known to have oil reserves in which US companies might find opportunities in more propitious political circumstances. Also the humanitarian issues of the Horn would continue with varying intensity and cause concern around the world with calls for action of various kinds.

Though the interests were still present, there appeared no longer to be a focal point like the Cold War as the context in which US policy in the Horn would be pursued. In fact there was one potential focus incubating in the Cold War, and partly growing out of it, namely the question of Islamism. Its roots lay on the fringes of the Horn, in Egypt, Saudi Arabia and Iran, but all were linked to the Cold War and grew within the Middle Eastern context that it had helped to foster. The Muslim Brotherhood in Egypt had been repressed by the secular Arab socialism of Nasserism supported by the Soviet Union, but had both become more radical in the process and spread its ideas and organizational example to in the region, including Sudan. Saudi Arabia was a staunch ally of the US and fostered its own Islamic agenda partly to counter the regional challenge of Arab nationalism, and from the oil hikes of the 1970s had large reserves to back it. From the 1970s it and its smaller Gulf allies were pumping money for Islamic causes, including charitable activities, banking and business enterprises, into Sudan in particular, to a lesser extent into Somalia, and even supporting opposition forces in Ethiopia. Iran was a newer force emanating from the revolution of 1989 that had been in part the product of the relationship between that country and the US Though more distant from the Horn, the success of its revolution both spurred its own regional ambitions and gave a fresh impetus to Islamists in their own countries. The incubating Islamism, in the Horn and elsewhere, thus drew on old roots in Muslim societies, new ideological and organizational developments within them, and perceptions of the US as a major component of all aspects of their predicament nationally, regionally and globally.

References

Anderson, N. (1999), *Sudan in Crisis: The Failure of Democracy*, Gainesville, University Press of Florida.

Burr, J. and Collins, R. (1995), *Requiem for the Sudan: War, Drought and Disaster Relief on the Nile*, Boulder, Westview.

Burr, J. and Collins, R. (1999), *Africa's Thirty Years' War: Chad, Libya and the Sudan, 1963-1993*, Boulder, Westview.

Cohen, J. (2000), *Intervening in Africa: Superpower Peacemaking in a Troubled Continent*, Basingstoke, Palgrave.

El-Affendi, A. (1991), *Turabi's Revolution: Islam and Power in Sudan*, London, Grey Seal Books.

Korn, D. (1986), *Ethiopia, the United States and the Soviet Union*, London, Croom Helm.

Laitin, D. and Samatar, S. (1987), *Somalia: Nation in Search of a State*, Boulder, Westview.

Lewis, I. (1998), *Saints and Somalis; popular Isalm in a clan-based society*, London, Haan.

Lewis, I. (1999), *A Pastoral Democracy*, Oxford, Oxford University Press.

Samatar, S. (1991), *Somalia: A Nation in Turmoil*, London, Minority Rights Group.

Simone, A. (1994), *In Whose Image?: Political Islam and Urban Practices in Sudan*, Chicago, Chicago University Press.

Woodward, P. (1979), *Condominium and Sudanese Nationalism*, London, Rex Collings.

Chapter 3

Facing Sudan's Islamist Regime

Although it was not immediately recognized in the international community, the seizure of power by army officers in Sudan in June 1989 was more than just another coup. It was to reveal itself as the second country in the Muslim world (after Iran) in which Islamists had taken power. The Iranian revolution a decade earlier had been greeted as a far more significant event, not least because America's policeman of the Gulf, the *Shah*, had been overthrown. Any revolution that had achieved that, let alone an Islamist one, had to be taken seriously. Sudan may have appeared a less threatening place for Islamists to have taken power, but nonetheless it was important. The new rulers were the first Islamists to come to power in the *suni* Muslim world, a far larger branch of the religion than the *shia* of Iran; and they also saw themselves as an Arab regime rather than the more confined nationalism of Iran with its distinctive historic identity and tensions with Islam's Arab heartland.

Moreover there were few clear policy precedents to follow with regard to the changing world of Islam. The Iranian revolution had contributed significantly to the trials and tribulations of the Carter administration, and indeed to his electoral defeat. The Reagan administration had started with caution towards Iran but moved on to a degree of accommodation, though less from any change of assessment of the regime itself than a recognition of a common enemy in the USSR following the latter's invasion of Afghanistan in 1979. The same sentiment had also led to US cooperation with Islamists in the *mujahadin* fighting against the Soviet forces in Afghanistan itself. This struggle was largely conducted with the active assistance of Muslim Pakistan; while the US also maintained the closest of relationships with Saudi Arabia, the home of one of the most puritanical and militant strains of Islam.

Such pragmatic relations with the Muslim world and the lack of any consistent policy with regard to the Islamist trend, reflected deep seated uncertainties. One was how seriously to take the whole question of Islamism when compared with the threat posed by the USSR and the growth of the Second Cold War in the 1980s, besides which officials in Washington were 'largely perceiving the new Islamists as a mere nuisance rather than a serious threat' (Gerges, 1999, p.60)? A second uncertainty was that attitudes towards the Muslim world were divided. In policy making and surrounding circles, such as the think tanks and the academic establishment, there were sharply divergent voices. 'Confrontationists', as they were sometimes known, had been staking out their case of the dangers of the growing Islamist movement and the need to meet it head on, and they were to be reinforced by Huntington's development of his thesis of the 'Clash of

Civilizations'. At the same time there was also an 'accomodationist' view that saw the West and the Muslim world as closely intertwined and which believed that by greater mutual understanding and cooperation the roots of Islamism could be addressed and mutually advantageous advances made. When there were queries over the quantity and quality of intelligence it was understandable that it would be used in policy making, in part at least, on the basis of the practitioners' various outlooks towards Islam in general and Islamism in particular.

By the time of the Bush administration in 1989 the challenge to clarify its policy in practice lay less with the new regime in Sudan, than the success of the Islamic Salvation Front (FIS) in the Algerian elections of 1991. This success was swiftly crushed by the existing military regime, and its move was broadly accepted by the US Democracy might have been generally favoured in Washington, but in the Muslim world could hand power to people whose commitment to it once in power was far from assured. From this was to emerge a general view that Islam should not be the new demonized 'ism' now that Marxism-Leninism was virtually dead, but rather that a distinction had to be made in practice between 'good' and 'bad' Muslims. The former were essentially allies of the US, and in the crucial Middle East that meant governments such as those in Egypt and Saudi Arabia; while the latter were predominantly the Islamists who appeared to hold anti-Westernism as part of their increasingly active and challenging ideology.[1] However, there was no clear foreign policy formulation that resulted from such an analysis, rather policy consisted largely of reacting to events in and emanating from the Muslim world. This brought assessment of policy from the realm of Islam in general down to particular developments in particular places; and that in practice was often to lead to conflicting views and policy making tensions, based less on general approaches than assessment of the particular situation and especially how 'good' or 'bad' the Muslims involved might be.

Islamists in Power: Sudan

At the time of the coup in Sudan in 1989 it was by no means clear what the consequences would be. While the Muslim Brotherhood was clearly well organized and had prepared its ground, ideologically it was far from certain what policies it would pursue, because the movement had never published a full and coherent programme before seizing power. Rather, its thinking had been deduced largely from the scattered writings and speeches of its leader, Hasan al-Turabi. While influenced by modern Islamic thinkers such as Hasan al-Banna and Abu al-Mawdudi, Turabi had always argued that intellectuals themselves, from whatever disciplinary background, should develop their own understanding of Islam, working from the application of the first principles of the Quran and sunna to the context of the modern world. He was thus dismissive of appointed and official *ulama* (religious scholars), who he believed had been weak in Sudan; nor did he follow one of the long-standing Islamic schools of law. What he had to say before 1989 was generally regarded as liberal and, according to some of his critics, even heretical (Niblock, 1991). His support for multiparty liberal democracy appeared clear in the 1986 elections (in which the other parties conspired to ensure that he did not win a seat), though later he was to develop more ambiguous interpretations centred around interpretation of *shura* (consultation).[2] However, as one of Turabi's followers made clear before the coup of 1989, far from relying on the long march of liberal democracy and/or *shura* to achieve eventual power, the NIF leaders were preparing 'to make a bid to control the state and impose their norms on society and hoped to succeed where their opponents had failed by defining a new Sudanese community based on Islam' (El-Affendi, 1991, p.163). It is in this light that the developments in Sudan after 1989 must be seen.

The NIF-backed military rulers practiced a form of vanguardism that had a number of dimensions. The first was the transformation of the state itself. The army was extensively purged after it had seized power, with up to 40 per cent of the officer corps dismissed (about 2,000 men). Attempted coups were ruthlessly crushed, although intermittent reports of unrest in the army persisted. At the same time a number of new security networks were established that appeared at times to be a law unto themselves, and an atmosphere of suspicion and repression was developed. Arbitrary detention and torture leading to mutilation and even death were authoritatively recorded by Sudanese and international human rights organizations, including the Sudan Human Rights Organization (SHRO) (which was itself forced into exile), Amnesty International, and the UN. In addition, the regime established its own Islamic force, the Popular Defense Force (PDF), numbering up to 150,000, to defend the National Salvation Revolution. PDF training was made compulsory for higher education candidates and for civil servants. The PDF was to supply fighters for the war in the south, and it would also be a potential counterweight to the army in the event of trouble from the ranks of the latter. The judiciary, the civil service, and educational institutions all saw extensive resignations and purges as the regime sought to impose its Islamism in all branches of the state.

Formal changes were also made in the political system. The NIF's commitment to the *sharia* was fulfilled with a revised version of the 1983 laws being introduced in 1991. Federalism also was adopted, with the number of regional states rising to 26, though with effective NIF control of top appointments in all states. A 'no-party' parliamentary system of a pyramidal character was established, inspired by the Libyan model, with power supposedly flowing up through the local councils and the states to the National Assembly. At the top, the Revolutionary Command Council (RCC) of military officers set up in 1989 was dissolved in 1993, and Omer al-Beshir was formally made president: however, most of the former RCC were given seats in the cabinet which was dominated by the NIF. At the same time, it was widely believed that the formal structure of government hid the real core of power: that was to be found in an NIF group known as the Committee of Forty, Chaired by Ali Osman Taha, former Deputy Secretary-General of the NIF who was later to become Vice-President. In practice, decisions were taken by a small clique within it, and for several years it was thought that the most influential figure in the general direction of events, if not necessarily detailed policy, remained Hasan al-Turabi operating largely as an *eminence grise*. In 1996 he was elected Speaker of the National Assembly, a post that he sought to turn into a major power base.

In urban and rural areas, Popular Committees were set up to operate in parallel with the local administration. Their significant powers included distributing rationed goods and acting as surveillance networks; and under their aegis, a plethora of local groups were encouraged, including organizations for women and youth and various Islamic groups. These activities were formally managed by the new Ministry of Social Planning, headed by Ali Osman Taha, which set out to achieve nothing less than the re-shaping of the Islamic character of the country. Under the guidance of the ministry, Islamic NGOs such as the Islamic Jihad Dawa, the Association of Southern Muslims, the Society for Enjoining Good and Speaking Against Evil, and the Islamic Africa Relief Agency, appeared in many areas of the country, rural as well as urban. Such activities contributed to the wider goal of Islamic renewal that sought to recapture the allegedly more authentic traditions of Islam in Sudan before they had become overlain and corrupted with the superstitions and other-worldliness of Sufism. This Islamic renewal had, in Turabi's view, to be central to the broader Muslim community, the *umma*, in the modern world. There was also a major drive toward Arabization and Islamization of education at all levels. New colleges and universities opened, but resources were severely limited while political control was tight less the student body pose a challenge to the new regime. In spite of Turabi's past comments on female emancipation, there was a crackdown on women at work in the name of defending an Islamic conception of the family, and the numbers of women active in the professions dropped sharply. A conservative dress code for professional women and students was enforced, and the free movement of women was restricted.

The NIF also pressed on with its economic penetration that had begun before 1989. Islamic banks, and NIF dominance of the business sector both grew (Shaaeldin and Brown, 1991). In addition to supporting more small businessmen the old interests of Umma and Unionist party supporters were targeted for various forms of adverse discrimination. At the same time the previously free press (into which the NIF had also been buying before the 1989 coup) as well as the national radio and television networks, were commandeered and used for propaganda purposes. And when, in spite of liberalization measures, international credit to Sudan was restricted as a result of Sudan's indebtedness and failure to reach agreement with the IMF, the regime turned to Arab sympathizers as well as to Asia, with countries such as Malaysia and China welcoming the new opportunities that were available. One American journalist was to describe the emerging picture as, 'An ingenuous hybrid between a theocracy and a Mafia Syndicate' (*New York Times*, 3 March 1996, quoted in Khalid, 2003, p.207).

The state was thus seeking to re-make all areas of civil society, and this included a sustained attack on those often referred to in Sudan as the 'modern forces': the professional organizations and the trade unions that had long been regarded as relatively developed and dynamic, having played a leading part in the popular revolts against military rule in 1964 and 1985. Perceived by the NIF as bastions of Western liberal standards or, worse, as communists and Baathists of various hues, the modern forces constituted the major ideological challenges to the new regime and had long contributed to a relatively free, pluralistic, and tolerant atmosphere in the country. In addition to dismissal and detention, many thousands of professionals and others went into exile, together with many former politicians. In their place, the regime encouraged alternative bodies, often claiming that they were independent organizations.

The extent of the success of this attempt at social engineering has been questioned. Though research activities were controlled, studies that have been done suggest that the impact was limited if not sometimes negative. A study of the Islamization programme in the burgeoning shanty towns around Khartoum and findings from rural Upper Blue Nile indicate that society was not as malleable as the new regime appeared to believe (Simone, 1994; De Waal, 2004, pp.90-7). After 1992, there were also regular reports of anti-government demonstrations in a number of urban centres generally as a response to the declining living conditions of the majority, though these were contained by the well-trained security forces often with loss of life. The demonstrations of September 1995 were the largest since the overthrow of Nimeiri ten years previously. As indicated, many left the country, especially those with professional skills; however, the opposition in exile appeared disunited and apparently incapable of organizing a major challenge from outside.

The trigger for the coup of 1989 had been the possibility of a peace agreement with the south that could have brought the end of *sharia* in the country; thus the question of the south was a major part of the NIF agenda once in power. The Islamists saw the war as not only inevitable, in view of their intention to build an Islamic state, but a reflection of the fact that the south was not merely non-Muslim but actually had evolved an identity that was anti-Muslim as a result of the activities of Christian missionaries. Thus pushing a programme of Islamization, and also Arabization, on southerners was a necessary move to seek to win back lost Sudanese brothers (El-Affendi, 1990). Under the NIF Sudan was becoming more polarized and war instead of halting intensified.

The conflict largely intensified because the NIF had hopes of victory. The regime threw all that it had into the war, including the PDF, who often became its front line forces indeed sometimes its cannon fodder. Not that that was a suffering since the NIF made much of a cult of *jihad*. *Jihad* is capable of wide interpretation from appropriate effort in any particular sphere to a call to arms and war (De Waal, 2004, pp. 21-70). The new military rulers certainly made the most of its extreme interpretation, and linked it also to martyrdom. Thus as the casualties mounted the slain on the government side were hailed as martyrs and their families enjoined to rejoice in their status and the glories of the after life, though few appeared to share the enthusiasm for death of their new rulers. The glorification of war also led to accusations of ethnic cleansing and deliberate rape of women in Nuba Mountains and Bahr al-Ghazal in particular. However on the battlefield all did not go the way of the government and after initial successes they encountered setbacks by 1994; and much of the thrust and fervour the government had endeavoured to arouse after

1989 receded into the routines of the long and brutal conflict. In spite of this the government remained reluctant to take peace talks seriously, though under pressure various attempts were made.

The US Response to Sudan's Domestic Developments

The NIF may have laid plans well before 1989, but the US was not prepared for the new regime, nor had there been much reason to have been. The US had focused for years on the Cold War and was struggling to adjust its understanding of, and organization for, the new world. In so far as a policy towards Sudan emerged, it inevitably began as a matter of playing catch-up with the developments outlined above. At first there had even been some hope in the coup of 1989. Herman Cohen, Assistant Secretary of State for Africa, records that, 'An audible sigh of relief rippled through the Africanist community in the US government, welcoming the departure of Sadiq's hopelessly inept regime' (Cohen, 2000, p.65).[3] The US was also impressed that its close ally Egypt initially welcomed the coup, believing that it was essentially a new military regime (rather than NIF-dominated) and that Egypt would be able to work with it. Apart from claiming to know the new ruling officers, in its many years of involvement in Sudan successive military-backed governments in Egypt have generally found it more congenial to work with counterpart military regimes than the confused party politics of the democratic eras. Among those in the US State Department concerned with the Muslim world there were some who expressed an interest, if not some sympathy, for the ideas of Turabi. He was seen by them as a genuinely new and liberal thinker with growing respect across the Muslim world. For his part Turabi visited the US in 1992 and used honeyed – though challenging – words, even being invited to appear before a Congressional committee. At one think tank he was critical of what he saw as Western dominance remarking that it was necessary, 'To correct the equation on which on which the world order is based ...We are sharing this world ... We would like the West to surrender something' (*Public Diplomatic Query*, 13 May 1992).[4] However, such initial hopes as there were in the US became increasingly dissipated in the face of the developments mentioned above. There was also uncertainty about Turabi's position in the power structure, especially his relationship with President Beshir who had led the actual coup of 1989, and of consequent divisions and struggles, but by the end of 1993 the US embassy in Khartoum at least recognized him as the primary figure in the regime (Petterson, 1999, p. 85).

While there had been American criticism of Sadiq al-Mahdi's governments from 1986-1989, they were at least elected governments. Under US law the very fact of a military coup meant that there could be no American development aid to such a regime and it was immediately stopped: only specific executive action to override the legal ban could have maintained it, and in view of the way the new regime was emerging that was highly unlikely. However humanitarian aid continued to flow. Indeed humanitarian aid was a particular concern and occasional excursions by journalists into southern Sudan brought horrific images that surfaced briefly in US and international news media.[5] The US continued to be the major supplier of food aid. It was the primary responsibility of the Office of Foreign Disaster Assistance and USAID, and much of it was delivered via the UN's Operation Lifeline Sudan (OLS), the largest UN humanitarian operation in the world that had started in 1989 (Karim et al, 1996). USAID's involvement in southern Sudan in particular helped to shape attitudes in Washington. OLS became in practice divided into two parts: the north, where it effectively came under government control; and the south, where in the name of the UN it was influenced by USAID and associated NGOs. USAID's experience highlighted the intensifying horror of the south, and thus added a particular dimension to appreciation in the US of developments in Sudan as a whole, not only in government circles but also in many humanitarian groups. However, there were some in America who feared that in practice the provision of food aid to such a war torn country was also reaching the parties to the conflict thus prolonging the suffering and perhaps even strengthening the combatants.

The ending of democracy in Sudan for the third time led to a return to military government that was a particular concern to the US following the end of the Cold War and the perceived triumph of a liberal-democratic order that many believed should be actively spread. The loss of liberal democracy was in turn closely linked to the abuse of human rights across the board. While Sudan had never had a good record on human rights, the situation deteriorated rapidly after 1989 and was a constant refrain in US representations. The situation was being monitored by international human rights organizations, and the issue was taken up periodically in Congress. This concern extended from the detention and torture of many members of the elite, through to the inhumane treatment of the hundreds of thousands of internally displaced people, many in shanties around the capital itself. Particular concern was expressed following the summary execution of local staff working for USAID in Juba, capital of the south, in September 1992. Almost immediately the Congress passed a Joint Resolution condemning the Sudan government and called on the State Department to seek a UN meeting to discuss the situation. In May 1993 feeling had risen to a point where there was an overwhelming Senate resolution condemning abuses of all kinds by both the government and the SPLA, and it was supported by the House of Representatives as well. Feeling in Congress indicated that while human rights abuses were carried out by both sides, the government was more to be condemned since it was seen by then as the more aggressive side in the conflict. The resolution also called for the expansion of US humanitarian relief in the south as well as for a UN special representative for Sudan. In response the administration did introduce such a UN resolution and pushed its adoption strongly. It was critical of all parties to abuses in Sudan and led to the appointment of the UN Special Representative for the country to investigate the situation on the ground. At the same time the US stressed that its stance was not anti-Muslim as such. George Moose, the new Assistant Secretary of State for Africa, testified that the government's:

Islamic orientation is not an issue. Our objection, rather, is to a state-sponsored effort to impose a specific religion and religious law, and to use religious criteria as a standard for higher education and government positions. These policies result in the violation of basic human rights.[6]

By implication the NIF was an example of a 'bad' Muslim regime. However, though some action had been taken, there was not yet the concern in government or non-government organizations in the US that Sudan was a significant threat.

There was, though, sufficient commitment for the US to support peace making in the civil war. Post-Cold War US policy towards Africa had a particular focus on conflict, and especially the large on-going wars in Ethiopia, Angola, Mozambique and Sudan. While Angola had top priority for the State Department, the pressure from Congress as a result of the war-related humanitarian suffering and growing allegations of slavery in Sudan meant that that country had the early attention of Cohen, following his appointment as Assistant Secretary by the incoming Bush administration in 1989. Following the success of his predecessor Chester Crocker with 'constructive engagement' in southern Africa, Cohen used the same term for his efforts to move peace forward in Sudan. Cohen himself appeared to favour a regional approach to peace in Sudan. This fitted with his involvement in the establishment of the new order in Ethiopia in which there was both the independence of Eritrea, and a new regional constitution in Ethiopia itself often known as 'ethnic federalism'. Speaking with a delegation from a northern Sudanese opposition movement in Washington in 1992, Cohen was reported to have said that should Sudan eventually be divided, that would be an outcome that would be acceptable to the US (*Indian Ocean Newsletter*, 12 September 1992). Later, appearing before the House Sub-Committee on Africa, he was to suggest the possibility that if there was no peace agreement in Sudan, there might be UN action to create a safe haven in southern Sudan, comparable to that established for the Kurds in northern Iraq (*Indian Ocean Newsletter*, 10 March 1993). Such remarks understandably made the Sudan government wonder about the possibility of outside intervention of some kind in the country.

From 1989 both Cohen and former president Jimmy Carter tried separately to bring about peace in the south. Within weeks of the coup feelers towards peace talks were emerging and it was notable that on balance Cohen depicted Garang and the SPLA as more openly intransigent than Beshir and the Sudan government (Cohen, 2000 pp. 68-85). At least that was how it appeared to him in the personal dealings with the two men that he sustained in the hope of a peace process starting, but since serious head-to-head negotiations never took place from his initiative this may have had more to do with style and appearance than reality. The possibility of serious talks was complicated on the government's side by its decision, after internal wrangling, to side with Iraq in the Gulf conflict of 1991; and on the SPLA's side by a split in its ranks a few months later in July 1991 that was to see the emergence of a new faction, SPLA United, led by Riek Machar (possibly with Sudan government connivance). It was to lead to the beginning of serious south-

south conflict, often with ethnic dimensions. In 1993 the Congressional Select Committee on Hunger even invited the SPLA and Machar's faction to Washington to try to reconcile them, but to no avail. The split in the SPLA in 1991 and the downfall of Mengistu's regime in Ethiopia in the same year that had backed the SPLA meant that the Sudan government believed that the time was propitious for a military victory. Nevertheless, there was a succession of peace talks, often in response to outside pressure, as with the attempts of Jimmy Carter and the talks in Abuja hosted by Nigeria; but there was little seriousness, especially on the government side (Wondu and Lesch, 2000). In 1994 USAID launched its Greater Horn Initiative to promote regional development including, 'crisis prevention, response and conflict resolution'. It admitted that regional organizations were weak but nevertheless backed the then moribund Inter-Governmental Authority for Drought and Development (IGADD) as a potential vehicle. In the same year the US appointed a special envoy, Ambassador Melissa Wells, to seek to facilitate the new IGAD peace process. Her appointment, rather than that of one of the higher profile names canvassed, such as Senator George McGovern and Congressman Steven Solarz, was an indication that Sudan was still well down the US agenda and she made little impact. Cohen remarks that given the failure in successive talks, and the ever more critical view of the Sudan government in Washington, 'We flirted with the idea of providing assistance to the SPLA but backed away because of the inter-factional fighting and the SPLA's reported human rights violations' (Cohen, 2000, p.82).[7] However though the IGAD talks were unsuccessful at the time they resulted in IGAD outlining a Declaration of Principles (DoP) that was to be of lasting significance. The core of the DoP lay in peace through agreement on a secular Sudan, or failing that acceptance of the right of self-determination for the south that could result in secession.

In an interesting *mea culpa* Cohen was later to reflect upon those efforts at peace and wonder whether the US had gone about it the right way (Cohen, 2000, pp.83-5). In particular the relationship between conflict resolution and humanitarian concern had long been confused, since in practice some relief supplies were siphoned off by both sides thus sustaining the conflict however virtuous the intent may have been in providing it. 'We could have limited ourselves to the humanitarian side and left conflict resolution to others such as the UN or the OAU. Or we could have worked only the conflict resolution side, leaving the humanitarian issues to the multilateral agencies and the NGOs' (Cohen, 2000, p.85). Cohen also felt that perhaps direct talks between the two leaders shortly after the 1989 coup should have been pushed further, 'In retrospect, we should have insisted more strongly that Garang accept Beshir's offer of direct government-to-SPLA negotiations'.

International Dimensions of Islamism

If Sudan's Islamist regime had been content to confine its activities to the domestic scene it would have been disliked by the US but not seen as a significant danger.

However it regarded itself as revolutionary, and like many such regimes an active foreign policy was part and parcel of its *raison d'etre*. The legitimacy of such a regime in the eyes of its followers depended in part on its being the standard bearer of the revolution abroad as well as at home. At the same time an active foreign policy strengthened the regime's self-identity by showing the world that it was an example for others. In addition ideological regimes generally tend towards Manichean views with the enemy identified not just at home but abroad as well. In short traditional realism in international relations was not enough for a regime of this nature (Armstrong, 1993). It was the activities arising from this revolutionary agenda that the US came in time to see as a real threat to its interests in both the Middle East and Africa. To determine how Sudan's attempt to build an Islamic state relates to the country's external environment, it is useful first to review once more the thinking of Hasan al-Turabi.

Muslims, he believed, should relate to each other at a number of levels; from households and local communities to their country and to *dar al-Islam*, the Muslim Commonwealth. This was not to be regarded as a monolithic structure but as the entity to which Muslims aspire (and that can incorporate non-Muslims, as has always been required by Islam). The last great pan-Islamic enterprise, the Ottoman Empire, had finally succumbed to the 'onslaught of European imperialism', which had also disestablished the *sharia*. However, pan-Islamism had been growing from the outset of that experience in the form of such developments as the revolt of Ahmed al-Mahdi and the teaching of Jamal al-Din al-Afghani. Later came movements such as the Muslim Brotherhood in Egypt and Jamaat-i Islami in the Indian subcontinent. However, in much of the Muslim world, imperialism had given way to a model of the nation-state that Turabi regarded as having been a 'resounding failure'. Nationalism and a range of other secular ideologies had all proven unsuccessful and left deep disillusionment. That was the context in which Islamic revivalism had developed throughout the Muslim world to challenge the failure of the 'national enterprise', the driving force of Westphalian international relations. True, the Organization of the Islamic Conference (OIC) had been established, but it was led by states that remained manipulated by the West (as exemplified during the Gulf War) and was seen as 'politically impotent and totally unrepresentative of the true spirit of the community that animates the Muslim people'. Instead of remaining within that framework, 'as Muslims tend towards their common ideals, they would per force move towards closer unity; and that would undermine the moral foundation and the positive structures of the present national state'. Instead of this being achieved by force, it would come from the bottom up: 'However once a single fully-fledged Islamic state is established, the model would radiate throughout the Muslim world', and it would become 'a focus of pan-Islamic attention and affection'. Turabi declared that he believed that Sudan was in the process of becoming such a beacon and that the country was being led in the right direction by the revolutionary government.[8]

Turabi's views were not just talk. Even before the coup he had been involved in a putative international organization, and in April 1991 the Popular Arab and Islamic Conference (PAIC) was established in Khartoum. The timing was directly related to the Gulf War to liberate Kuwait from Iraq that had taken place shortly before as the organizers felt that the time was ripe to seek the mobilization of pan-Islamists across the Muslim world in the face of the demonstration of Western might and the collaboration of many Arab governments with the US and Israel. Some 200 representatives of the pan-Islamic movement from 45 countries attended together with 300 Sudanese, and Turabi was duly installed as secretary-general. It was funded by private donors and was thought to have Iranian backing as well since Turabi was anxious to unite *suni* and *shia* Muslims. In December 1993 a second conference was held at which Pakistan, then backing the rise of the Taliban in neighbouring Afghanistan, was strongly represented. The major outcome of the conferences was networking amongst the Islamist groups that participated, and many of those connections were to remain obscure but to become relevant to activities in various areas of conflict as the decade unfolded. As well as bringing the Islamists to the centre of his web in Khartoum, Turabi also travelled widely to promote the cause. His activities, however, were not always appreciated in other Muslim countries, and as a mark of their concern the OIC in 1992 cancelled a meeting of foreign ministers of Islamic states to be held in Khartoum following which Sudan broke with the OIC though it later re-joined.

The PAIC's activities did not stop at the Muslim world. It was in keeping with Turabi's expressed views that he, as its secretary-general, should seek to enter into dialogue with the West, and particularly with Christian churches. Talks with British and US government officials in 1992 had not achieved much progress, but with the Vatican relations grew and in 1993 diplomatic relations were established. From the Vatican's perspective, it was doubtless a means to try to help Catholics in Sudan. However, an attempt to achieve a similar rapprochement with the Anglican Church proved less successful.

While Turabi liked to project himself to the West as a man of peace seeking to reconcile Islam and Christianity, the PAIC was providing a catalyst for the growth of armed movements. In this the timing was perfect for there were hundreds of 'Afghans' available for recruitment. In the war waged by the *mujahadin* guerrillas in Afghanistan against the Soviet-backed government, there had been many volunteers from the Arab and Muslim world who had mainly been trained in Pakistan by the local security forces and the CIA. With the war over many were rootless with strong Islamist commitments and a reluctance to return to their home countries which they often regarded as in the hands of repressive and unIslamic governments. For some Sudan was the one place to welcome them when there was nowhere else to go; for others it offered a base from which they were encouraged and aided in their attempts at armed confrontation with the governments in power in their countries of origin. Sudan was keen to attract these 'brothers in Islam' as they were known, admitting them without visas, and distributing Sudanese diplomatic passports when required. Once in Sudan, as well as planning activities abroad they were used to train and lead in battle Sudanese forces, especially the PDF in the war in the south. The secret training camps established worked with men from a variety of groups from across the region. They included: Hizbollah of Lebanon; Islamic Jihad from Egypt; Hamas, the Popular

Front for the Liberation of Palestine (PFLP) and the Palestine Liberation Organization (PLO); the Islamic Salvation Front (FIS) from Algeria; al-Nahda from Tunisia; as well as dissidents from Eritrea, Yemen, Libya and Saudi Arabia.[9] There were also freelance groups and individuals such as Abu Nidal and Ilich Ramirez Sanchez, better known as Carlos the Jackal, though the latter was handed over to France in a murky deal in 1994.[10]

Less well known at the time than the above groups was an organization called al-Qaeda led by Osama bin Laden. Bin Laden, the son of a Yemeni who had made a fortune in the construction business in Saudi Arabia, had joined the 'Afghans' and established al-Qaeda (the base) whilst he was in Pakistan. However with the end of the war in Afghanistan there was uncertainty how to proceed. Following the Gulf War of 1990-1991, bin Laden had protested to the Saudi authorities at the stationing of US troops on Saudi soil, and offered to raise an 'Afghan' force instead, but to no avail: the Saudis had no wish to house a new radical Islamist force, much to bin Laden's disgust. After the coup in Sudan in 1989 Turabi and a small NIF delegation had visited bin Laden and persuaded him that following success against the Soviet Union, the international Islamist movement could take on the US, thus in 1991 bin Laden and some 500 of his followers made their headquarters in Khartoum.

Once in Sudan al-Qaeda continued with its international organization and activities, including training camps and the shipping of arms to Islamist groups around the world. It also worked closely with Sudanese security on a number of projects including experiments for the manufacture of chemical weapons. Bin Laden also helped with financial arrangements for the Islamist movement, especially following the collapse in 1991 of the Bank of Credit and Commerce International (BCCI) that the network had relied upon heavily hitherto. A new bank, al-Shamal, was established in which bin Laden invested $1 million, and he also became involved in a variety of business ventures with some 30 companies in Sudan in activities that ranged from agriculture to road construction. In all, he was creating a 'hybrid capitalist-terrorist network' (Benjamin and Simon, 2002). He also mixed socially with the NIF leaders and took as his third wife a niece of Turabi, though he was not well known in the country more generally. In 1994 there was an assassination attempt on him, allegedly involving Saudi Arabia, and in the same year he was stripped of his Saudi nationality and cut off from the country as a result of al-Qaeda activities there. Following that attempt he kept an even lower profile in Sudan, though he continued with his activities and, 'Without Sudan bin Laden could not have incubated the networks that … caused such devastation in subsequent years' (Lesch, *Current History*, May 2002, pp. 203-9). Pigeons were coming home to roost: 'With hindsight, the US-backed Islamic guerrillas in Afghanistan would come to haunt the United States and it allies' (Gerges, 1999, p.71).

In Sudan's global outlook, the NIF felt particular responsibility for developing its Islamist program in its African neighbors. Most of these had significant Muslim communities, but they generally lacked the militancy and level of activity of the groups targeting the Middle East. They now had to be mobilized as a new part of the worldwide movement whose aim, according to Turabi, was no less than the creation of linked Muslim countries stretching from north Africa to the Indian Ocean. One of the most obvious areas for action was in Sudan's eastern neighbors, Eritrea and Ethiopia. Since the early 1960s, Sudan had been host to Eritrean liberation movements (as well as refugees). Later, the Eritrean People's Liberation Front (EPLF) assisted the formation of the Tigrean People's Liberation Front (TPLF). Sudanese security helped both these movements in the final assaults on the regime of Mengistu Haile Mariam, which resulted in his downfall in 1991 and led to the formation of the independent state of Eritrea and the establishment of governments both there and in Ethiopia based on the former liberation fronts. The core groups in the interim governments in both Ethiopia and Eritrea consisted of former leftists who were still secularist in outlook and came from the traditionally Coptic Christian areas of northern Tigre on either side of the new international border.

These African neighbors were not only a convenient target for Sudan but also useful in the fight against the West and Israel since these enemies had long recognized the Horn's strategic importance. Sudan's attention was to focus on support for terrorism, while throughout the region there was also a good deal of activity by Islamic charitable organizations that were always a vital part of the movement as a whole and which, wittingly or not, were sometimes connected to the violent activities. At the first PAIC conference it was agreed to aid Oromiyyah Islamiyyah among the Oromo community in Ethiopia and Jihad Eritrea among the Muslims of western Eritrea. This provoked understandable alarm within the new governments and even public denunciation by Eritrean leader Issayas Afwerki. Tensions rose until in 1994 diplomatic relations with Sudan were broken, after which Eritrea called openly for the overthrow of the regime in Khartoum and even handed over the empty Sudanese embassy to the opposition movement. With regard to Ethiopia the situation was initially somewhat different: for Sudan maintaining relations with the new government took precedence over being actively committed to the Islamists since the Sudanese army was initially allowed access to western Ethiopia which facilitated its attack on SPLA positions in eastern Equatoria. However, as with Eritrea, relations with Ethiopia deteriorated with the attacks of Islamist movements in the regions, in particular in Oromia and Ogaden, and even terrorist incidents in Addis Ababa itself. Somalia was a third area of the Horn targeted by Islamists, as will be seen in the following chapter.

On Sudan's southern flank, the situations in Kenya and Uganda were also important. The fall of Mengistu in Ethiopia had the immediate impact of weakening the SPLA: it lost its major source of supplies, fragmented into competing factions, and suffered a series of reverses at the hands of government forces (Nyaba, 1997). This made the main SPLA faction (John Garang's 'Mainstream' as it was often called) more dependent on East Africa, where there had long been a natural sympathy for southern Sudan's 'African' fighters struggling against the forces of Islamism and Arabism. The continued supplies to the SPLA came to depend largely on the friendship of these two states, especially Uganda. Sudan in return sought to exert diplomatic pressure and threatened to encourage the Muslim minorities in both countries. In Uganda the Tabliq Youth movement was active and carried out terrorist acts around the country; while Sudan was also accused of supporting the 'Christian' Lord's Resistance Army (LRA), terrorizing the north of the country (Woodward, 2002).

While the NIF saw Africa as a new area of activity, the Middle East was also central to its concern. The PAIC was about 'Arabism' and Islamism', and Sudan's new rulers did little to acknowledge their country's 'African' south, but they did see its role as linking developments in the Middle East with East Africa. One such link was the war in the south, in which the NIF looked for the assistance of certain Middle Eastern countries. The first country to which Sudan turned was Iraq, but it did so less for Islamist ideological reasons than for Arab solidarity in the face of the SPLA's threat to the 'Arab' north. Iraq, having just ended the long war with Iran, was in a position to supply much-needed arms, and Saddam Hussein was keen to promote himself in the Arab world generally. The link had begun before 1989 and contributed to Sudan being one of the few states in the Middle East that refused to condemn Iraq's invasion of Kuwait, and continued to support it during the subsequent Gulf War of 1990-1991. After the war Iraq was in less of a position to support Sudan, while most Arab states were critical of its stance: Kuwait and some of the Gulf Arab states cut aid as a punishment and expelled numbers of Sudanese working there.

While support from Iraq declined relations with Iraq's former enemy Iran grew strongly. As the first Islamic revolution of the modern era Iran appeared to be an obvious ally for Sudan from 1989; however, while the Sudanese Muslim Brothers recognized the Iranian revolution, they had also had their criticisms of it. In particular, as indicated, Turabi's concept of an Islamic state was not of a theocracy run by mullahs. Indeed, those to whom he felt closest had been the leaders of the Iran Freedom Movement, who were crushed as the revolution unfolded (El-Affendi, 1991, p.146). However, shortly after seizing power the NIF had started to woo Iran, with Turabi providing the ideological justification that the Islamist movement embraced *suni* and *shia* alike; whilst Iran proved willing to assist Sudan in its post-Gulf War isolation. From Iran's standpoint, it was an opportunity to demonstrate a continued commitment to Islamism, which was appealing to most militant elements within the regime. In addition, having supported Islamist groups in the Middle East through the arms and training provided by Hizbollah in Lebanon, Iran now saw a chance to use Sudan for the penetration of Africa's Muslim communities that had always been one of the revolution's objectives. The growing relationship led to President Rasfanjani visiting Sudan in 1991.

Iran, like Iraq before it, had weapons to spare after the years of war; and it also financed deliveries of new equipment to Sudan from China. There were also military instructors with experience from the Iraq war and Afghanistan. In 1993 Sudan's armed forces and police were reorganized along the lines of the Iranian security forces, and there was talk in international circles of a 'Khartoum-Tehran axis' that was training and sending Islamist terrorists to various fronts, from Bosnia in the north to Somalia in the south. However, Iran had its own domestic problems and a declining economy; and by 1994 enthusiasm for struggling Sudan was waning.

Improved relations with Iran in the early 1990s inevitably brought tension for Sudan with Saudi Arabia, an implacable opponent of the *shiite* revolution, even though Saudi Arabia had been for years a backer of the Islamist movement in Sudan. In part, this had been to contain the influence of Egypt, especially in the late 1970s, when Saudi Arabia's oil wealth was deployed to contain the spread of Egyptian influence in the Nile Valley. From National Reconciliation in Sudan in 1977, money flowed to the Islamists from Saudi Arabia and the smaller Gulf states, most obviously to the Islamic banks. However, after 1989, there was growing concern. Saudi Arabia presented itself as an Islamic state but now found it was increasingly castigated particularly for its relations with the US Matters came to a head with Sudan's attitude toward the Gulf War, after which Saudi aid was sharply reduced and many of the numerous expatriate Sudanese in the country were expelled. Then there were the activities of bin Laden and al-Qaeda. There were a number of attacks in the Kingdom itself and though al-Qaeda claimed no credit publicly, privately it was seen as the perpetrator through its Saudi supporters. In response Saudi Arabia regularly hosted members of the Sudanese opposition and was in turn accused by Sudan of supporting even the SPLA in the south. Meanwhile, links between Sudan and the Islamist movement in Yemen had been increasing, allegedly aiding al-Qaeda terrorists in Saudi Arabia.

The agenda for Sudan also embraced North Africa where a combination of returning 'Afghans' and high unemployment amongst youthful populations contributed to an increasingly volatile situation in which Islamism appeared to have a very active part to play. Islamist leaders from Algeria and Tunisia in particular had been amongst the participants at the PAIC conferences; and in the former a low level civil war was starting following the aborted elections of 1992. Even Libya, which at first had been hopeful of useful relations with the new regime, was disconcerted to find that its own Islamist opposition was finding succor in Khartoum and from 1993 to 1995 there were a number of attacks in Libya that Qaddafi blamed on Sudan.

However amongst Sudan's North African neighbors by far the most important was Egypt. Relations have always been of a special nature for both countries. Egypt, a former ruler of Sudan, continued to regard the country as something of a southern hinterland; and it also had special concern for the Nile waters, which, though not rising in Sudan, flow through it for much of their course. From Sudan's viewpoint, one of the continuing points of reference in its politics for decades had been whether governments, parties, and politicians were broadly pro- or anti-Egyptian. After an initially favorable Egyptian response to the coup of 1989, apparently due to an initial misunderstanding of its perpetrators, the Islamist agenda adopted by the NIF soon put it in the anti-Egyptian camp. Egypt denounced Sudan for supporting Islamist terrorists, especially as the Islamic Jihad movement stepped up its attacks in Egypt. Egyptian Islamists had taken refuge in Sudan, including Umar Abd al-Rahman, a leader of Islamic Jihad who later went to New York where in 1996 he was jailed for his connections with the bombers of the

World Trade Center. Some Egyptians did receive military training in Sudan and weapons were smuggled to Egypt. The deterioration in relations between the two countries contributed to the revival of their border dispute over Halayab, which had been dormant since 1958. Its origin lay in ambiguity over the border from the days of British imperialism, but in 1992 Egypt moved decisively effectively annexing the disputed region, a move that Sudan could do little to reverse. In other areas too relations deteriorated over matters that were at least partly concerned with Islamism. Egypt had long retained a cultural and educational presence in Sudan, especially through the Khartoum branch of the University of Cairo and a network of schools. These were all closed in 1993, and Egypt complained about the treatment of its nationals in the process. Sudan in reply accused Egypt of seeking to be involved in Sudanese life, including political activities, and pointed to such incidents as Egypt's hosting of John Garang, of the SPLA (Mainstream) and permitting various northern political exiles to operate in Egypt.[11] Egypt was concerned by the possible implications of the establishment of IGAD, especially if it might presage greater exploitation of the Nile waters by upstream states. In consequence, Egypt secured observer status with IGAD but still saw Sudan as a potentially threatening force within it. At the same time, fears that a new regime in Sudan might permit the eventual secession of southern Sudan with possible implications for Egypt's water supply maintained a note of caution in the latter's policy.

Relations with Egypt came to a head in June 1995 with the attempted assassination of President Mubarak in Addis Ababa where he was to attend a meeting of the OAU. The well planned attack, that came very close to success with Mubarak's car sprayed with heavy machine gun fire, was carried out by Egyptians from Islamic Jihad, but it was soon clear that they had been trained in Sudan and elements in the regime there (though not all members of the government) were complicit in the attack. The attack was also linked to al-Qaeda (Lesch, *Current History*, May 2002, pp. 207; Gunaratna, 2002, p. 160). The attack brought together Sudan's Middle Eastern and African activities, for while it took place in Addis Ababa it was intended to be linked to further action in Egypt that had to be aborted in the light of the failure against Mubarak, and to an attack on US personnel in Riyadh that went ahead successfully (Bodansky, 1999, pp. 121-135). Mubarak was furious, understandably; Ethiopia was humiliated that it could have happened on its soil; and the international community more broadly was horrified that such a major figure could have been so close to assassination. There was also shock that Turabi's response was such as to imply that Mubarak had deserved the attempt on his life: 'When Mubarak dared to got to Addis Ababa to attend the OAU summit, the sons of the Prophet Moses, the Muslims, rose up against him, confounded his plans, and sent him back to his country'(Petterson, 1999, p. 179). Sudan was soon to feel the full weight of regional response to its programme of regional disorder in the name of revolutionary Islamism.

US Policy

It was not only Sudan's neighbours that were learning more about the new regime and its international ambitions, so too was the US Nevertheless the US initially had something of an open mind, and endeavoured initially to work with the new rulers. However the US was increasingly alarmed at Sudan's hosting of active terrorists, especially when their operations extended into neighbouring states with which America had good relations, notably Eritrea, Ethiopia, Uganda and Egypt; while Sudan was also remembered for siding with Iraq in the Gulf War of 1990-1991. Intelligence agencies in these countries particularly highlighted the actual or potential threat of Islamist terrorism and contributed to growing concern in the CIA that fed into its reports on Sudan.

Sudan's involvement in terrorism was hotly denied by the government but the evidence appeared overwhelming. There was clearly the ideological justification, and directly or indirectly there were links between many of the individuals and groups given shelter in Sudan and acts of terrorism perpetrated in various parts of the world. However amongst the acts most debated was the first attack on the World Trade Center in 1993 that caused a number of fatalities and considerable damage to one of the towers. It was alleged that the UN building was also targeted, since the collapse of the 'Western dominated' UN was another Islamist aim. Much discussion has taken place over the years and it appears that there were connections between the perpetrators and Sudan, with possible assistance from both the Sudan Embassy in Washington and Sudanese diplomats at the United Nations in New York. However, the investigations have still left some uncertainty about just who knew what in American circles. Ambassador Petterson's memoirs reveal that he was not able to see all the evidence on which charges of involvement in terrorism were made; nor was he convinced, at least initially, of the correctness of the allegations being made by the CIA (Petterson, 1999, p.69).[12] It was also notable that during his time he at least did not see bin Laden as a leading figure (Petterson, 1999, pp. 42-3).

However in spite of the ambassador's views it was believed in Washington that the evidence was compelling and in 1993 Sudan was placed on the US list of states supporting terrorism, alongside Libya, Iran, Syria, Iraq, North Korea and Cuba.[13] The Office of Counterterrorism made it clear that Sudan would have to fulfill five conditions in order to come off the list. First, it would have to close down the offices and activities of groups regarded by the US as terrorists. Second, it would have to halt the issuing of Sudanese passports or identity papers to suspected terrorists. Third it would have to extradite a number of listed terrorists to the US for trial. Fourth, it would have to suspend the deportations of people taking place especially of internally displaced in squatter camps around the capital; and halt the attempts to Islamise southern Sudanese. Finally, it would have to expel the Iranian ambassador to Sudan (*Indian Ocean Newsletter*, 31 July 1993). Such a list was hardly one that Sudan was likely to accept, especially at a time when the Islamic regime still had high ambitions both nationally and internationally. Instead it accused the US of supporting the SPLA which it branded a terrorist organization.

Being placed on the US list of states supporting international terrorism also resulted in economic and financial restrictions. Arms related exports and sales were banned and any goods that might be used in an ancilliary way for weapons production (so-called 'dual-use' goods) were subject to tight control, and the US also opposed World Bank and IMF loans to Sudan. While in spite of Cohen's claim that the US had 'backed away' from supporting the SPLA there were repeated stories in the press, especially sourced from Uganda, of US and Israeli materiel reaching the SPLA (Petterson, 1999, p. 213). Reconnaissance was also being carried out of possible facilities for military use in southern Sudan and northern Kenya. Fears of terrorism even led to the withdrawal of the families of US government personnel from Sudan in 1993. The US ambassador to the UN, Madeleine Albright, summed up her country's feeling towards Sudan in April 1994, immediately after a brief visit to the country: 'Sudan has set itself apart from the community of nations by its support for international terrorism, its gross human rights violations, and its failure to take steps to resolve the civil war that has created a massive humanitarian crisis throughout Sudan.' She also condemned Sudan's alleged support for international terrorism, and 'the arbitrary detentions, torture, and repression of political opposition and unions' (Petterson, 1999, p.106).

However, for the US, as for so many others, the final straw was the attempted assassination of President Mubarak in 1995. The US with the rest of international community backed the imposition of UN sanctions on Sudan, rejecting all the latter's protestations of innocence. It was to open the way for a period of isolation of Sudan that was at marked variance to the initial US reception of the regime, and Cohen's attempts at constructive engagement. But as for the possibility of the US doing any more, Petterson has two quotations that illustrate the limits of its power – that lay more in the US than in its potential capabilities in Africa.

> The United States, for its part, had force to spare that could have been applied to Sudan if the political will to use it existed. I knew, from talks I had with senior officials in the State Department, Anthony Lake and some of his staff at the National Security Council, and Under Secretary of Defense Frank Wisner- a Foreign Service officer who was outraged by the killings of the US government employees at Juba and the behavior of the Sudan government- that there was a desire to do something to force Sudan to behave better. However, once faced with options that amounted to active US intervention, policymakers backed off (Petterson, 1999, p.88).

> ... Powerful sanctions were not possible. There would be neither domestic nor international support for a measure like imposing and enforcing a total trade embargo, which would have required involvement of the US Navy. Ultimately it was not the administration but the US public that narrowed the range of actions the United States might have taken against Sudan. Following the debacle in Mogadishu in 1994, Americans were not keen to see their soldiers going into possible harm's way in the absence of a clear threat to major US interests. Certainly Congress would be in no mood to endorse direct US

intervention either to put great pressure on the Sudanese government or to end the war in southern Sudan (Petterson, 1999, p.178).

In the international community, Sudan remained in an isolated position. It was shunned by most Arab states and remembered for its position in the Gulf War; and among its African neighbors hostility arising from allegations of Islamist activities also grew. It was also formally condemned for its human rights record by the UN Special Rapporteur, Gaspar Biro, who was himself obstructed and vilified by Sudan; while the European Union also took a continuing interest and a comparable view.

Conclusion

With US policy seeking to re-define itself after the Cold War and Sudan after the Islamist-backed coup of 1989 seeking to move in hitherto unparalleled directions, it was not surprising that there was uncertainty in Washington over the relations between the two countries. Within Sudan the imposition of the Arabist and Islamist agenda not only brought greater political repression and economic discrimination, but the intensification of civil war in the south. In foreign policy the changes were in some ways even more dramatic. For the first time since independence in 1956, Sudan had sought to set itself up as a major actor in regional and international politics. It had acted as a mediator in the past, with the activities of Mohamed Ahmed Mahjoub at the Khartoum summit after the Six Day War of 1967, and Nimeiri's attempt at mediation in the first civil war in Lebanon, but on these occasions it was the marginality and unobtrusiveness of Sudan that made it acceptable, rather than its pretensions to international leadership. In 1969, Sudan also sought to be part of a new union with Libya and Egypt, but very much in the shadow of Nasser and it effectively died with him a year later. Only since 1989 had Sudan sought to become a guide to the Arab and Muslim worlds. This was a challenge to US friends and interests in the region- both old ones, including Egypt and Saudi Arabia, and also new rulers such as those in Eritrea, Ethiopia and Uganda. However, while proclaiming itself to the Arab and Muslim worlds, Sudan was seeking to appear non-threatening to the West. In Turabi's contacts with the West it was Islamic renewal and adjustment of relations that he appeared to seek rather than confrontation, but was this really credible?

It took time for the US to appreciate the unfolding character of the regime. The initial relief Cohen had mentioned at the ousting from power of Sadiq al-Mahdi heralded a willingness to give the new rulers a chance. Islamists they might be, but perhaps they would be 'good' Muslims rather than 'bad': from an American perspective at least. Over the following years appreciation of the harsh realities of the new regime grew so that Cohen could write of Turabi, 'The man we saw essentially as a harmless intellectual was in reality the mastermind of a dangerous web of terrorism and subversion' (Cohen, 2000, p. 85). The US had eventually responded on all fronts, from cutting development aid to listing Sudan for its support of international terrorism, but it had failed in the first half of the 1990s to bring any significant shift in Sudanese policy either at home or abroad. As Ambassador Petterson summed it up, all that had emerged was a 'barren status quo' of mutual suspicion as the National Salvation Revolution sought to advance its programmes at home and abroad (Petterson, 1999, p. 89).

Notes

[1] Edward Djerejian, Deputy Assistant Secretary of State, speaking on US relations with the Middle East said, 'Religion is not a determinant – positive or negative – in the nature or quality of our relations with other countries. Our quarrel is with extremism, and the violence, denial, intolerance, intimidation, coercion and terror which too often accompany it' (Public Diplomacy Queries, 3 June 1992).

[2] For a full discussion of Turabi's views see Mishal Fahm al-Sulami, (2003), *The West and Islam:Western liberal democracy versus the system of shura*, London, Routledge Curzon.

[3] There were though dissenting voices, including some in the US embassy in Khartoum, who regretted the passing of democracy.

[4] Academics in the US were equally divided in their views on the new regime when called on for their advice (Burr and Collins, 2003, p.109).

[5] One journalist who has produced a very vivid picture of the southern Sudan in the 1990s is Deborah Scroggins (2003), *Emma's War: Love, Betrayal and Death in the Sudan*, London, Harper Collins.

[6] Statement before the Senate Sub-Committee on African Affairs, 4 May, 1993.

[7] It was a repeated accusation by the government-controlled Sudanese media that the US supplied the SPLA.

[8] Address by Hasan al-Turabi to the Royal Society of Arts (RSA), London, 27 April 1992.

[9] Rashid Ghannouchi, leader of the al-Nahda movement in Tunisia, was one of the prominent figures in Suda: he traveled on a Sudanese diplomatic passport until Sudan was pressured to withdraw it, after which he took refuge in Britain. Turabi was a personal friend of Yasir Arafat and sought to mediate between the PLO and Hamas, though without success.

[10] The handing over of Ilich Ramirez Sanchez, 'Carlos the Jackal', was a complex deal with France, and though a noted international terrorist he was not an Islamist (Burr and Collins, 2003, pp.156-63).

[11] Former President Nimeiri, then in exile in Egypt, was permitted to call for a popular uprising, apparently without any hint of irony in view of the fact that he had been overthrown by just such a movement.

[12] In the 1980s Khartoum had been a centre for CIA surveillance across the Horn and Chad, and even in part for Yemen but this capability fell sharply after 1989.

[13] With a lack of intelligence available to the embassy in Khartoum, and the neighbouring states ready and able to make their intelligence available the difference in assessment is perhaps understandable, though the apparent failure to coordinate positions is less excusable.

References

Armstrong, D. (1993), *Revolution and World Order: the revolutionary state in international society*, Oxford, Clarendon Press.

Benjamin, D. and Simon, S. (2002), *The Age of Sacred Terror*, New York, Random House.

Burr, J. and Collins, R. (2003), *Revolutionary Sudan: Hassan al-Turabi and the Islamist state, 1989-2000*, Leiden, Brill.

De Waal, A. (ed.) (2004), *Islamism and its Enemies in the Horn of Africa*, London, Hurst.

El-Affendi, A. (1990), 'Discovering the South: Sudanese dilemmas for Islam in Africa', *African Affairs*, 86, 356.

El-Affendi, A. (1991), *Turabi's Revolution: Islam and Power in Sudan*, London, Grey Seal.

Gerges, F. (1999), *America and Political Islam*, Cambridge, Cambridge University Press.

Karim, A. et al (1996), *Operation Lifeline Sudan: A Review*, UN Department of Humanitarian Affairs.

Khalid, M. (2003), *War and Peace in Sudan*, London, Kegan Paul.

Niblock, T. (1991), 'Islamic Movements and Sudan's Political Coherence', in Bleuchot, H., Delmet, C. and Hopwood, D. (eds), *Sudan: History, Identity, Ideology*, Reading, Ithaca.

Nyaba, P. (1997), *The Politics of Liberation in South Sudan: an insider's view*, Kampala, Fountain.

Petterson, D. (1999), *Inside Sudan: Political Islam, Conflict and Catastrophe*, Boulder, West View.

Scroggins, D. (2003), *Emma's War: Love, betrayal and death in the Sudan*, London, Harper Collins.

Shaaeldin, E. and Brown, R. (1988), 'Towards and understanding of Islamic banking in Sudan', in Barnett, T. and Abdelkarim, A. (eds), *Sudan:State, capital and transformation*, London, Croom Helm.

Simone, T. (1994), *In Whose Image?: Political Islam and Urban Practices in Sudan*, Chicago, Chicago University Press.

Wondu, S. and Lesch, A. (2000), *The Battle for Peace in Sudan: An analysis of the Abuja Conference 1992-1993*, Maryland, University Press of America.

Woodward, P. (2002), 'Religion and Politics in the Southern Sudan: the Uganda dimension', in Hassan, Y. and Gray, R. (eds), *Religion and Conflict in Sudan*, Nairobi, Pauline Press.

Chapter 4

Intervention in Somalia

While seeking to define its policy on Sudan, the US was to appear, at first sight, more decisive on the other side of the Horn in Somalia. The general image of Somalia is that of an African state which of its own volition had plunged into anarchy by the early 1990s, when along came the UN and the US – like knights in shining armour – in 1992. But alas in the murky world of Somalia finding the dragon, let alone rescuing the maiden proved more difficult than anticipated; and the knights were unexpectedly burned before riding off again and leaving the Somalis to their own violent devices. Reality is rather more complex, of course, not least the fact that the UN and the US had been contributing to developments in Somalia for many years and should have amassed considerable experience of the country and its complex problems.

Somalia has been, in its own way, as artificial a state as most others in Africa. While the country was unusual, in that mainly pastoral Somali clans had common cultural and religious traditions, there had been no experience of indigenous state formation; and the imperial division of the continent in the late nineteenth century meant that Somalis were left in a number of separate independent states rather than being brought together in one. Britain, France and Ethiopia all absorbed swathes of Somali-occupied territory into their imperial states, but the largest area and number came under Italian rule. It was Italy's defeat that had made its former Somali territory the responsibility of the UN Trusteeship Council at the end of World War II: but there were few covetous glances at it, and in 1950 it was returned as a trusteeship to Italy to be prepared for independence ten years later, for such was the flow of international and UN politics at the time.

Like most former European colonies independence brought liberal democracy and, as in most of the rest of Africa, that gave way to authoritarian rule – in this case via the military coup of Siad Barre in 1969. Few tears were shed and, indeed for a while, it seemed that Barre might bring Somalis together for development in the 1970s more than the fractious politicians of the previous decade. The UN Development Programme (UNDP) certainly seemed to think so, becoming one of a number of donors that invested generously in rural development in particular.

However, the hopes of the 1970s were to be a false dawn, especially after Barre sought to take advantage of the turmoil of the Ethiopian revolution to capture Somali-occupied territory in eastern Ethiopia in 1977. Defeated the following year by Ethiopia's Soviet-backed army, the clan-based resistance to Barre began which was to grow through the 1980s and eventually lead to his downfall in 1991. Somalia's defeat in 1978 opened a new chapter in UN involvement, for hundreds of thousands of refugees poured into the country from Ethiopia (estimates ranged from 600,000 to 2 million). It gave Somalia the highest concentration of refugees to indigenous population (5 million) in the world. The UN High Commission for Refugees (UNHCR) was swiftly involved, and by the early 1980s was spending $70 million per annum. The impact of the refugee camps was most important: they were a major source of foreign exchange; numerous jobs were provided for educated Somalis; and the rations distributed eked out into the poor Somali communities in which they were situated. As Somalia deteriorated politically in the late 1980s, Barre took military conscripts from the camps, looted refugee supplies and extorted protection money, much in the manner of which the 'warlords' were to be accused when the UN Operation in Somalia (UNOSOM) began in 1992. Yet, in spite of this background of involvement, the UN from 1992 was to appear to have learned little: perhaps one of its characteristics as an international organization is a lack of, or an unwillingness to draw upon, collective memory on the part of the various agencies already experienced in Somalia.

UNOSOM

The events that were to lead to the decision to undertake UNOSOM date from the downfall of Barre in January 1991. The violent overthrow of one autocrat and his replacement by a new ruler would have been of no particular significance in contemporary Africa, but in Somalia's case was to lead to state collapse. Barre had been opposed for several years by a number of clan and sub-clan based militias. The collapse of the Somali state, and coincidentally the downfall of Mengistu in Ethiopia, had released a mass of arms and the civilian population was awash with guns. The eight main militias identified after Barre's downfall were commanded by emerging leaders swiftly labelled 'warlords' as they competed for power. In addition to these militias, generally of 2,000-3,000 men, there were numerous smaller bands, often of youngsters, who appeared beyond any form of authority.

Amidst this confusion there were attempts by Islamist groups to carve out their own areas of activity. Best known and most radical amongst them was al-Ittihad al-Islaami (Islamic Unity), often referred to simply as 'al-Ittihad', which developed as both a social and military group. It had financial support from Sudan and Iran, with the former also arranging links between Somali and Saudi Arabian financiers (Burr and Collins, 2003, p.113). In addition, some 'Afghans' arrived to assist with training; augmenting a number of Somali 'Afghans' already back in the country (Medhane, 2002, p.33). With its ambition to be a pan-Islamist movement, rather than another clan-based militia, al-Ittihad endeavoured to spread its organization across Somalia and into the Muslim peoples of Ethiopia, notably the Ogadeni and Oromo in the east. However, it was very loosely structured and although it established its own militia it found itself the target of more powerful clan-based groups that perceived themselves as every bit as Muslim as al-Ittihad. Forced away from Mogadishu by the clan-based factions in 1991, Islamist groups associated with al-Ittihad moved to other towns, including Kismayo to the south and Bosaso in the north-east. Driven out of the former, in Bosaso they made headway for a while before once more falling foul of the more powerful clan-based militias. Remnants of the movement retreated to more rural centres, especially in Gedo in the south-west where they carved out areas of local control that were to last for some years.

While the warlords appeared to be essentially political rivals, amongst whom efforts at conciliation and mediation proved abortive, many of the other armed men were little more than bandits. Barre's men had increasingly looted and their example was continued in the vacuum left behind. Continuing commercial activity, especially the trade in the popular narcotic *qat*, attracted violence, as did the agricultural areas of the south. Soon refugees were pouring into Kenya and Ethiopia. Foreign aid organizations had long been working in Somalia, and as the crisis deepened, so the need for emergency relief rose as well. The international community responded to what was depicted as 'famine', but the relief itself became a target. Supplies arriving at the port of Mogadishu, in particular, came under attack and the relief agencies were forced to hire protection from among the armed groups that threatened them.[1] As it was later put, 'The relief effort had begun to generate its own pernicious dynamic; food had become the main item of commerce, to be commandeered at the point of a gun without regard to the effects on the general populace' (Woods, 1997, p.154).

It was as this situation intensified that the UN was drawn in. Somalia was very much in mind when the UN Department of Humanitarian Affairs was established in 1991; and Under Secretary-General James Jonah arrived in Mogadishu in January 1992 to assess the situation. His task was to facilitate the flow of aid, but he also appeared to make some headway towards a ceasefire between two of the leading warlords contending for power in Mogadishu, Mohammed Farah Aideed, leader of the new Somali National Alliance (SNA), and Ali Mahdi, of the United Somali Congress (USC). He even suggested a UN force to separate the warring factions, but the suggestion was stillborn: there was great reluctance in the Security Council, especially from the US and Russia, largely due to the organization's rising commitments. Eventually as the situation continued to worsen 500 UN troops did arrive in the country, but they remained in camp at the airport effectively hemmed in by the militias and uncertain of their role. In an effort to improve relief aid the umbrella of UNOSOM was established under Security Council Resolution 751 of 24 April 1992, but the situation remained very difficult.

At this stage the position adopted by the US proved crucial. The Under Secretary of State for Africa, Herman Cohen, has given an account of the decision making process in Washington that is a fascinating insight into how the US involvement developed. One dimension was the different assessments of the various agencies about how the situation should be perceived. The Africa Bureau argued from the outset that the root of the problem lay in the security crisis in Somalia. Cohen was supported in this diagnosis by Andrew Natsios of the Office of Foreign Disaster Assistance; and later by James Bishop, a former ambassador to Somalia, then Deputy Assistant Secretary for Human Rights. Against this view, and perceiving of Somalia essentially as a 'food problem', were other important voices. In many areas of the administration there was a reluctance to take on another responsibility at a time when there were several competing calls, including the costly operations in Cambodia. Amongst these doubting voices was the State Department's Bureau of International Organization Affairs, without the support of which the US was never going to take an active role on Somalia at the UN (Cohen, 2000, pp. 206-17).

The stalemate in the US administration was especially galling for the new UN Secretary General, Boutros Boutros-Ghali. He had particular concern for Somalia from his years as Deputy Foreign Minister of Egypt with special responsibility for Africa. He also took seriously the notion of a more active role for the UN in the New World Order proclaimed by George Bush; and he wished to show that such actions were as relevant in Africa as in European areas of conflict, notably the Balkans. But hard as he tried to raise the UN's concern with the deteriorating situation in Somalia, he was at a loss without US support. There was, however, a groundswell of support for action in American society. The television station CNN gave growing coverage of the crisis while the charities working in Somalia campaigned more actively, with the result that pressure started to be felt in Congress where various committees, most notably the House Select Committee on Hunger, held hearings as the situation worsened. This pressure was particularly significant given the uncertainty in the highest reaches of the administration.

In March 1992 the US had agreed to support the sending of a UN special representative to Somalia. An experienced Algerian diplomat, Mohammed Sahnoun, was sent to take charge of UNOSOM, and soon evolved his own approach. He tried to develop relations with the leading warlords, and not just Aideed and Ali Mahdi (though the former, in particular, was highly suspicious of the UN). Any attempt to deploy UN forces Sahnoun thought should have their agreement and cooperation. He also endeavoured to support other elements in Somali society, such as clan elders and women's representatives. In an effort to deflect the concentration of attention on Mogadishu, and rivalry for control thereof, he proposed dividing the country into a number of zones for the delivery of relief, each to be supplied by different routes. These were to be around Bassosa, Berbera, and Kismayo, as well as Mogadishu. In addition to relief, the zones would become centres for regional reconciliation, which would involve local leaders such as clan elders, as well as the warlords whose importance would be slowly eroded in a process that would require time (Sahnoun, 1994, p. 27).

Meanwhile there were further developments in Washington. Within the administration the various agencies met in the Policy Coordinating Committee on Africa. One regular participant was Walter Kansteiner, a Republican political appointee serving as Director for African Affairs on the National Security Council Staff. Apparently through his reports to Brent Scrowcroft, the National Security Adviser, news about Somalia was reaching President Bush, who was also aware of the growing 'CNN effect' on the general public. In consequence by July 1992 Bush instructed the State Department to be '"forward leaning" on Somalia' (Cohen, 2000, p.209). On 18 August 'Operation Provide Relief' was established based in Mombasa, Kenya, to airlift relief supplies into Somalia. As Cohen wrote:

That the president acted shortly before the 1992 Republican presidential nominating convention, against a backdrop of increasing demands to do something, did not escape us. We did not question his motives. We welcomed wise decisions from our leaders any way we could get them.

Throughout the autumn the coordination of planning for possible US operations in Somalia had been underway right up to senior levels.

At the top level, although formal National Security Council (NSC) meetings were very rare, the secretaries of state and defense, the national security adviser and the chairman of the Joint Chiefs of Staff (JCS) conferred frequently and at length on Somali courses of action and apparently had full access to the president when needed (Clarke and Herbst, 1997, p.156).

In the State Department a Somali Working Group was officially established in November to facilitate inter-agency cooperation as preparation for US intervention.

On the ground in Somalia the situation continued to be bad, and by late 1992 Sahnoun had become increasingly frustrated with UN headquarters in New York and expressed his criticism publicly. He felt that in practice his policy of regionalism was being undermined by UN agencies concentrating their presence in Mogadishu to the neglect of other zones, partly due to lack of staff to work outside the capital. He was also critical of other aspects of the agencies: the headquarters in New York was overly bureaucratic; there was a lack of cooperation between agencies; while some agencies were failing to fulfil the commitments that they had made. For his part Boutros Boutros-Ghali felt that Sahnoun was acting too independently, and some suggested favouring Aideed in the Mogadishu area (Gurdon, 1994, p.58). The clash between the two former friends led to Sahnoun's resignation, and his replacement by an Iraqi diplomat, Ahmed Kittani, a much less flexible personality who did as New York told him. At the same time relief aid came under more attacks and reports indicated that the levels of famine and disease were rising fast. A major humanitarian crisis appeared to be looming once more, in spite of the efforts of UNOSOM, which, in its existing form, was widely regarded as inadequate.

UNITAF

Developments in Somalia were having a growing impact in two places in particular. In New York Boutros Boutros-Ghali reviewed the options. Existing operations under Resolution 775 would permit the deployment of a further 2,400 UN peacekeepers, but this was thought to be an inadequate number in the deteriorating situation. On the other hand total withdrawal of UN forces was seen as a retreat that would have disastrous consequences in the worsening security situation. Third there could be a show of force in Mogadishu, the main area of violence, but this might only provoke the well-armed main faction leaders, and not help elsewhere in the country. Fourth there could be a countrywide operation at the behest of the UN but led by a member state. A fifth option was for an enlarged UN force to takeover from the existing UNOSOM operation, but this was thought beyond its existing capacity. In reality Boutros-Ghali himself was becoming ever keener on armed intervention by the UN (Gurdon, 1994, p.53).[2] In part it was because he judged it the only way to deal with what appeared to be a deteriorating situation in on the ground; and in part because he had greater ambitions for the UN internationally in the wake of the end of the Cold War (Sahnoun, 1994, pp.53-4).

Meanwhile, in Washington, the rivals for the White House in the forthcoming presidential elections were also moving in the same direction. The press coverage of the deteriorating situation was causing American politicians to take Somalia more seriously than any concern for normal understanding of national interest required; and George Bush in particular, the incumbent candidate, had long prided himself on being a foreign policy president. After his success in the Gulf War in particular he was much given to speaking of a New World Order, a concept that however remained largely undefined (Hurst, 1999). Moreover he was frustrated with the perceived lack of European action in former Yugoslavia and sought to show by the example of decisiveness in Somalia what could be achieved in a disintegrating state. It would also show that the US was concerned about the situation in a Muslim state even though America was a predominantly Christian country. Although there were doubting voices about the need for armed intervention and the objectives, Bush was moving in that direction even before his electoral defeat. And once he had lost to Bill Clinton, intervention was one last chance to demonstrate his decisiveness in foreign policy, and show America what it was losing with his departure.

As it moved towards a commitment in principle, the US was also reviewing what it meant militarily. One possibility, known as option 'A', was greater American support for a traditional UN peacekeeping operation by expanding the existing UNOSOM force to 3,500 or more, with heavy arms and the authorization to use force if necessary. Option 'B' was the organisation by the UN of an international force of 15,000. This would not involve US ground troops, but America would provide logistical support, and a rapid reaction force with helicopter gunships offshore in case of emergencies. Thirdly, under option 'C', US troops could take the lead in an international operation, as had been the case in the liberation of Kuwait (Cohen, 2000, p.211).

While many officials expected option 'B' to be adopted, because of the delay there would be in getting the UN force together Bush and his advisors went for 'C'. Though it would involve a US military commitment on the ground, it was apparently seen as comparatively easy to do with minimal casualties. As Speaker Foley remarked after Congressional leaders met with President Bush in December 1992, 'The impression we had today strongly from the military leadership is that they do not expect major confrontations with armed forces' (Public Diplomacy Query, 8 December 1992). The lead in the thinking of the military came from the Chair of the Joint Chiefs of Staff, Colin Powell (Halberstam, 2002 p.251). His readiness for military involvement in Somalia surprised some but he clearly thought that with sufficient force, and a strictly defined agenda leading to an exit strategy via the UN, humanitarian relief was manageable as well as necessary. Action in Somalia would also relieve the US of pressure for action in Bosnia, which Powell and other military leaders judged to be much more risky. Instead the comparison suggested by some, including Paul Wolfowitz, Under Secretary of Defense and a keen supporter of action, was with northern Iraq where a protected area permitted the delivery of humanitarian aid (CBS, 10 December 1992). There were though some notes of caution. Privately Cohen warned of the, 'combative nature of the Somali nomadic tradition' (Cohen, 2002, p.213). More public were the warnings of the outspoken US ambassador to neighboring Kenya, Smith Hempstone, who wrote, 'If you liked Beirut you'll love Mogadishu ... I do not think Somalia is amenable to the quick fix so beloved of Americans', and that the US should, 'Inshallah [God willing], think once, twice and three times before you embrace the Somali tarbaby' (Hempstone, 1997, p.230).

Clinton was understandably cautious being newly elected and not so interested in foreign affairs as Bush. However it was difficult to deny the humanitarian pressure, and in the presidential election campaign he had tried to spoil Bush's foreign policy achievements by doubting his morality in the face of situations such as those in Bosnia and Somalia. Faced with this new moral maze Clinton too gave his agreement to US leadership of Operation Restore Hope. It was suggested to him that in any case the US military involvement in the operation would be largely over by the time of his inauguration (Clarke, 2004, p.85).

The alliance of the UN secretariat and the US was followed on 3 December 1992 by the passage of UN Resolution 794 that called for the establishment of a safe environment for humanitarian aid in Somalia. It was a double first for the UN. The intervention would take place without the permission of the government of the member state of the UN involved, for though Somali faction leaders claimed to rule none was recognized internationally as the legitimate ruler. Furthermore it was to be a Chapter VII operation, by which the Unified Task Force (UNITAF) would be required to make peace among the disputing parties rather than simply keeping the peace between them. The following day, 4 December, President Bush announced that US troops would be committed to Somalia: in the last resort it appears that it was very much his own decision and the last major foreign policy decision that he took.

There had been some debate about how the forces should be deployed. One suggestion, that seemed to reflect Sahnoun's viewpoint, was for a flexible force to operate outside Mogadishu delivering aid to small ports and using helicopters if necessary thus bypassing the main Mogadishu-based warlords and their militias. Though it won some support among the aid professionals of the NGOs, it was swiftly scotched by the military. Instead the plan was for overwhelming military force to cow the warlords, and this required an operation that could only be conducted through the port of Mogadishu itself (Clarke and Herbst, 1997, pp.157-8).

Television cameras were already set up on the shore to record the arrival of the first UNITAF forces on 9 December 1992. Eventually they built up to 37,000 troops (28,000 of whom were from the US), who were deployed to take control of the southern ports of Mogadishu and Kismayu and ensure that relief could get through to the urban and rural distribution centres. Originally Bush had spoken of this being completed by 20 January, but this optimistic timetable was extended to 120 days; after which UNITAF, would withdraw to be replaced by UNOSOM II (a mixed international force with a smaller US presence) which would then be responsible for peacekeeping and further UN operations.

In terms of improving the supply of aid UNITAF did have initial success with raids on humanitarian relief supplies diminishing. Subsequent claims for a measure of success in Somalia lay largely on the number of people claimed to have been saved by UNITAF's intervention – which has been estimated at as high as 100,000. However this was disputed by some on the ground who claimed that mortality rates had already dropped before the US forces arrived: the World Food Programme spokesman was reported as saying, 'what you have now are just pockets of famine' (Alagiah, 2001, p.108). Whatever the truth about the figures UNITAF's main problems soon turned out to be political. On the UNITAF side differences appeared with regard to dealing with the militias. Boutros-Ghali thought that a secure environment for relief necessarily required a commitment to disarm the gunmen, but the Bush administration reflected the thinking of the US commanders on the ground that this was neither necessary to ensure relief nor was it practicable.[3] It was not deemed necessary, since it was a humanitarian operation to permit aid to flow to Somalis and not a strategic exercise to takeover Somalia. It was not thought practical, since it was not clear how much disarmament would be necessary, especially since arms were so widespread in the country; large scale disarmament might result in clashes and casualties on both sides which would be politically damaging; and such a large operation would be very expensive. The possibility of guns for food was contemplated, but with so many weapons that was also deemed impractical. This position on armaments was to cause friction between the UN and UNITAF, especially when Boutros-Ghali and Kittani were still actively, if somewhat ambiguously, involved in Somalia.[4] Furthermore, elsewhere in the country, especially while the Australians were in Baidoa, more progress on disarmament was achieved (Patman, 1997).[5] Though the US eschewed systematic disarmament, when the crime situation again deteriorated sharply in January 1993 and a number of NGO relief operations were suspended there were intermittent ad hoc seizures of arms in Mogadishu.

However the uncertainty and inconsistency surrounding the UN and UNITAF on disarmament from the outset served to alarm the Somali factions more than they secured the environment for relief. This was particularly damaging when the US special envoy, Robert Oakley, a diplomat with considerable experience in comparable difficult situations, was trying to take a political approach towards the warlords. Initially the leading figures in Mogadishu, Aideed and Ali Mahdi, had welcomed UNITAF's arrival. Conferences involving them and thirteen other leaders from elsewhere in the country were held in Addis Ababa in January and March, and Oakley hoped that if agreement could be fostered then there might be an agreed beginning on disarmament, demobilisation, and the reintegration of the militias into Somali society (Hirsch and Oakley, 1995, p.105). But tensions surfaced. Politically the warlords rivalries remained intense, with Aideed in particular appearing determined to prevent Ali Mahdi from being recognized as interim leader. Militarily Aideed was particularly unwilling to hand over weapons, though Ali Mahdi did initially surrender some armoured trucks known as 'technicals'. The outcome of resistance to disarmament by the SNA in particular was some heavy but brief clashes in the capital. At the same time all factions were continuing to receive more arms from Ethiopia and Kenya (Lewis, 2002, p.269).

Although UNITAF was not supposed to be involved in 'trusteeship-type' activities to bring about some restoration of the Somali state, the rising crime at the beginning of 1993 encouraged it to make some efforts to restore a semblance of law and order. Police were trained and some began to be deployed, as well as a few courts beginning to function. There was also some encouragement of local elders to try and restore an element of authority that had been much weakened by the militia conflicts. However in total these efforts were to have little effect.

All these moves were in any case only beginnings. UNITAF claimed to have established a safer environment for relief and that was really all that it was for or that it achieved. UNITAF was coming to an end less because of complete success than because its limited time span was running out. Boutros Ghali, for one, claimed that UNITAF's work was incomplete and called for a continued US presence at a similar level, but the UN-US alliance that had started the operation was now essentially the voice of the US and it was determined that by the end of March UNITAF would be winding down.

UNOSOM II

In theory UNOSOM had never stopped. UNITAF was an additional short term measure and Ahmed Kittani had continued as UN Special Representative. But in reality UNOSOM had been side lined, and with UNITAF's withdrawal a new operation, UNOSOM II, was established. The major difference in aim was that under UN resolution 814 of 26 March 1993 UNOSOM II was specifically intended to give greater emphasis to disarmament than had been the case under the more ambiguous UNITAF. The confrontation that the American leadership of UNITAF had sought to avoid was now to take place. Yet though there was to be a tougher line it is claimed that there was in fact no proper UN planning of how to tackle the whole disarmament issue. This may have been due partly to the hostility between SNA and Boutros-Ghali (the latter had been forced by an SNA-organized demonstration to cut short a visit to Mogadishu) who was reluctant to delegate the handling and planning of operations. Furthermore the absence of Kittani, who was away for medical treatment in the early weeks of UNOSOM II, did not help the development of policy. In March he was replaced as UN Special Representative by an American, Admiral Jonathon Howe, former Deputy National Security Adviser to President Bush.

What Howe was supposed to be doing, as far as the Clinton administration was concerned, was far from clear. In the White House itself there was a lack of engagement with the unfolding situation, reflected in the fact that no senior policy figure visited the country as the crisis developed. At the same time Boutros-Ghali was calling for more committed intervention, a theme apparently taken up by the

US representative at the UN, Madeleine Albright, who spoke on behalf of a UN resolution calling for, 'the rehabilitation of the political institutions and economy of Somalia' (Halberstam, 2002 p.256). Halberstam remarks that, 'Her speech, so different from the original mission concept, was a clear sign that Washington was not taking events in Somalia seriously enough, and that no one was really in charge' (Halberstam, 2002, p.257). On the ground Admiral Howe, always more a military than a political thinker, felt that a show of strength was required.

Howe perceived his main protagonist on the Somali side in the unfolding conflict as being Mohammed Farah Aideed and his SNA faction in south Mogadishu. Aideed saw himself as the real destroyer of Siad Barre and consequently the rightful leader of a new Somalia. He was rightly suspicious that UNOSOM II would not share this evaluation: indeed Howe soon came to see Aideed's destruction as the central aim of his policy. For his part Aideed accused UNOSOM II of favouring his rival claimants, with whom UNITAF had tried to arrange pacts in the past. Since Aideed's claim lay in his military capacity, the new mandate of disarmament was another major challenge, and one to be tested to see if UNOSOM II was any sterner than the first feeble UNOSOM force of the previous year had been. A successful challenge to the UN would also strengthen the SNA's position. It was also noticeable that with 28,000 troops UNOSOM II was substantially smaller than the UNITAF force that had not attempted systematic disarmament. Weapons that the SNA had moved out of Mogadishu at the time of UNITAF's arrival were smuggled back in; and SNA's Radio Mogadishu was used to whip up civilian hostility to the UN.

It was Aideed's group that was most actively connected to external Islamism, particularly through links to Sudan and Iran. Aideed was not himself sympathetic to Islamism ideologically, but pragmatically it was useful to him. For its part the Sudan government thought that it was the real US target, and Somalia only the first step. The situation in Somalia thus offered an opportunity to check the expected US attack. The main links, which went to the top of the NIF leadership in Sudan, were with Aideed and his branch of the Habre Gidr clan. Support took the form of training by experienced 'Afghans' of both Habre Gidr forces and members of the Somali al-Ittihad group. Other groups were also involved, and as well as al-Ittihad, Harakat al-Islah (Reform Movement), Moujama'a al Ulama (Congregation of Islamic Scholars) and Widhat as Chabab al-Islami (United Islamic Youth) were invited to Khartoum for a planning session in February 1993 (*Indian Ocean Newsletter*, 27 February 1993). One source claims that 3,000 fighters were flown from Yemen at a cost of $3 million to help Aideed's faction (Lesch, *Current History*, May, 2002, p. 205). Training included the use of hand held missiles against helicopters. There was also financial support that was organised by Osama bin Laden himself, as well as assistance with communications. The fighting itself was conducted predominantly by Somalis, but the claim is made that the violence confronted by US forces was not simply random, or the product of Aideed alone, but rather was an operation planned by senior Iranian and Sudanese officials to trap and defeat US forces (Bodansky, 1999, pp.78-90; Bowden, 1999, p.167; Gunaratna, 2002, pp.154-5; Kepel, 2002, p.317).[6]

Tension rose in the weeks after UNOSOM II's deployment as its patrols tried to find weapons' dumps, and conflict came to a head on 5 June when 24 Pakistani troops and scores of Somalis were killed in a single clash. From then on it became open warfare. UNOSOM II was to place its highest priority on capturing Aideed, and a price of $25,000 was placed on his head. Heavy weapons and even helicopter gunships were provided by the US, which also sent units of its crack special forces from the Rangers and Delta Force. Indeed, it began to look as if the US rather than the UN was in charge of the operation to hunt down Aideed with the chain of command running from Washington rather than the UN in New York. The use of force was making the UN look like the biggest warlord of all; and, with the help of SNA radio propaganda, the population of south Mogadishu, in particular, was turning against it. It was notable that the propaganda now included rallying calls to Somalis to fight in the name of Islam, a move apparently encouraged by Sudanese support (Lewis, 2002, p.272). UN forces were scarcely able to leave their quarters, even in vehicles (particularly since they were short of armoured personnel carriers after UNITAF withdrew). Firepower and aerial domination were proving unable to defeat the SNA on the ground, or to capture Aideed. It later became apparent that, amongst other sources of information, Aideed was in contact with his son, Hussein Maalim Aideed, a young man who had grown up in America and who had been unwittingly recruited as an interpreter with UNITAF. In contrast US intelligence was weak, especially following the death of the top CIA agent in Mogadishu. As a result information coming in was often erroneous, and the intelligence staff was aware of its weakness, though scarcely able to communicate its shortcomings to the force commanders (Peterson, 2001, pp.105-8). Realization of this emerging bloody deadlock was driven home by a clash between the SNA and US troops on 3 October that left 18 American dead and countless Somali victims in one of the largest battles ever involving UN peacekeeping forces. Political opinion in the US, already concerned by events, was now outraged and demanded that something be done to clarify UNOSOM II's objectives and the US role in particular.

President Clinton's response was confusing. He was furious at the way operations had been conducted, but determined not to be seen to run away and US forces in UNOSOM II would be strengthened. However he was also coming under growing pressure from Congress, which hitherto had been generally supportive of US involvement in the UN operations. The upshot was to reinforce American troops, but also to announce that they would also be pulled out entirely by 31 March 1994 (Clarke, 2004, p. 87; Clinton, 2004, pp.550-4; Hendrickson, 2002, p.34).[7] The impression was thus created that the US would be involved in one last effort in Somalia, but would then wash its hands of UNOSOM II.[8] Furthermore, Clinton announced that there would be a greater involvement of neighboring states in peacemaking, a move which was generally welcomed since the neighbors had long offered their services but hitherto had been neglected by the UN and the US At the same time the return to the kind of talks between factions attempted by Oakley at the start of 1993 meant abandoning the demonizing and pursuit of Aideed. Oakley was sent back to Mogadishu and contact with Aideed was restored: in December he was even flown to one meeting in Addis Ababa in a US plane (having refused a seat on a UN flight as unsafe). For his part Aideed had responded by producing his own thoughts on the future of Somalia, which linked local Somali politics ('the most democratic people in the world') with a national system of non-clan based parties, which would compete on the basis of proportional representation in order to ensure stable coalition governments (Aideed and Ruhela, 1993; Ruhela, 1994).

While the Americans prepared to leave as scheduled, the political initiative was passed to the UN, the factions and to neighboring states that sought to broker peace. But nothing substantial had been achieved by the time that the US forces had finally pulled out, or even a year later in March 1995 when the remaining UN forces were withdrawn. They had spent much of the intervening period shut in their compounds scarcely able to move out around Mogadishu and surrounding areas. Meanwhile the factional rivalry in Mogadishu and southern Somalia continued with occasional outbreaks of heavy fighting. After declaring himself president in 1995 (a claim recognised only by Libya and Sudan) Aideed himself died after being wounded on 1 August 1996, and was eventually succeeded as leader of the SNA by his son Hussein.

UNOSOM II had been not only a military and political debacle for the UN, it was also damaging operationally. Even the military operations had shown up major problems of coordination. The pull out of UNITAF had placed a heavy burden on Pakistani forces in UNOSOM II in south Mogadishu for which they were ill prepared and equipped. It also became clear that US troops remaining with UNOSOM II were taking their orders from Washington rather than the UN commander on the ground. The French were accused of unilaterally withdrawing their forces from Mogadishu to avoid taking casualties; while the Italians, who as the former colonial power felt a special affinity for Somalis, were alleged to be bribing SNA supporters to obtain a quiet life for their troops.

UN operations had been being so dominated by what had become a military confrontation with the SNA that other aspects of its work were being neglected. In particular humanitarian work, supposedly the original reason for intervention, was reduced. Efforts at further promoting the restoration of some basic attributes of statehood, often referred to as the 'trusteeship' side of the operation, were also beyond the capacity and resources of the UN. Some work did continue, especially after the ending of confrontation with Aideed, but it was always limited and fragile in the face of the continuing factional rivalry that remained the dominant characteristic of Somali politics. A further major weakness of the UN lay in its bureaucratic incompetence and waste. There was little effective coordination of the military, political, humanitarian and institution-building sides of the UN's work. Combined with the embarrassments caused to the US militarily, this aspect of the UN's shortcomings in Somalia was a major contribution to the growing criticism in the American administration of the Secretary-General, Boutros Boutros-Ghali. In his defence it could be argued that there were some efforts to improve the bureaucracy, and that with a number of operations simultaneously across the world the UN was under funded (partly due to US deficiencies in payment) and understaffed.

After UNOSOM II

At the time of the UNOSOM II pull out in 1995, Somalia was similar to conditions before UNOSOM in 1992. The two major faction rivals for control of the largely destroyed capital of Mogadishu were still those of Aideed and Ali Mahdi. There was still a UN presence and its civilian personnel, as well as those of the remaining NGOs, were as constrained in their activities as they had been for much of the time since Barre's downfall in 1991, with or without foreign troops. There were continuing efforts to facilitate political reconciliation between the factions, but the latter appeared as implacable as ever, and deadly clashes occurred from time to time. Some hoped that Aideed's death in August 1996 might improve the situation. His SNA was already weakening following the defection of his main financial backer, Osman Ato, to Ali Mahdi Mohammed and the development of fresh clan and sub-clan rivalries within it, and Aideed's death might now accelerate decline. A weakened SNA might lead to a consolidation of power around Ali Mahdi and the SSA which had been less belligerent and shown considerable capability to develop a climate for business.

Away from southern Somalia, the situation in the country was less violent. In the central and north eastern areas local faction leaders, especially the Somali Salvation Democratic Front (SSDF), emerged to participate in the management of stateless society. Local leaders were joined in this by clan and sub-clan leaders, particularly from the Mijerteyn; as well as by influential Muslim figures. However the most remarkable transformation was in the region of former British Somaliland in the northwest. It had suffered terribly in the unsuccessful uprising of 1988, but after Barre fell the Somali National Movement (SNM) assumed full control. In May 1991 President Abdel Rahman Ali Tour announced the formation of the state of Somaliland and repealed the Act of Union that had joined the former British- and Italian-administered territories in 1960.

There were predictably faction, clan and sub-clan tensions, but Somaliland did not descend into the violent anarchy of the south. In part this seemed due to the devolution of power with local leaders being actively involved in administration. Traditional processes of mediation and dispute settlement were revived, as well as *guurti* (councils of elders) that could arbitrate between clans on sensitive subjects such as grazing and water rights. This local involvement in political life culminated in a national *guurti* or conference at Boroma that lasted from February to May 1993. Amidst criticism of the new 'national' government the local representatives voted for a new leader, former prime minister, Mohammed Ibrahim Egal, to replace President Tour. Alongside this new state with its considerable reliance on local leaders, a vibrant commercial dynamic was growing including a growing trade with neighbouring countries.

Yet, internationally, Somaliland remained unrecognized and an important factor in that was the attitude of the UN. From the outset of UN involvement Boutros-Ghali, in particular, had opposed recognition.[9] Sahnoun had hoped to bring Somaliland back into the regionalized fold of a re-built Somalia but, after he had gone, the UN was seen as actively hostile to the self-proclaimed new state. Other countries followed suit, including neighboring states much involved in

Somalia such as Ethiopia and Djibouti. It all appeared to stand in sharp contrast with the readiness of the international community to recognize the independence of Eritrea, formerly part of Ethiopia, following its referendum in 1993. The lack of international recognition deprived Somaliland of official aid, though some NGOs resumed work there. It also left some Somalis in the south hoping that in some way the former regions of the country might be brought together once more in the future.

Conclusion

Almost from the outset of operations, and certainly from UNOSOM II, Somalia was described as one of the worst ever UN interventions anywhere in the world, and with at least part of the blame due to the US (Clarke and Herbst, 2001). As indicated at the start, Somalia was not unknown territory either for the UN or the US, which was to become the major operational arm. As a former UN Trust Territory, and a US client in the later years of the Cold War, there was no lack of experience of the country. Yet the first line of criticism is that in spite of past experience opportunities for that desirable alternative to intervention – 'preventive diplomacy' – had been missed. Mohamed Sahnoun has argued the case for three wasted opportunities (Sahnoun, 1994, pp.3-12). The first was in 1988 when the uprising in the north was met by savage butchery from Barre. The US did subsequently cut military aid as a result largely of an outcry by human rights groups, but there was insufficient action to demonstrate concern for the victims directly and to address the political issues. The second came in 1990 when intellectuals in Mogadishu sought reform through the presentation of a manifesto that could have been supported by the international community. The third chance was the failure of the reconciliation conference in 1991. On none of these occasions was there sufficient international concern and pressure; indeed the international response was more to cut and run, as with UN personnel in the north in 1988, than to engage positively in preventive diplomacy.

Once there was international recognition of the scale of the problem of Somalia there was little criticism of the decision to embark on UNOSOM in 1992, but much of the way it was handled. In particular the public clash between the Secretary General Boutros Boutros-Ghali, and UN Special Representative Mohamed Sahnoun, did much to undermine confidence. While Sahnoun was not above criticism, especially for his alleged emollience towards Aideed, there was wide support for his ideas for targeting intervention regionally, and trying for local support including 'traditional' authorities.

Criticism of the US involvement stemmed largely from uncertainty of action. Bush himself had seemed initially uncertain about sending American forces, but more importantly once that decision had been taken the purpose of the mission appeared unclear. While Boutros Ghali wanted disarmament to be at the centre of UNITAF operations, the Bush administration chose to leave the issue to US commanders on the ground and went along with their view that disarmament was unnecessary and impractical, and that a conciliatory approach to the warlords would reduce tension and facilitate the relief operations. Instead of using its apparently overwhelming force of 37,000 well-armed troops UNITAF talked to all of the warlords when it could have detained them, and then allowed them to return to their factions whose weapons were only intermittently and ineffectively raided. At the same time the disarmament carried out in Baidoa by Australian forces suggested that more could have been achieved in Mogadishu with stronger leadership from Washington.

The sense of a missed opportunity on the part of UNITAF became greater once UNOSOM II was in place. Now that there was a more determined effort to pursue disarmament the warlords had had several months to prepare to resist militarily and to build popular support against what was in effect military occupation. Thus when challenged by Admiral Howe Aideed was able to hit back to embarrassing effect. The appearance of mission creep from 'peace-keeping' to 'war-fighting' damaged the UN intervention overall and later gave rise to the phrase the 'Mogadishu line' (Farrell, 2002, p.289). Yet while it was trying to do more than UNITAF, UNOSOM II had fewer forces; and displayed marked fragmentation and signs of national rather than UN command.

As well as growing criticism of the Clinton administration there was also a turning against the UN. The active involvement of the Secretary-General himself was seen by many as unfortunate. He was personally associated with Egypt's backing of the former Somali dictator, Siad Barre, who had contributed so much to his country's debacle; and was also known to have a personal dislike of Mohammed Aideed. Widely criticized for sacking Sahnoun, that decision also led to the concentration on operating through Mogadishu to the detriment of a more regionalized approach and alienated Somaliland in particular. UN headquarters in New York remained overly bureaucratic; while on the ground in Mogadishu there appeared to be a lack of expertise and co-operation amongst a staff who spent much of the time confined to their bunkers.

Following the final withdrawal of US troops in 1994 UNOSOM II was a listless operation in its final year, and any prospect of effective international action to help the people of that failed state was now finally dashed. In addition the experience of the US in the Somalia and its reluctance to commit its troops again in a humanitarian emergency was to contribute to the lack of international action in the face of the Rwanda genocide of 1994.[10] There was also no longer any question of the US contemplating direct military action in Sudan. Though al-Qaeda did nothing to claim a victory in Somalia at the time (in line with its normal policy), the involvement of various Islamist groups was later to emerge.[11] In the eyes of the Islamists they had gained a victory in contributing to the forced withdrawal of US forces from Somalia, and also heading off possible intervention in Sudan. As for the US, with problems in Somalia and Sudan, continuing policy would focus less on direct military action than working with friends in the region to protect America's interests.

Notes

[1] Lewis notes that this situation was similar 'to the old *abbaan* protector-agent system' that was well known in Somalia (Lewis, 2002, p.267).

[2] Boutros Boutros-Ghali had outlined his thoughts in 1992 in a UN publication entitled *An Agenda for Peace*. Three years later he published a *Supplement for an Agenda for Peace* with more emphasis on consent and the non-use of force.

[3] A lengthy and revealing account of Defense Secretary Cheyney's views was given on Meet the Press, 6 December 2002. See Public Diplomacy Query 7 December 2002.

[4] Critics, and some Somalis, believed that Boutros-Ghali was pursuing an Egyptian as much as a UN agenda.

[5] Clarke and Herbst also argue that disarmament of heavy weapons would have been possible (Clarke and Herbst, 2001, p.60).

[6] There is still dispute with regard to the degree of Islamist involvement in the fighing in Mogadishu and its significance for Aideed's faction in particular (Burke, 2003, pp.134-6).

[7] Madeleine Albright entitled the chapter of her memoirs that included Somali 'The New World (Dis)Order' (Albright, 2003).

[8] Sidney Blumenthal recalls, 'In a telling performance, after the Somalian carnage, Secretary of State Warren Christopher and Secretary of Defense Leslie Aspin trooped before a congressional hearing to present no policy at all and beseech the legislators for ideas: the Congress as suggestion box' (Blumenthal, 2003, p. 61).

[9] Boutros Ghali was remembered in Somaliland for having backed Barre's repression of the region in 1988 when he was Egypt's Deputy Foreign Minister.

[10] De Waal mentions that the lessons were formalised in Presidential Decision Directive 25, written by Susan Rice (De Waal ed., 2004, p.219).

[11] Osama bin Laden did later claim successful involvement in Somalia. By 1998 his involvement was recognised in the US and cited in condemnation of him.

References

Aideed, M. and Ruhela, S. (1993), *The preferred development in Somalia*, New Delhi, Vikas.

Alagiah, G. (2001), *A Passage to Africa*, London, Little and Brown.

Albright, M. (2003), *Madam Secretary: A Memoir*, Basingstoke, Macmillan.

Bodansky, Y. (1999), *Bin Laden: The Man Who Declared War on America*, Roseville, California, Prima.

Bowden, M. (1999), *Black Hawk Down*, London, Corgi.

Blumenthal, S. (2003), *The Clinton Wars*, New York, Farrar, Strauss and Giroux.

Burke, J. (2003), *Al Qaeda: casting a shadow of terror*, London, Tauris.

Burr, J. and Collins, R. (2003), *Revolutionary Sudan: Hasan al-Turabi and the Islamist State, 1989-2000*, Leiden, Brill.

Clarke, R. (2004), *Against all enemies: Inside America's war on terror*, New York, Free Press.

Clarke, W. and Herbst, J. (eds) (1997), *Learning from Somalia: The lessons of armed humanitarian intervention*, Boulder, Westview.

Clinton, B. (2004), *My Life*, London, Hutchinson.

Cohen, H. (2000), *Intervening in Africa: Superpower peacemaking in a troubled continent*, London, Palgrave.

De Waal, A. (ed.) (2004), *Islamism and its Enemies in the Horn of Africa*, London, Hurst.

Farrell, T. (2002) 'Humanitarian Interventions and Peace Operations', in Baylis, J. *et al* (eds) (2002), *Strategy in the Contemporary World*, Oxford, Oxford University Press.

Gunaratna, R. (2002), *Inside Al Qaeda: Global Network of Terror*, London, Hurst.

Gurdon, C. (ed.) (1994), *The Horn of Africa*, London, University College London Press.

Halberstam, D. (2002), *War in a Time of Peace*, London, Bloomsbury.

Hendrickson, R. (2002), *The Clinton Wars: The Constitution, Congress and War Powers*, Nashville, Vanderbilt University Press.

Hirsch, J. and Oakley, R. (1995), *Somalia and Operation Restore Hope*, Washington, US Institute of Peace Press.

Hurst, S. (1999), *The Foreign Policy of the Bush Administration: in search of a new world order*, London, Cassell.

Kepel, G. (1993), *Jihad: The Trail of Political Islam*, Cambridge, Massachusetts, Belknap.

Lewis, I. (2002), *A Modern History of the Somali*, Oxford, James Currey, 4th ed.

Medhane, Tadesse (2002), *Al-Ittihad: Political Islam and Black Economy in Somalia*, Addis Ababa, Meag Printing.

Patman, R. (1997), 'Disarming Somalia: the contrasting fortunes of United States and Australian peacekeepers during United Nations intervention, 1992-93', *African Affairs*, 95.

Peterson, S. (2000), *Me Against My Brother: At war in Somalia, Sudan and Rwanda*, London, Routledge.

Ruhela, S. (ed.) (1994), *Mohamed Farah Aideed and his vision of Somalia*, New Delhi, Vikas.

Sahnoun, M. (1994), *Somalia: The missed opportunities*, Washington, US Institute of Peace Press.

Smith, Hempstone (1997), *Rogue Ambassador: an African Memoir*, Sewanee, Tennessee, University of the South Press.

Woods, J. (1997), 'US Government Decisionmaking Processes During Humanitarian Operations in Somalia', in Clarke, W. and Herbst, J. (eds) *Learning from Somalia: The Lessons of Armed Humanitarian Interventions*, Boulder, Westview.

Chapter 5

New Friends for the US?
Ethiopia, Eritrea and Djibouti

While the US was experiencing failure in Somalia and setbacks in Sudan, it was all the more important that it should consolidate itself in the new states that it had befriended as the Cold War ended and one of the USSR's last bulwarks, the Ethiopian regime of Mengistu Haile Mariam, collapsed. And the auguries looked good since the US's involvement in the final stages of the rise to power of the EPLF and the TPLF/EPRDF in Eritrea and Ethiopia respectively appeared to ensure a strong influence in both countries. The US involvement was directly related to the end of the Cold War for the USSR had been making it clear from the end of the 1980s that it wanted out of Ethiopia and was prepared to cooperate with the US to achieve that objective. (This disillusionment on the part of the USSR with its client in the Horn mirrored the growing US disillusionment with Somalia. The two moves, and their aftermaths, well illustrated the impact of the end of the Cold War on Africa.)

The regime in Ethiopia struggled to the end to maintain itself, even endeavouring to transfer itself from the retreating USSR to the US In 1989 Herman Cohen became the first senior US official to visit Addis Ababa for 15 years, and finding Mengistu willing to negotiate for US involvement, decided to recommend a policy of 'constructive engagement' (Cohen, 2000, pp.17-27). Some political prisoners were released; and under Jimmy Carter's auspices there were peace talks though they soon came to nothing. In return the US was looking for progress with expatriating to Israel the 30,000 Ethiopian Jews commonly known as Falasha, who remained a concern of Jewish groups in the US and to President Bush who had overseen the earlier movement in 1984.[1] However with the peace talks failing and Mengistu suspected of trying to buy time in order to obtain new arms (now denied him by the USSR), possibly from Israel, the opposition forces went on the attack in 1990. At the same time US officials believed that regime change was the likely outcome of the struggle and that the concern should be to try and mitigate the degree of suffering that would be entailed especially if humanitarian relief was cut as a result of the intensifying conflict; as well as seeking to extract the Falasha in the process, but without Israel supplying arms in return as Mengistu wished. With both the USSR and the parties to the conflict apparently seeking US involvement, the latter decided to be active in the evolving change of power.

An important decision for the US was to adopt a position with regard to Eritrea. The EPLF's claim was that Eritrea was not simply a rebellious territory seeking independence from the state in which colonial history had placed it. Rather it was a former Italian colony that had moved from being a colony and then UN trust territory to confederal status with Ethiopia in 1952 without proper consultation with its population by way of an exercise in self-determination. Furthermore, in 1962 Haile Selassie had unilaterally abrogated the agreement contributing to the growing resentment and hostility in Eritrea. There was therefore an argument for considering Eritrea a special case when placed within the context of the OAU's principled opposition to secession. In early 1991 the US hosted talks in Washington, but with little progress since the regime offered only a weak form of federalism, while the EPLF sought self-determination for Eritrea. However the US did have one success, as while negotiations were underway it managed to assist Israel in arranging the exit of the Falasha who had already been brought from their homeland near Gondar to Addis Ababa in preparation. In the event, continued successes for the insurgent forces, and the flight of Mengistu to a prepared refuge in Zimbabwe effectively terminating his regime, opened the way for the final act in which the US played a role.

The final moves took place in London and Addis Ababa. In London the US convened a conference in May that brought together the EPLF, the TPLF and the Oromo Liberation Front (OLF). Although the OLF had not been heavily involved in the fighting (they made a contribution to the latter stages), the Oromo people were arguably the largest ethnic group in the country and therefore not to be overlooked if an agreement was to stick. The three groups agreed that there would be an all-party conference in Addis Ababa shortly to establish a transitional government. Meanwhile in that city the US sought to ensure that the inevitable takeover of the TPLF should be a 'soft landing' to limit bloodshed (Cohen, 2001, p.53). Nevertheless Ethiopian critics were to see America's actions as effectively anointing the TPLF as the new rulers of their country.

Overall it appeared that the US had played a significant part in the changes underway in Ethiopia. The end of the Cold War, and with it Soviet assistance, might have made the collapse of the Mengistu regime inevitable but the US played a role in the way that the events turned out. It had cooperated with the USSR in helping the latter to extract itself from a situation well past its sell-by date; assisted with the removal of the remaining Falasha to Israel; convened the conferences that led to eventual agreement of the three major factions to the formation of a transitional government as well as eventual self-determination for Eritrea; and helped to avoid major bloodshed in the capture of Addis Ababa. The installation of a new government in Ethiopia was also followed by the establishment of full diplomatic relations with the US To many it looked like the restoration of an old relationship that flowered after World War II under the Emperor, but which had not survived the rivalries of the Cold War. It could now be restored in an era of only one superpower, and when a friendly Ethiopia might still be useful in a troubled region. At the same time as supporting peace, the US had also sought to impress on the new rulers that issues such as democratization and human rights were high on its agenda and that it would be monitoring the way that 'good governance' developed.

In practice the most controversial policy adopted by Ethiopia's new rulers was the one that became referred to widely as 'ethnic federalism'; though this was not a term welcomed by the new rulers. For them the central question was the 'national question', or, in their own phrase, that of the 'Nations, Nationalities and Peoples' of Ethiopia. The issue had of course been central to the long conflicts beginning in Eritrea and Ethiopia that had helped to weaken the Emperor's rule and then brought the downfall of Mengistu's regime. Both had taken an essentially centralist view of the subject. In the Emperor's case that had been demonstrated by his absorption of Eritrea in 1962, while Mengistu had taken a Stalinist approach of regionalized centralism, only belatedly offering a weak form of federalism. It meant however that an ideological response was central to the new rulers' approach. At the core of the new government was the leadership of the old TPLF that had put self-determination at the heart of its thinking. Indeed even its former praise for Albanian Marxism was later explained as being because Albania was perceived as trying to find its own solution rather than accepting Soviet leadership. In TPLF thinking the repression of the former systems had been not simply one of class domination, but central repression and exploitation of the 'Nations, Nationalities and Peoples'. It was that which had resulted in revolution, and it had to be met by decentralization and recognition of the elements comprising Ethiopian society. Alongside decentralization would have to go democracy at all levels to ensure popular consent and participation, without which the new policy could not survive. There remained the question of what self-determination would mean and whether or not it included the right of secession? Constitutionally this was to be possible (as it was in the USSR), but it was to be offset by the success of 'ethnic federalism' in the Ethiopian context. Early in the struggle the TPLF had spoken of fighting for the independence of Tigray, but this had later been changed to seeking autonomy. Thus the aim was to establish units that would provide sufficient self-determination to address the aspirations of the various peoples of Ethiopia without leading to centrifugal forces that would destroy the country, i.e. something more devolved than the USSR had been, but less than it became after its collapse.[2]

In contrast the EPLF in Eritrea had not fought for a redefinition of its place within Ethiopia but for full self-determination including full independence. As seen, this was because the EPLF had never accepted the legitimacy of the formation of the confederation in 1952 or its full incorporation by Ethiopia ten years later. It regarded itself as a colony that had never been granted the opportunity to decide its own future. The domestic consequence of this was that the EPLF had not found it necessary to place particular emphasis on the communities comprising Eritrea. The fact that the EPLF had seen itself as containing elements of the whole of Eritrea, and not a particular region as the TPLF had inevitably done, also helped in relegating the question when compared with the emphasis it received south of the Eritrean border.

An early step along the path to ethnic federalism had lain in the transformation of the TPLF into the Ethiopian Peoples Revolutionary Democratic Front (EPRDF). As it moved beyond its heartland the TPLF sought to broaden. The first step was the absorption of the Ethiopian Peoples Democratic Movement

(EPDM) into the new EPRDF in 1989, and the following year an alliance was made with the Oromo Liberation Front (OLF) that was the start of a series of Peoples Democratic Organizations (PDOs). In 1991 a national conference was organized at which the existing EPRDF and various other groups, several of which were hastily constituted, came together to establish the Transitional Government of Ethiopia (TGE) that was to run for two and a half years. A 17 strong Council of Ministers was set up which included members from seven ethnic groups. At the same time the country was divided into 14 regions (later reduced to 10) based primarily on ethnic identities.

The process was dominated by the EPRDF and it was soon clear that the outcome was not without challenge. Throughout the transitional period there was to be a significant challenge from forces critical of what was seen as EPRDF manipulation. Prominent amongst these were groups in the lowlands of the country, especially to the south and east in the new Oromiya and Ethio-Somali National Regional States. Here clashes occurred both between local armed factions and between them and forces of the EPRDF which had now established a new army to replace the former force that had disintegrated with the fall of Mengistu. It was also notable that these parts of the country had largely Muslim populations that became targets of the Islamist movement encouraged by Sudan. Criticism was also expressed by defenders of strong central government in Ethiopia, a position often associated with the Amharas, who feared that the EPRDF was playing a dangerous game that could easily lead to the fragmentation of the country.

The tensions all came out in the 1992 local and regional elections. These disputed elections resulted in the predictable domination of the regional PDOs encouraged by the EPRDF, but also the loss of the OLF which left the TNG making the latter appear far less inclusive thereafter. The EPRDF also dominated the commission drafting the new constitution. In 1994 there were elections for the Constituent Assembly, and in the following years fresh elections at federal and regional levels marked the final chapter in the transitional period. By this time the military challenges to the EPRDF had largely been contained (though some incidents of terrorism were to recur); while political opposition had taken to boycotting the elections making it a matter of conjecture where the balance of support lay. The EPRDF appeared firmly in charge, but how democratic the process had been, or how far it was a classic example of 'guided democracy' was left for others to judge.

The structure of ethnic federalism was eventually enshrined in the new constitution, presented to the people for ratification as part of the 1995 elections. Its writing had involved a variety of Ethiopian and foreign experts, and great efforts were made to disseminate it to the population as widely as possible. Among its more novel and controversial features was the way that sovereignty was placed not with the citizens of the Ethiopian state but with the 'Nations, Nationalities and Peoples'. As well as the House of Peoples Representatives, the Constituent Assembly also included an upper House of the Federation that was also the highest constitutional court in the land. In delineating the National Regional States, great emphasis was placed on culture, especially language. The fear that this would unleash centripetal forces in the country was magnified by the feature that the critics of the new constitution raised most frequently, namely the right of secession. To the critics it was an open invitation to separatism, but to the writers of the constitution it was a vital element guaranteeing the reality of vesting sovereignty in the Nations, Nationalities and Peoples. However what was constitutionally possible was not what the new rulers of the country wished to see develop. Thus the political system sought to strengthen the grip of the EPRDF and its associated PDOs. To supporters of the system there was a balance of constitutional and party political power: to its opponents the former was a façade and the latter smacked of Leninist vanguardism.

One way to judge the direction Ethiopia was taking lay in assessing the degree of independence actually attained by the component parts into which the country had been divided. As indicated the number of units was reduced from 14 to 10 to try to increase viability: eight were National Regional States and two were the self administering cities of Addis Ababa and Dire Dawa. While all of them were intended to develop their own resources there were significant differences in economic development from the outset, and for the poorest in particular there was heavy reliance on budget allocations from the centre. There were also accusations of favouritism, especially that with Tigre the heartland of the leaders of the EPRDF it was given particular aid and investment. Arguable though that was, it was clear that the highland regions such as Tigre, Harari and Amhara made stronger progress than the lowland Afar, Somali and Benshangul/Gamuz regions, while the largest region, Oromiya, had a mixed record as well as continuing signs of resistance. There were also continuing efforts by the centre to encourage regional cooperation, the means of which could vary from organizing seminars for state officials to deploying the national army when major security threats arose. However desperate poverty persisted in many areas with continuing need for international humanitarian aid, and it was a matter of debate how far this was due to aspects of nature and how far it reflected inefficiencies that some said were products of an over-ambitious faith in ethnic federalism?

The Ethiopian experiment also had to be judged on the issues of freedom. The situation regarding human rights was central and there were some disturbing developments from the outset. An obvious question was how to treat survivors of the old regime that had been responsible for large numbers of abuses? Unlike situations in which a transfer of power is negotiated and some provision regarding the method of tackling past abuses is agreed, the remnants of the old regime were in the hands of the outright victors. While keen not to be seen to be wreaking vengeance, the new rulers were nevertheless slow to bring the accused to justice. A Special Prosecutor's Office was established in 1992 to try members of the old regime, but several years later hundreds of people were still languishing in detention awaiting trial. For ordinary civilians there were also questions about justice. International monitors such as Amnesty International and Human Rights Watch/Africa compiled reports of apparent injustices, as did the newly formed Ethiopian Human Rights Council (EHRC). The Ethiopian government was inclined to remind the international bodies that the new system emphasised group rights as much as individual human rights. It also conceded that there were problems in the administration of justice especially since much of the system had been devolved to the regions. Often it was the regions with the most problems that had the weakest judicial systems thus contributing to a vicious circle. As for EHRC, this was depicted by the government as a voice of opposition and it even suggested that it should be classified as a political party.

Education was another area that tested freedom. Under both the Emperor and Mengistu education had been closely controlled, and it would be an important test for the new rulers. At the level of higher education the universities and colleges brought together concentrations of young people. In many countries in Africa and elsewhere students had been a political force and Ethiopia was no exception. The University of Addis Ababa in particular had a bloody history of involvement in national politics. For the new government both staff and students were somewhat suspect, and on occasions the former were purged, while armed forces were sent against the latter sometimes giving rise to fatalities. At other levels of education it was the teachers, and especially their trade union, the Ethiopian Teachers' Association (ETA), that clashed with the government on a number of occasions.

Lacking industrialization or a developed infrastructure other forms of trade unionism were generally weak in Ethiopia. Nevertheless there had been some record of labour organization at the end of the Emperor's time, while as a Marxist-Leninist Mengistu had established state run unions. The EPRDF also recognized trade unionism while wanting its cooperation in the project of developing ethnic federalism. In the circumstances it was unsurprising that clashes occurred and with them charges of attacks on workers' rights.

One of the areas that gained most attention was the freedom of the press. Here too there was an uneasy relationship between the new rulers and a press that sought to test the limits of its freedom. As so often in such circumstances the rulers tended to equate the press with political opposition and a number of struggles ensued with neither party gaining the upper hand.

Overall the new rulers had taken over a country in which human rights and the judicial system had never been strong, and in which there had been widespread conflict and abuses. In principle the EPRDF favoured the growth of civil society organizations, but it also wanted their participation in its own project and was always seeing the hand of opposition in the clashes that occurred.

Perhaps it is surprising that amongst those hands, Islam seemed comparatively insignificant. With Ethiopia having the largest population in the Horn, and up to 40 per cent Muslim, there might have appeared to be fertile soil for Islamists.[3] But while Islamists had come to power in Sudan, and were a factor in Somalia, their presence in Ethiopia seemed minimal. The largest Muslim community was amongst the Oromo people, but their opposition movement focused on a nationalist rather than an Islamist call, though there were small splinter groups claiming allegiance to Islam mainly in the east of the region, such as the Islamic Front for the Liberation of Oromia (IFLO).[4] In addition the Oromo as a people were scattered and difficult to unite in collective action. In any case the government was alert to the possible challenge from the Oromo and combined assimilating the elite with repressing opposition. The latter had attempted armed resistance in the early 1990s and was blamed for terrorist incidents in 1997, but it was largely contained. In the Ogaden there was also the possibility of Islamist sentiment, but here too a combination of clan and sub-clan rivalries, and a willingness on the part of the government to use force, made sure that any possible challenge was contained. When al-Ittihad claimed responsibility for bombs in Addis Ababa in 1996 it was the Somali base of the movement that the government attacked rather than sites within the Ogaden itself.

While there had been similarities and close political connections between the TPLF and the EPLF, the situation in Eritrea after 1991 was very different to that in Ethiopia. Instead of a coalition of forces under the leadership of one region of a vast country with the second largest population in Africa (68 million), Eritrea had a unified command of a small state and population (3.5 million). In addition while the newly formed EPRDF found itself responsible for areas of the country with which it had had little contact hitherto, the EPLF had had years of operating across the whole of Eritrea. Thus the Ethiopian experiment with ethnic federalism was largely irrelevant to Eritrea. True a system of regions was inherited and then re-drawn in 1996, but it was essentially a devolved system and firmly under the overall control of the centre. Though the population was heterogeneous, Eritrean nationalism did not have to be combined with a formula such as Nations, Nationalities and Peoples.

In other respects there were similarities between Eritrea and Ethiopia, especially in the consolidation of the leadership of the civil war. While the new constitution was to speak of democracy and pluralism, this was not to lead to what the country's new president, Issayas Afwerki, termed 'pseudo-multipartyism' (Leatherbee and Bricker, 1994). The EPLF was re-born as the People's Front for Democracy and Justice (PFDJ) and the country became a de facto single party state. Afwerki himself and his old EPLF colleagues maintained a strong hold on power, and the inner workings of the elite remained secretive.

Formal opposition was prohibited and, in the circumstances, it was understandable that there were underground activities. Some of these came from Islamic groups. Remnants of the original Eritrean Liberation Front (ELF), generally from the Muslim-populated lowlands of western Eritrea surfaced occasionally; while a newer Islamist movement, Jihad Islamiya Eritrea, supported in the early 1990s by Sudan, posed a growing threat. There were also indications of ethnic unrest, especially from the Afar in the north-east, who now found themselves divided into three states, Ethiopia, Djibouti and now Eritrea.

The prevention of the emergence of a recognized opposition was also affected by the control of civil society that resembled developments in Ethiopia. Tales of restrictions of human rights, and tough measures against the independence of the press occurred, while little freedom was accorded to the workers, including many of the former EPLF soldiers. There was encouragement of women's groups and growth in education, but all under the management of the new state.

Just as political liberalism was limited, so too was economic liberalism in spite of well-intended pronouncements. Land had been central to the EPLF's success and continued to be ultimately under the control of the state. There were complex arrangements for the allocation of land, and there was a form of inheritance permitted, but it was far from establishing a free market in land. Some of Eritrea's limited industries had been taken by Ethiopia after 1952 and there was re-building, but the industrial and trading activities came largely under the management of the PFDJ's commercial arm, the Red Sea Trading Corporation.

The US Response

In both Ethiopia and Eritrea the US found itself dealing with regimes that had made concessions to the post-Marxist era ushered in by the collapse of the Soviet Union, but still had many characteristics that reflected the old ideological colours of the leaderships that were entrenched after independence.

While Eritrea liked to see itself as the big brother of the two new regimes for historical reasons, it was clear that the most crucial position for the US would be Ethiopia. It was by far the larger of the two states, with the deeper historical roots. It had been a useful ally of the US in the past, and though the strategic position of the country was not as crucial as it had been in the Cold War, especially now that the country was landlocked, it remained a potentially dominant power in the troubled Horn. The US was therefore keen to support Ethiopia, and saw at least a part of its new development as very appropriate. Undersecretary of State for Africa, Herman Cohen, had expressed his belief that regionalism appeared to him to be a viable way forward not just for Ethiopia but the Horn in general. Thus there was approval in US policy making circles for the new policy of ethnic federalism. However the question of democracy posed greater problems. Cohen had said at the outset that he favoured elections within six months of the establishment of the new government (*Indian Ocean Newsletter*, 25 April 1992). The 1992 elections were generally perceived by international observers as less than satisfactory, but it was early days. In the build up to the 1995 elections the US was to make greater efforts to improve the quality of democracy, especially by bringing the opposition parties into the political process. For its part the opposition, mainly a number of ethnically-based groups who believed that the alliance of the EPRDF and the PDOs dominated the apparent decentralization, was reluctant to participate on what it saw as a playing field that was far from level. Thus in March 1993 six opposition groups met in Paris and were prepared to talk to the EPRDF there, though predictably the latter declined to be seen to have to leave the country for talks with fellow Ethiopians.

As the 1995 elections approached new efforts were made. Former president Jimmy Carter, who sometimes appeared to conduct a private foreign policy not always in line with the existing administration (Clinton was inclined not to listen to his Democratic predecessor to Carter's chagrin) became involved. As an old friend of Ethiopia's primeminister, Meles Zenawi, Carter believed that he would be able to mediate. Meles listened and appeared ready to act, but in the end declined to make the moves Carter suggested to the latter's disappointment.

Official US pressure was also being applied. Morse informed the House sub-committee on Africa that 'Neither exclusionary attitudes by those in power nor boycotts by those in opposition serve the cause of democratization', while at the same hearing Cohen declared that, 'boycotts and organizing for violence are not what Ethiopia needs right now' (*Indian Ocean Newsletter*, 27 August 1994). In October 1994 a task force was set up in Washington by former Congressman Harry Johnson to try to mediate between the government and the opposition. The US ambassador to Ethiopia, Irving Hicks did chair talks, but without success and the opposition duly boycotted the 1995 elections.

The US was not uncritical of the Ethiopian government. Officials commented on their concerns for human rights and called for greater freedom of the media. They also felt that the government could do more to encourage opposition participation in the political process by making facilities and funding available. However the US still appeared unwilling to pressurise the government. It has been described as a 'Jekyll and Hyde' situation because any US criticism of progress towards liberal democracy was more than offset by the view in Washington that Ethiopia was key to America's regional policy, especially after the Somalia episode and with growing realisation of Sudan's threat.[5] Meles paid an official visit to Washington in 1994 where he was received by Clinton, and in the following year they also met on the fringe of the UN's 50th anniversary celebrations. Ethiopia was also the second largest recipient of US aid in Africa, behind post-apartheid South Africa. In addition the IMF was generally understanding of the new government's position, and prepared to assist, in spite of slow privatization of Ethiopia's economy.

Thus the EPRDF and its allies easily won the 1995 elections, but there were worrying signs. In addition to the boycott of the opposition parties, there was a growth of Islamist activity. Islamist tracts and videos were appearing and there were fears that the situation could worsen. Yet these stirrings were as nothing compared to the shock of the attack on President Mubarak in Addis Ababa in June 1995. Much as the US may have wished to see changes in the direction of a more liberal political system, it had to balance that against the threat to its ally from the possible growth of Islamist violence.

An Unexpected War

The one development that nobody had expected was that the new friends of the US, Ethiopia and Eritrea, would engage in a war of their own (Lata, 2003). Though the EPLF and the TPLF had not always seen eye to eye for most of their years as guerrilla movements they had had intimate connections. That appeared to have been consolidated after independence when Ethiopia was willing to see the independence of Eritrea, even though it meant that the former was then the largest landlocked state in the world with all the attendant problems that might arise with regard to access to the sea. Most of the world was therefore surprised when what appeared to be a minor border dispute suddenly exploded into one of the bloodiest international conflicts in Africa since the end of colonialism. There had already been indications that the borders of the new state of Eritrea were a touchy subject, and that Eritrea was generally assertive when issues arose. Border problems had already occurred with regard to Djibouti, and with Yemen over the Hanish Islands, but both seemed little more than a storm in a teacup. Eritrea had also seen relations with its western neighbour, Sudan, deteriorate, but most put that down to the latter's backing for Islamists. Although Eritrea had appeared belligerent in its relations with these three neighbours, conflict with Ethiopia seemed very different both in cause and scope.

However analysts were soon pointing out that though open warfare was an unwanted surprise, there had been a number of differences building up over the years since Eritrea became independent in 1993. The precise demarcation of the border was indeed an issue. It had been known in 1993 that it existed and reflected the differences in where certain maps had placed the border between Ethiopia and the then Italian colony of Eritrea; but it was expected that it could be negotiated amicably. However during the course of the negotiations differences exploded into violence. Eritrea claimed that Ethiopia was administering territory around the small town of Badme that maps showed as Eritrean, and it advanced its army into the disputed region, whereupon Ethiopia responded with force. In days fighting spread along much of the border and though there was a ceasefire tension continued and there was a further round of fighting in the following year. The conflicts were intense, as large as any in the world in those two years, with thousands killed on both sides and many more of the population displaced on both sides of the border.

Another issue behind the conflict was that of the economic relations between the two countries. With the decline of the railway from Addis Ababa to the port of Djibouti, Ethiopia had become particularly dependent on the port of Asab that lay now in Eritrea. Differences arose about the special position of Ethiopia in the use of the port. A further problem arose over the new Eritrean currency of the *nacfa*. As an independent state it was understandable that Eritrea should want its own currency, but Eritrea still expected it to be on a par with the Ethiopian *birr*. However Ethiopia did not accept that and, as the *nacfa* soon sank against the *birr*, demanded that trade be conducted in hard currency, of which Eritrea had little. A further source of discontent was that Eritrean traders seemed to be becoming more prominent in Ethiopia.

It all added up to a burst of aggressive nationalism on both sides. Eritrea appeared as a small state trying to act like a big one. Its rulers appeared to have an inflated value of their own significance that had worsened relations with all the neighbours. Ethiopia however had its own problems. EPRDF rule was associated with acceptance of Eritrea in some quarters, such as the Amhar, against the interests of the ancient state that they thought had an historic right to it, and especially to a port on the Red Sea. Anything less than a firm response to Eritrea's sending of troops into the disputed border region smacked of weakness and might be exploited by forces critical of the government. The resulting burst of nationalism in both countries was accompanied by mass expulsions of the other's nationals, which in practice included many of the traders from Eritrea residing in

Ethiopia. The fighting itself was extremely bloody with both sides prepared to sustain large losses. And as well as the high human cost, the war was estimated to have cost over a billion US dollars by 2000 (US Congressional Research Service, 21 November 2000).

For the US the outbreak of war between its two major allies in a deeply unstable region was a dreadful development. Almost immediately Susan Rice, Assistant Secretary of State for Africa, set off on the first of two trips to the region in an effort to halt the guns, and the US also involved Rwanda in the drawing up of a joint plan. (Rwanda's ruler, Kigame, enjoyed a degree of trust with his Ethiopian and Eritrean counterparts.) The plan produced called for: agreement to settle the dispute by peaceful means; an observer mission to be placed in Badme, with Eritrean troops withdrawn; binding de-limitation of the border; and demilitarization by both sides along the whole of the border region.

Ethiopia was prepared to accept the plan, especially since it called for the withdrawal of Eritrean forces, but Eritrea was more circumspect. In part it said that the US-Rwanda plan had exceeded the brief of the two governments which was to act only as facilitators. It was also said that many issues had still to be resolved and that in consequence the proposals already put forward could not be accepted in that form. But behind whatever measures of substance were raised, there was also a question of diplomacy. Rice was seen as young, inexperienced and very forceful in her approach; while her entourage contained at least one figure known to be close to the Ethiopian prime minister. One interviewer was told that, 'The Eritreans felt that they were "overrun" by the US-Rwanda delegation' (Negash and Tronvoll, 2000, p.57). According to the same source, the US team even tried to use the problems of the Ethiopian prime minister (and the need to help a previously close ally of the Eritrean leadership 'for fear of finding something worse') to persuade the Eritreans to make concessions: an argument that was hardly likely to cut much ice in the circumstances. Negash and Tronvoll conclude:

> The US-Rwanda proposal was formulated and presented in a manner that put the blame for the conflict on one of the parties only [Eritrea], or, at least it was perceived as such. Since all subsequent negotiations attempts build on the US/Rwanda [sic] peace plan, this cemented the positions of the parties, making it even more difficult to create space for the two governments to manoeuvre within (Negash and Tronvoll, 2000, p.60).

This conclusion largely reflected the subsequent efforts of the OAU to make progress, for when a High-Level Delegation visited the two countries they found that the different positions of the two sides to the US-Rwanda plan was still the bone of contention, and the delegation was unable to make progress.

The US had maintained a low profile while the OAU was about its work, but did have two small successes. It managed to broker a moratorium on the use of military aircraft, though it lasted only until fighting resumed in February 1999; and it backed a UN embargo on arms to the belligerents to the particular annoyance of Ethiopia that still liked to present itself as the aggrieved party. The US also made it clear that it would not provide financial aid to either government while the conflict continued. In October a new delegation was sent, this time headed by Anthony Lake as special envoy, rather than Rice.

Lake and his team made four visits to the region, but still found it hard going. They were reported to have made new suggestions, especially about Ethiopia's access to the port of Assab and also the currency question, but there was no breakthrough, and shortly after Lake's last visit in January 1999 war resumed on a large scale. By late February Badme had fallen to Ethiopia, after which Eritrea announced that it accepted the US-Rwanda plan, though fighting continued along the front for several more months before eventually grinding to a halt. The US, Algeria, the OAU and the UN were all involved in efforts to establish a proper cease-fire and then move towards a solution. There was also a further visit to the region by Lake and Rice as they tried unsuccessfully to move the process along. Eventually in June 2000, after a further round of fighting in May, the two sides agreed an OAU initiative for a cessation of hostilities, but relations between the two governments remained extremely rancorous and it was clear that there was little immediate chance of the US re-building the working relationship it had had with both before the outbreak of war. However, by the end of 2004 it appeared that Ethiopia at least was expressing the wish to avoid a further round of conflict and there was thus hope of greater stability at the centre of the Horn (*Ethiopian News*, 3 November 2004).

While war dominated US relations with Eritrea and Ethiopia, its ambassadors in both countries continued to express their concerns on governance issues such as the opening up of more inclusive democratic practices and human rights issues. But in the heated nationalistic atmosphere in both countries, and with each seeking to undermine the rival camp, the timing was far from propitious and little progress was made. It all added up to grave disappointment for the US, but one in which there was a greater danger should it seriously contemplate disengaging from the region.

Djibouti

In time the situation in Eritrea and Ethiopia made the US appreciate the significance of Djibouti, sandwiched between Eritrea, Ethiopia and Somalia/Somaliland. Like the rest of the region, its identity went back to imperial activity in the late nineteenth century. France may have ended up with much less territory than Britain or Italy in the Horn, but it had not been without ambition. The establishment of French Somaliland in and around the port of Djibouti had one eye on the interior. In befriending Ethiopia, and establishing a railway from Djibouti to Addis Ababa, France hoped to advance its position in the Horn more broadly. In fact direct control was limited to French Somaliland, but its position at the southern end of the Red Sea still made it a very valuable position for the French navy from which it could operate into the Indian Ocean. Djibouti contained a number of different ethnic communities, the two largest of which were the Issas (a Somali clan) and the Afars. In 1967 the name was changed to that of The French Territory of the Afars and Issas in an attempt to make it appear more inclusive than it had previously. At independence ten years later it became simply the Republic of Djibouti.

For years after independence in 1977 Djibouti seemed rather like the calm at the eye of the storm. While conflict went on in all its neighbors, Djibouti appeared comparatively quiet and stable. President Hassan Gouled Aptidon ran a one-party state, but it seemed to endeavour to balance the main communities in terms of posts and to be pursuing cautious policies both domestically and internationally. Its tiny population of around half a million were poor, and the economy depended heavily on the port, the French garrison and the rail link to Addis Ababa, though the latter was a declining asset. However by the end of the 1980s trouble was growing, especially amongst the Afars and in 1991 they formed the backbone of the Front pour le Restauration de l'Unite et la Democratie (FRUD) that grew into a guerrilla force of about 3,000 men.

In addition to claiming oppression by the Issas, the FRUD was probably encouraged by the success of the EPLF and TPLF; while the Afars in both Eritrea and Ethiopia were also showing signs of restlessness at a time when the fall of Mengistu was making a new wave of arms available across the region. Finally, the arrival of the post-Cold War era of democratization appeared to favour a challenge to Djibouti's one-party state. President Gouled responded with carrots and sticks. There was constitutional reform, but he also strengthened his army and attacked the FRUD determinedly. Gouled finally retired from the scene in 1999, but power was passed to his nephew Ismail Omar Guelleh.

On the face of it Djibouti held little significance for America and was very much a French base serving the latter's offshore interests in particular. The US in contrast had had a close relationship with Somalia, including access to the nearby port of Berbera. However, the Gulf War of 1991 had shown the US the potential value of Djibouti. The French had used it as a base for their forces in the Gulf and its significance was not lost on the US which welcomed the helpful position taken by Djibouti and showed greater interest and aid thereafter. Indeed Bush invited Gouled to Washington to meet him personally. There was regret when the troubles associated with the FRUD occurred, but the US did show support by sending a small contingent to help with training; and once they were over it continued to show general approval. The strategic importance of Djibouti for the US was shown when the Ethiopia-Eritrea war broke out, and it was to grow subsequently in the face of the rising threat of international terrorism in the region.

Conclusion

After years in the Cold War, in which the US had competed with the USSR in the Horn, it had seemed that a new era had arrived. The US hoped that it would be possible to work with both the new governments in the Horn, the EPRDF in Ethiopia and the PFDJ in Eritrea. Both were led by 'renaissance' rulers, and both were secular. There was some opposition from Islamists in both, including terrorism, but both seemed capable of resisting that challenge. However in the face of US desire to see democratization, both rulers had as their first concern their consolidation in power. At the same time both were more than willing to tackle the major source of regional Islamist terrorism in Sudan and the US would have been more than happy for them to succeed, but it was they who were taking the lead and the US that was hitching a ride rather than directing developments.

However, it was not to be the Islamist regime in Sudan that fell before the isolation from its neighbours and the international community more generally, but US policy that was undermined by the unexpected war between Ethiopia and Eritrea. Try as the US might it could not check the war once it had started, and in its failure its enemy in the region, Sudan, was able to contrive its escape and largely turn the tables diplomatically.

Notes

[1]   It was also in 1994 that the US began supplying food to the EPLF and the TPLF, whilst trying to ensure that food did not reach Ethiopian government forces.

[2]   One writer has put this forward as a choice from three routes. The assimilationist route attempted by Haile Selassie and Mengistu; the secessionist route taken by Eritrea and favoured by some Oromo nationalists; and the accomodationist route chosen by the EPRDF (Berhe, 2004).

[3]   The official figure was put at 29 per cent Muslims but many think this too low (Shinn, 2002).

[4]   I am grateful to Kjetil Tronvoll for this point. Amongst students of the history and politics of Ethiopia there has been a lack of focus on the country's Muslim communities when compared with the Coptic Orthodox church.

[5]   I am grateful for this point to David Shinn, former US ambassador to Ethiopia.

References

Berhe, A. (2004), 'Diversity and state-building in Ethiopia', *African Affairs*, 103, 413.

Cohen, H. (2000), *Intervening in Africa: Superpower peacemaking in a Troubled Continent*, London, Palgrave.

Lata, L. (2003), 'The Ethiopia-Eritrea War', *Review of African Political Economy*, No. 97.

Leatherbee, L. and Bricker, D. (1994), *Balancing Consensus and Dissent: Prospects for Human Rights and Development in the Horn of Africa*, New York, Fund for Peace.

Negash, T. and Tronvoll, K. (2002), *Brothers at War: Making sense of the Eritrean-Ethiopian War*, Oxford, James Currey.

Shinn, D. (2002), 'Ethiopia: Coping with Islamic fundamentalism before and after September 11', *Africa Notes*, 7 February.

Chapter 6

Confronting Sudan

The involvement of the US in Somalia had been on a far larger scale than anything that had happened in Sudan, and the outcome of the intervention in Mogadishu effectively ensured that American troops would not be deployed elsewhere in Africa for a significant period of time at least. However, while events in Somalia were seen in the US as primarily indigenous, there was awareness of the accusations of Islamist complicity linked to Sudan and there was thus unlikely to be any form of rapprochement. Instead Sudan had remained on the US list of states sponsoring terrorism and the (relatively mild) consequences of that remained in place. Sudan's place on the list was, in US eyes, amply justified with the attempted assassination of President Mubarak in Addis Ababa in 1995 which was to open a new chapter intensifying confrontation by the US and its allies towards the country. If the years from 1989 to 1995 had consisted largely of the US responding to Sudan's Islamist foreign policy, positions were now largely reversed with the US seeking ways to bring about change in Sudan. However it had to be by policies short of direct military engagement: what would they be, and how far would they work?

Sanctions

Following the assassination attempt the US strongly supported Egypt's decision to seek UN sanctions against Sudan: the first time that the UN adopted mandatory sanctions for the attempted assassination of a political figure, and only the second that they had been adopted in response to terrorism, the first being Libya (Osman, 2002). The grounds given were not simply the general accusation of supporting terrorism, but that three fugitives from the failed attempt had gone to ground in Sudan, and should be extradited to Ethiopia where their alleged offence had taken place. It was Sudan's failure to produce them that led to the sanctions resolution being adopted. For its part Sudan claimed that it had tried to apprehend them, and later said that they had probably left the country rather than remain in hiding there. Although the sanctions resolutions were put before the UN Security Council by Ethiopia and Egypt, as the aggrieved parties, it was clear that they had the enthusiastic support of the US as well as significant backing in Africa and the Middle East.

In all, three sanctions resolutions were passed during 1996. In January Resolution 1044 not only called for the extradition of the three suspects, it also called on Sudan to cease supporting or sheltering terrorists, a reference that caused serious concern in the Sudan government of possible international action. Resolution 1054 called for diplomatic sanctions that would include member states reducing the number of accredited Sudanese diplomats and restricting the movements of Sudanese officials. Resolution 1070 was intended to restrict the international activities of Sudanese airlines (allegedly the carriers of the would-be assassins and some of their arms and equipment).

When compared with other sanctions imposed on the states of the region – notably Libya and Iraq – at Egypt's behest the sanctions against Sudan were light (Niblock, 2001). While Egypt was highly critical of the Sudan government for the attempted assassination, it was very sensitive to the feelings of the Sudanese people with whom Egyptians had long and close relations. It had no wish to see sanctions imposed like those in Iraq that would bring further distress to a population already experiencing long term economic deterioration, and with extreme conditions in several parts of the country. In addition Egypt opposed any weapons ban on Sudan that might restrict the government's ability to maintain the coherence of the state and that could lead to its break up with grave consequences for Egypt itself. As Mubarak himself put it, 'We could agree on any sort of sanctions except an arms embargo, which means Northern Sudanese would be unable to buy arms to defend their country while those in Southern Sudan could buy arms anywhere. This can lead to the division of Sudan, which we reject and refuse' (*Africa Confidential*, 37, 8, 1996). From Egypt's point of view the sanctions were primarily a warning to the Sudan government to mend its ways rather than a serious attempt to inflict pain on the country. Even these mild sanctions were barely enforced (though officially mandatory as they were passed under Chapter VII); and Resolution 1070 was never enforced at all, in part because of the need for humanitarian aid flights to Sudan. Indeed, it appeared that Egypt was regarded as soft by the US and criticised for its support of such weak sanctions: the US permanent representative at the UN, Madeleine Albright, was said to have 'chastised Egypt for the weakness of its resolution'; while her deputy was quoted as saying that, 'In failing to impose more meaningful sanctions against Sudan, we risk further insecurity and instability for the people of eastern Africa, the Middle East and the Sudan' (Niblock, 2000, p.10). For its part the US expressed such concern for the security situation in Sudan, which it feared might be exacerbated by sanctions, that shortly before the first resolution was passed it withdrew its ambassador, Tim Carney, and his remaining staff, even though Carney himself protested at the decision. He was later to claim that it was based on a CIA recommendation, accepted by Secretary of State Warren Christopher, but which itself had accepted false information. Its falsity, and that of over 100 other reports, lay in that it 'had either embellished or wholly fabricated information': the error became known quite quickly but the decision to withdraw staff from Khartoum was not revoked (Carney and Ijaz, *Washington Post*, 30 June 2002). Thereafter Carney was reduced to covering Sudan from the US embassy in Nairobi with only occasional visits to Khartoum.

The frustration that the US had displayed with the mildness of the UN sanctions not merely persisted but worsened as even those sanctions were scarcely applied. In 1997, as the Clinton administration's policy towards the regime in

Sudan tightened, the US decided to impose its own sanctions. These included blocking the movement of US technology to Sudan, the stopping of US bank loans to Sudan, and seizing Sudanese assets in America. Unlike the UN sanctions, these measures were enforced in the subsequent years, but their impact was very limited since economic and financial links between the two countries were comparatively few. The State Department in Washington was aware of that reality, but could do little more by the sanctions route. Largely frustrated by the limitations of the impact of UN sanctions, especially when compared with the grip of sanctions on Libya and Iraq, the US had to rely more on other measures in its growing confrontation with Sudan.

Destabilization

Even without any possible US encouragement, it was clear that Sudan had raised a great deal of concern amongst its neighbours. Eritrea, Ethiopia and Uganda in particular felt both threatened by the subversive activities of Islamists that they saw as sponsored by Sudan, and in a position to make an active response. However, while they were in time to coalesce in their support for Sudan's opposition movement, each had its own particular axe to grind.

The most outspoken in denunciation of Sudan was Eritrea's leader Issayas Afwerki. This was in part because of his real sense of grievance for what he alleged to be Sudan's support for Islamists, but was also due to his own sense of his country's importance. Although Eritrea was, in reality, small and impoverished it had grown from a long and difficult conflict and saw itself as something of the David of the Horn that had slain the Ethiopian Goliath and was not prepared to tolerate a challenge, following the coup of 1989 by Islamists, on Eritrea's western border. By 1995 Eritrea was quite open about its desire to see the regime in Sudan overthrown, and actively supported the Sudanese opposition. This consisted not only of encouraging the exiled politicians of the NDA, now installed in the former Sudan embassy (where they were visited by the American ambassador to Sudan, Donald Petterson), but also the Sudan Alliance Forces (SAF), a new northern Sudanese armed force led by a former army officer, Brigadier Abdel Aziz Khalid Osman. In December 1995 the SAF began its first operations in eastern Sudan.

Meanwhile to the south relations between Sudan and Uganda had also been deteriorating. President Museveni was an old friend of SPLA leader John Garang, added to which Uganda's support had become especially vital following the collapse of Mengistu's regime in Ethiopia. Uganda's support for the SPLA remained as firm as ever, but it was to contribute to growing conflict in northern Uganda. Though less widely acknowledged, problems of 'north' and 'south' in Uganda are as much a part of that country's politics as they are of Sudan's. The years of turmoil under both periods of Milton Obote's rule as well as that of Idi Amin were periods of northern domination that were reversed by Museveni's victory of 1986. Resulting partly from new northern Ugandan alienation, especially amongst the Acholi, bizarre religious cults emerged claiming Christian inspiration. The first in the 1980s was the Holy Spirit Movement led by Alice Lakwena, but far more enduring was to be the movement in the 1990s led by Joseph Kony known as the Lord's Resistance Army (LRA). The LRA became noted for abduction of children in northern Uganda, and extreme violence; so much so that one investigation commented that the 'LRA leaders appear to regard violence as a way of purging society of impurity' (Amnesty International, 1997, p.6). By 1996 it became apparent that the Sudanese army had links to the LRA, and that the latter had bases in southern Sudan. The relationship not only allowed the Sudan government to respond in kind to Ugandan support for the SPLA by destabilizing parts of northern Uganda, it also on occasions encouraged LRA activities directly against the SPLA and southern Sudanese refugee camps in northern Uganda. The Sudan government was not only backing Islamists in Uganda, much more important in terms of the impact on Ugandan politics, it was supporting a bizarre and grotesque 'Christian' movement as well. The Ugandan government's anger increased and with it the openness of its support for the SPLA (Woodward, 2002).

Ethiopia was slower to show its displeasure with Sudan. Though aware of Islamist activities it was less vocal in its response and less active in support of the Sudanese opposition. However the attempted assassination of Egypt's president in Ethiopia's capital while on his way to attend a meeting of the OAU was both a grave offence and an embarrassment to the country. More discretely than Eritrea or Uganda, Ethiopia began to allow SAF and SPLA forces to establish bases on the country's border with Sudan.

In addition to their individual grievances towards the Sudan government, Eritrea, Ethiopia and Uganda had a collective identity. Their three leaders, Afwerki, Museveni and Meles Zenawi, had all come to power through successful armed struggles against despotic regimes. Even before attaining power they had gained some international admiration, especially Afwerki and Zenawi, and once in control were regarded as dynamic new brooms (the name of Paul Kagame in Rwanda was also added to the select list). It was thus as like-minded leaders perceiving themselves as facing a common enemy in Sudan that Afwerki, Museveni and Zenawi were acting in concert in encouraging the attacks of the SPLA and SAF that stepped up at the start of 1997. From their own experience they knew that armed revolt in Africa could be successful; but at the same time they also knew that cross-border support was most important, and that on their own the various elements of the Sudanese opposition might well be unsuccessful. Their support was designed to engage Sudan's forces on the eastern front as well as in the south; and as more forces were deployed away from the capital and other major cities it was also hoped that a popular uprising could be encouraged, of the kind that had unseated two military regimes in Sudan hitherto in the 'revolutions' or '*intifadas*', as they were known, of 1964 and 1985.

The US, for its part, was not averse to the initiatives of these 'African Renaissance' leaders with regard to Sudan, but the emergence of the broad challenge to the Sudan government was to provoke renewed concern on the part of the relevant policymakers in Washington and in the region.[1] Officially US policy towards the region was the same as that towards the rest of Africa. As Assistant Secretary for African Affairs, George Moose, put it the four main concerns were: support for democracy, human rights and the rule of law; crisis and conflict prevention; environmental protection and sustainable development; and free trade. Unofficially some countries were better at that than others and the 'African Renaissance' leaders were seen generally as moving in the right direction. The US ambassador to Eritrea, Robert Houdek, remarked, 'Afwerki [sic], Zeenawi [sic] and Museveni are ideal leaders in the region, adhering to the democratic principle, espousing privatisation and co-operating towards achieving peaceful settlement to regional disputes such as the one lingering in Sudan' (*Sudan Focus*, 15 February 1995). Such a view was broadly held in Washington and amongst US officials in the region; but the crucial phrase was 'peaceful settlement'. As the three leaders named came to support more active measures by the Sudanese opposition to achieve an armed overthrow of the Islamist regime in Sudan, so US policy became more debated before finally moving to appear to support whatever change its allies thought possible. Ambassador Carney later claimed that in moving in this direction the US relied too much on second hand intelligence from Sudan's hostile neighbours 'rather than on its own eyes and ears' (*Washington Post*, 30 June 2002).

While anti-Sudan sentiment was building in American circles, it was far from clear what path to follow: should it be one of support for efforts to bring the existing regime to the negotiating table over the war with full diplomatic backing for IGAD, which in 1994 had produced the Declaration of Principles (DoP) for the ending of the conflict which the US could back; or should it be support for growing military confrontation? Reports from Washington suggested that the former route was that generally preferred in the State Department, while in Defense and CIA circles the latter course of action had most support (*Indian Ocean Newsletter*, 12 October 1996).[2] On the face of it the two paths were not incompatible: the US could support armed confrontation in an effort to drive the Sudan government to an agreement. However, even were that to be successful, it appeared to hold out the prospect of the same regime in power at least in northern Sudan, and able to continue on its Islamist ways, both internationally and domestically. As a generally pro-government publication put it at the time:

> The US, it can be argued, needs to see an end to the war in the southern Sudan and this has been the main thrust of its present Africa policy. But this view contradicts the widespread belief that the US is actually taking a calculated risk and sustaining the war in the hope that prolonged fighting will result in a change of government in Khartoum (*Sudan Focus*, 15 February 1996).

Policy might have been clearer if there had been less conflicting voices in Washington, and if Sudan had had a higher priority that would have focused minds; but even though Sudan still appeared to be fuelled by Turabi's grandiose ambitions it was well down the foreign policy agenda, as was Africa in general. However, with the presidential re-election completed safely, new steps were taken that were widely interpreted as indicating US support for the option of war as a path to regime change in Sudan. In November 1996 it was announced that $20 million worth of military aid would be going to Eritrea, Ethiopia and Uganda. While emphasis was put on the non-lethal character of the aid – uniforms, tents and other such material – and that it was for the defensive needs of the recipients, it was clear that those needs were in respect of the perceived threat from Sudan (the 'front-line states' as they were sometimes known), and that some at least of the supplies could end up with the SPLA and the SAF. A few weeks later these forces opened their new offensives in southern and eastern Sudan. At the same time the administration in Washington talked of a new Africa Crisis Response Force, to which friendly African states would supply 10,000 men which would be equipped by the US to act in crisis situations. The move was widely interpreted as a further challenge to Sudan, though it proved stillborn since events on the ground were soon to make the idea redundant.

Whatever the truth of the whereabouts of the military aid supplied by the US, the expectation of a clear commitment to a harder line on Sudan and support for the opposition grew with changes in the State Department in Clinton's second term. Madeleine Albright, who had already shown her feelings on Sudan when at the UN, moved to become Secretary of State. She in turn was soon joined as Assistant Secretary of State for Africa by a young African-American woman, Susan Rice, to whom Albright was close. Rice had already served in the White House as Special Assistant to the President for Africa and Senior Director for African Affairs at the NSC and was noted for having strongly critical views of the Sudan government, although she was no unreserved fan of the SPLA. Albright had sought the post for Rice, and obtained the backing of Hilary Clinton in the process. Through these personal connections Rice had greater access to both the President and Vice-President than other holders of her office have usually had. Close to Rice were Gayle Smith, who followed Rice in both her previous roles, and John Prendergast, who was director for African affairs at the NSC and then deputy to Susan Rice: both Smith and Prendergast had long experience of disasters in the Horn of Africa and of the success of liberation movements. Rice, Smith and Prendergast were to prove an influential team behind Albright, with Rice herself very much at the forefront. Shortly after taking office Rice announced the need, 'To apply additional pressure aimed at isolating the Khartoum regime in order to contain the threat it represents to US interests' (*Indian Ocean Newsletter*, 20 September 1997). In July 1997 it was reported that they had already won the argument in Washington against those favouring 'constructive engagement' with the Sudan government, in which Ambassador Tim Carney, from his exile in Nairobi, was generally seen as a leading voice backed by other State Department officials worried at the growing polarisation in the Horn.[3] This view was supported apparently by some in the CIA, concerned about lack of good intelligence with no official US representation in Sudan. An embarrassing example of the different voices at work came in the autumn of 1997 when it was announced publicly that the US Embassy in Khartoum was to be re-opened, only for the decision to be reversed two days later.[4]

The strongest message of all came from Madeleine Albright herself in December 1997 when she stopped in Uganda on a tour of Africa. After meeting Museveni she announced that, 'the United States and other regional states are deeply concerned over the situation in Sudan'; and then went on to meet the SPLA leader John Garang and other NDA leaders, and was reported to have given her support for the 'final onslaught' against the NIF regime and for the establishment of a government that would 'oppose terrorism' (*Indian Ocean Newsletter*, 13 December 1996). US policy had come full circle: in the early 1980s it had backed Nimeiri's regime, even when it had allied itself with the Muslim Brotherhood and and fought the SPLA then supported by Ethiopia, the Soviet Union and Cuba; now it was the US appearing to encourage the SPLA in its confrontation with the Islamist regime in Sudan. A long time academic observer of Sudan, interviewed shortly before Albright's visit to Uganda, reviewed attitudes in Washington from hard line Christian groups in Congress hoping for an SPLA victory to the more diplomatic voices in the State Department preferring a political solution, and concluded, 'I don't know of anybody in the US administration wanting to see the present government continuing to stand by itself' (*Sudan Focus*, 15 October 1997).

However, stand by itself it continued to do. While many were speculating about the likely fall of the Sudan government throughout 1997 and into early 1998 it managed to survive the military assault and prevent any popular uprising. Few put its survival down to the ability of its own armed forces, and more attention focused on the performance of the SPLA and the SAF, which appeared to have let a prospect of victory slip. Perhaps the failure was due to wishful thinking about the capacities of the opposition forces, but their limitations had always been known and that had been a reason for the support given by the 'front line states' – with US encouragement. The major failure, and the one that ensured that speculation about greater support for the opposition was effectively ended, came with the eruption of war between Eritrea and Ethiopia in May 1998. While war over a scrubby patch of border seemed both surprising and pointless to many, it was the culmination of a number of factors that had emerged as the former guerrilla partners (but not always the best of friends) led neighbouring independent states with perceived differing national interests. It was also the biggest blow since the Somalia debacle to American policy in the Horn. It was the US that had helped the transition from Mengistu's regime into the brave new world of two separate states, and that had supported both new governments in their early years. It was also the US that had supported them in the growing confrontation with Sudan. Now US objectives for the whole region appeared to fall as Eritrea and Ethiopia turned on each other, and US power and influence proved of little avail in the face of inflamed nationalism.

Sudan Responds

While its African neighbours had been supporting the SPLA and SAP, Sudan had moved to clean up its act, at least publicly. The help for the would-be assassins of Mubarak in Addis Ababa was rumoured to have been the work of loose cannon in security and the military establishment around President Beshir was keen to rein them in. Three leading Islamists in security were demoted and replaced by figures more aligned with the president. Sudan also went on a charm offensive under the overall management first of Foreign Minister Ali Osman Mohammed Taha, and later, when Taha became Vice-President, his successor, Mustafa Osman Ismail. The moves were to be on four fronts: the Arab world; the African neighbours;

Europe; and the US itself. In addition to these new moves Sudan consolidated its emerging relations with its new Asian partners in the moves to develop its oilfields (Burr and Collins, 2003, pp.231-252).[5]

In the Arab world the starting point was Egypt, since the attempted assassination of Mubarak had been such a shock. As seen Egypt had called for sanctions at the UN, but then been willing for these to have only a very limited impact. By mid-1996 Mubarak made it clear that he sought to improve relations with Sudan, or at least with President Beshir, since the hope had long existed in Egypt of exploiting differences between Beshir and the army on the one hand and Turabi and the NIF on the other. Central to the thaw in relations was the question of Egypt's list of Islamists that it claimed were being sheltered in Sudan, and on which progress was made. However it was not only Egypt that mattered for Sudan was seen almost as suspiciously in Saudi Arabia, from where Osama bin Laden emanated. In addition to measures to appease Saudi Arabia on terrorism, Sudan could also suggest that the support from its African neighbours for the SPLA and SAP was being encouraged by Israel. This opened up the spectre not only of the forces of Zionism seeking to destabilise Sudan, and perhaps separate the south of the country, but also of the growth of Israeli influence in the Red Sea, long a matter of particular concern to Saudi Arabia. While Egypt and Saudi Arabia were the Arab states with most obvious and direct concern for Sudan, others were also drawn in through suggestions that on Sudan's fringes the Arab world was being attacked. This view had played well for Sudan in the past and could now draw on the apparent strength of the Eritrea-Ethiopia-Uganda relationship with its backing from Israel's greatest patron, the US

The relations with the African neighbours were harder to build, at least until the war between Ethiopia and Eritrea, but even here there were opportunities. One such was the Sudan's need to at least appear more conciliatory on the war in the light of the advances made by the SPLA and the SAF in the early months of 1997. Internally the government had exploited the longstanding split in the SPLA by making an agreement with the breakaway group led by Riek Machar known as the Khartoum Peace Agreement (KPA), this included the proposed establishment of a coordinating council for the south in Juba and the right of secession. Externally the government accepted the idea of a new round of talks towards peace by the Inter-Governmental Authority for Development (IGAD) that had already laid down the aforementioned Declaration of Principles (DoP) to end the conflict in 1994.[6] Under pressure from its African neighbours, and fearing that rejection might provide an excuse for deeper intervention in Sudan of the kind underway by Uganda and Rwanda in Zaire (also believed to have received a green light from the US), the Sudan government appeared to commit itself to the DoP. However its agreement remained ambiguous since it suggested that it was agreeing to the DoP agenda rather than swallowing the principles whole. In the short term it took some pressure off the government without contributing to a direct success in further talks, though in the long term the government's acceptance of the DoP as an agenda was to be a significant step.

A major reason why peace talks between the Sudan government and the SPLA did not go further at that time was the outbreak of the Eritrean-Ethiopian war, of which Sudan was quick to take advantage. Both protagonists were keen to repair their relations with their western neighbour, and from Sudan's point of view Ethiopia was the more valuable of the two. Many in the international community saw Eritrea as the aggressor in the conflict; while the much larger Ethiopia, with its shared water and oil potential in the common field around Gambella that would require the cooperation of the two countries, was a more important friend for Sudan. Beginning with restrictions on the SAF, improved relations between Ethiopia and Sudan later went on to restrict the SPLA as well. Meanwhile Eritrea also sought improved relations, but more slowly than Ethiopia and only once the opposition threat on Sudan's eastern flank had been effectively contained. That left Uganda in the south where, in spite of third party attempts to bring agreement between the two countries over the LRA and the SPLA, the situation remained fundamentally unchanged. However, while militarily Uganda's support for the SPLA remained a problem for Sudan, politically its weight was less once the war to the north-east had collapsed the Eritrea-Ethiopia-Uganda relationship. As Susan Rice put it in testimony to a Congressional hearing:

> Since the conflict [between Ethiopia and Eritrea] began last year, Sudan has increasingly benefited from the hostilities between its former adversaries. Eritrea recently signed an accord with Sudan to normalize relations. Ethiopia has renewed air service to Khartoum and has made overtures to Sudan for improved relations as well. Both sides have moved to reduce support to Sudanese opposition groups (Negash and Tronvoll, 2002, App. 12, p.139).

The policy towards Sudan of pressure via African proxies had effectively collapsed.

A third region on which Sudan government focused was Europe. A number of European countries were supporters of the IGAD peace process, first as the Friends of IGAD and later as the IGAD Partners' Forum. There was also a feeling in some European capitals that the way to respond to Sudan's apparent attempt to row back from its international isolation was to enter into some kind of engagement. Germany, the Netherlands, Britain and Italy all seemed willing to review their attitudes towards the Sudan government, especially in the light of both the KPA and the government's response to the IGAD talks (International Crisis Group, 2002, pp.65-7). Cynics also pointed out that there were new developments with regards to Sudan's oil fields that were attractive for European companies with interests in the business, from which American companies were excluded by US sanctions on Sudan: Britain and France were Sudan's major European suppliers.

However, it was the US that mattered most as far as Sudan's international isolation was concerned, especially in the light of American backing for UN sanctions and its support for Eritrea, Ethiopia and Uganda. It was here that one of the most controversial aspects of US-Sudanese relations developed over an apparent offer from Sudan to hand over Osama bin Laden to America early in 1996. As seen, despite his protestations Ambassador Carney had already been instructed to move to Kenya because of an alleged security threat. Sudan had already gained improved cooperation from France by handing over Carlos the

Jackal, and there were some at least in the Sudan government who thought that a similar offer could be made to the US However, the US had only begun to focus closely on bin Laden shortly before the offer was made, and one reason for debating the offer to hand him over was apparently a lack of evidence in US files against him.[7] An alternative suggested was to hand him over to Saudi Arabia. While Saudi Arabia was keen to see bin Laden out of Sudan, it did not want him back in his native country: evidence against him was not the problem in this case, but his family was very well connected; while there might be danger of a terrorist backlash in the event of bin Laden being tried and executed for his actions against the Kingdom. There was also doubt as to the seriousness of the offer from Sudan, or whether, even if those making it were in earnest, others in the NIF, notably Turabi himself, would have allowed such an important figure as bin Laden to be extradited. It is also suggested that while the offer was on the table, bin Laden and many of his followers had been encouraged by Turabi, in May, to slip away to Afghanistan where bin Laden's old friends in the Taliban were coming to power in Kabul. Nevertheless Carney and Ijaz were later to claim that the failure to take bin Laden in 1996 had been a grave mistake; with the implication that had the US acted otherwise it is possible that the events five years later on 9/11 might never have taken place (Carney and Ijaz, *Washington Post*, 30 June 2002; *Jane's Intelligence Digest*, 14 January 2005). Clinton himself was reported to say after 9/11 that the failure to accept the offer of bin Laden in 1996 was the biggest mistake of his presidency (Gunaratna, 2002, p.157).

Even with bin Laden out of Sudan and inaccessible in the al-Qaeda training camps in Afghanistan, the US still had the opportunity to acquire significant intelligence on him and his organization, for from late in 1996 Sudan repeatedly offered it intelligence material. In addition to offering files, there were also invitations for US officials to have access to Sudan and go anywhere they wished to investigate alleged terrorist activities. There were officials in the State Department who believed the information on offer from Sudanese security sources could be valuable, as did members of the FBI; however they were refused permission to engage with the Sudanese authorities, apparently at the level of Secretary of State Madeleine Albright and her Assistant Secretary for Africa Susan Rice. Sudan also used informal channels in an endeavour to show its keenness to engage the US administration.[8] These included a Pakistani-American businessman, Mansoor Ijaz, a member of the Council on Foreign Relations who had links with the Democratic Party that went right up to Clinton himself, and experienced lobbyist Janet McElligott, but all to no avail. Ambassador Carney has since claimed, 'The US failed to reciprocate Sudan's willingness to engage us on serious questions of terrorism … the US lost access to a mine of material on bin Laden and his organization' ('The Osama Files', *Vanity Fair*, January 2002). The reason Carney gives for the resistance to engagement was that intelligence, mainly from the CIA, was 'politicized'. By this he appears to mean that Albright, Rice and others in the State Department had already had their minds made up that Sudan was continuing to support terrorism on the basis of faulty intelligence, fed according to a former CIA official by 'an organized ring whose motives were a mixture of malice and greed' ('The Osama Files', *Vanity Fair*, January 2002).

However others in the administration argued that the offers of cooperation by Sudan were no more than a diversionary tactic to take the heat off the government and cover up what was really happening.[9] In particular there was still a case to be made that Sudan had not broken all of its links with bin Laden or Islamist terrorism after his expulsion in May 1996. Though some Islamist training camps were shut down it was alleged that a number still remained and continued to train members of opposition groups from a range of Muslim countries, including Hamas, Hizbollah and Islamic Jihad, regarded in Sudan as in much of the Muslim world as freedom fighters rather than terrorists. The fullest published claims of these contacts is provided by Yossef Bodansky, Director of the House Task Force on Terrorism and Unconventional Warfare, who gave chapter and verse on activities both before and after bin Laden's expulsion from Sudan (Bodansky, 1999, pp.78-90).[10] While he cites various leading Sudanese NIF figures as involved, principle responsibility is laid at the door of Hassan al-Turabi himself. Bodansky claims that there was a meeting in Khartoum as late as August 1997 in which Turabi gave full backing to Islamist terrorist acts in East Africa, allegedly in response to his belief that the US was actively seeking to bring down the regime in Sudan with the assistance of the country's neighbours, and that an attack on US interests there would provide a message to those African governments as well as to America itself. This was only a year after Turabi had, at the pressing of Mansoor Ijaz, written personally to Clinton offering his assistance for anti-terrorist cooperation between Sudan and the US Such apparently contradictory behaviour is however credible given Turabi's repeated ability over many years to address Western and Islamist audiences in very different terms. Suspicions about Sudan and terrorism were also encouraged by continuing accusations from neighbouring states after bin Laden's departure from the country. Eritrea claimed that opposition groups based in Sudan continued to operate on its territory; as did Ethiopia right up to the time that the war with Eritrea started in 1998.

It could be argued that faced with conflicting pictures of Sudan- a public wish to cooperate with the US and alleged secret continuing support for terrorism- it was understandable that some in the State Department, backed by the CIA, still maintained their suspicions. It was also notable that certain of the go-betweens – notably Ijaz – had business connections with Sudan at a time of potential oil developments (Susan Rice, 'J'Accuse', *Elle*, May 2002). It has also been queried whether the US intelligence services had the capacity to deal with the large amounts of material in Arabic that Sudan appeared to be offering to handover. However, the biggest query of all concerns US ability to assess political developments taking place in Sudan. Rumours of rivalries within the ranks of the government, the NIF and the military were legion and also crucial. Was the regime looking for a showdown in terms of this new fount of Islamism versus the US (as Bodansky argues) or was there a pragmatic streak which, while wishing to maintain an Islamic state, was recognising that in the face of its international isolation, and with the support being given to the opposition, the government should try to make at least a tactical retreat? Such arguments frequently came down to personal assessments of the alleged rivalry of the NIF's founder, Turabi, on the one hand, and President Beshir on the other. Once more the US was in a difficult position to judge since it had no diplomatic staff of its own on the ground inside the country: a result of intelligence-led decisions in Washington that had been opposed by successive ambassadors, Petterson and Carney.

US Missiles on Khartoum North

If the confrontation of the US and Sudan really took off with the implication of at least some members of the Sudan government in the attempted assassination of President Mubarak of Egypt on 26 June 1995, then it came to a head when American Tomahawk cruise missiles rained down on the Shifa pharmaceutical plant in Khartoum North on 20 August 1998. The immediate motive for the attack was the allegation of Sudanese support for terrorism and the manufacture in the Shifa plant of chemicals capable of being used in weapons of mass destruction. The timing and the decision to act were linked to the attacks on the American embassies in Nairobi and Dar es Salaam that had taken place 13 days earlier on 7 August. They had killed a total of 224 people, including 12 Americans.[11] None of the accounts of the actual conduct of the attacks directly relates the events to Sudan, but there are references to past connections. The attacks themselves were organized through sleeper cells of al-Quaeda in both Kenya and Tanzania, that had significant Muslim communities where young recruits could be found, especially in Mombasa, Zanzibar, Dar es Salaam and Nairobi. The Nairobi cell also had links to Islamist activities in Somalia. All these sleeper cells went back to the international network that had centred on Sudan during the most militant and internationalist phase of the NIF regime, inspired by Turabi and partly organised by bin Laden. Preliminary thought about an attack on US positions in East Africa was undertaken as far back as 1994 and had involved bin Laden himself when he was in Khartoum. The plan had been to carry out the attacks in 1996, but they had been postponed, partly because bin Laden had de-camped to Afghanistan. Though none of the perpetrators of the attacks were Sudanese, it appeared that at various times beforehand they had passed through the country and some had Sudanese passports. Bodansky also claims that as late as May 1998, when all the plans were in place, bin Laden and his number two, Ayman al-Zawahiri, went to Khartoum for final talks on strategy with Turabi (Bodansky, 1999, p.248).

Whatever may have been going on behind the scenes (quite possibly unbeknown to at least some members of the Sudan government) as soon as the attacks took place the government roundly condemned them. It went on to offer the US cooperation in tracking downs the perpetrators of 'these criminal acts' as the Foreign Minister, Mustafa Osman Ismail, called them. However public condemnation was not to prove sufficient to deflect American suspicions away from Sudan, or to ensure the country's safety from retaliation via the bombardment of the Shifa factory. The legitimacy of the attack in Afghanistan was generally accepted in the international community since the connection between bin Laden and al-Qaeda with the bombings in East Africa was scarcely contested. However the justifications for the missile attack on Sudan, which destroyed the factory and killed a night watchman, were far more controversial.

A major claim was that the al-Shifa factory was making chemicals that were precursors of the VX nerve gas. The US claimed that it had soil samples from the site to back up this allegation. Much doubt was cast on the accuracy of this evidence, especially since none of the material allegedly analysed ever became available for neutral expert scrutiny.[12] It was also argued that, even if found, the chemical named EMPTA could have been used for commercial purposes.

Initially there were also claims from official sources, including National Security Adviser, Sandy Berger, that the factory was not a commercial enterprise at all, but a chemical weapons facility; and that as such it was guarded by the Sudanese military. This soon proved to be the most easily dismissed claim since it was indisputable that whether or not the factory was connected to the production of chemical weapons, it was a pharmaceutical factory. Indeed non-Sudanese witnesses came forward connected with its design, building and operation to confirm that fact, and several denied that it could have been used for chemical weapons at all. As for military guards, these too were denied, and there were clearly none at the time of the attack.

Suggestions were also made of links between Sudan and Iraq's alleged programme of chemical weapons. Indeed ever since 1989, and especially around the time of the Gulf War, there was talk of weapons links of various kinds between the two countries, but no evidence ever appeared connecting Iraq in any way to al-Shifa. In time it became ever more doubtful that there had been good intelligence supporting the attack: indeed at least one report not only queried the intelligence, but claimed that the Joint Chiefs of Staff were not informed of the attack; while at least some senior figures at the CIA were dubious (*Vanity Fair*, March, 1999). It seemed that, once again, Sudan's critics at the NSC and the State Department lay behind Clinton's decision to fire the missiles (cynics also noted that the timing coincided with Monica Lewinsky's appearance before a Grand Jury giving rise to 'wag the dog' accusations). In the longer term the judgement remained that if, as was quite possible, Sudan was making chemical weapons (like several other Middle East states) then it was probably not taking place at al-Shifa but at two other sites.

However there was also a non-technical argument advanced to justify the action, namely that bin Laden either owned the factory or had some financial connection with it. This too was questioned when it became clear that the pharmaceutical company was privately owned by a businessman named Salah Idris, of Sudanese origin and Saudi nationality. Though he had businesses in Saudi Arabia and Sudan, and appeared to have some links with the NIF, no connection was ever proven with bin Laden. This became clear when the US froze his assets in America, only to have to have to unfreeze them the following year: Salah Idris went on to open a case for compensation for the destruction of his factory. Whatever lay behind the US attack, in political terms it proved damaging. Many sceptical voices were raised internationally following Sudan's appeal to the UN; while the Republican critics made more mileage out of expressing doubts about the veracity of the Clinton administration than the president achieved by attacking an alleged enemy.

The Sudan government was worried that the bombardment might presage further attacks. A further round of peace talks with the SPLA in Addis Ababa in August had ended in predictable deadlock; while the opposition forces in the field were still a threat, if less so than the previous year. The SPLA and the NDA had proceeded from Addis to Cairo where there was talk of Egypt putting its weight behind the opposition in further negotiations. There had also been a wave of popular disturbances in the capital during which three students had been killed by the security forces. Was the US now intending to take advantage of the situation to turn its military force directly on the country? Its response was to come out with a barrage of righteous indignation at an unjustified and unprovoked bombardment; and it orchestrated public demonstrations of protest against the US and appeals to nationalism and Muslim solidarity. In the Middle East in particular it found considerable sympathy; and in time a number of European governments came to believe that on this occasion at least Sudan was more sinned against than sinning.

The attack on al-Shifa was both the high and low point of the Clinton administration's policy towards Sudan. High, because after appearing to seek to bring down the regime through largely covert means involving proxy neighbours, it had finally come out and used direct force. However the effect of not following up its strike on al-Shifa was to appear to be merely chastising and not challenging the Sudan government. Low, because the doubts about the legitimacy of the attack grew rather than diminished, and because the Sudan government was politically strengthened by the attack at home and made to appear the aggrieved party internationally.

Humanitarian Aid

Whatever the feelings in the US about the political reality in Sudan, there was another area of great frustration namely the continuing horror of the humanitarian situation. While drought may have contributed to famine in the mid 1980s, it was very clear that the continuing humanitarian crisis a decade later was overwhelmingly the outcome of conflict. This was particularly recognised by those with experience and expertise with regard to humanitarian issues in the Horn generally, most notably Smith and Prendergast.[13] They were aware too that some of the aid for humanitarian relief was being diverted to feed the armies in the conflict; thus contributing to a vicious circle of war and suffering. The humanitarian relief itself was being delivered overwhelmingly through the UN-run OLS: now nearly ten years old; the largest operation of its kind in the world; and with the US as the largest donor of food. It was little wonder that the situation created a great deal of frustration in America. For some, including Prendergast, the situation called for a re-think about humanitarian aid and a more politically aware analysis of delivery. In particular there was a perceived need to be more critical in addressing relations between armed political forces and indigenous communities whose human rights were so often abused and social organizations damaged, and to seek to engage more directly with the latter.[14] In the situation in the Horn of weak states in conflict there were opportunities to act to use humanitarian aid to promote local communities by cross border NGO operations that could more easily avoid the political niceties of diplomatic handling of abusive sovereign governments (Prendergast, 1997, pp. 139-152).[15]   In 1998, the year of the attack on al-Shifa, OLS was responsible for 4.2 million people in southern Sudan. To supply them it had to seek the agreement of the Sudan government and the SPLA, both of which were constantly trying to manoeuvre *vis-à-vis* OLS, even when they were also acquiring at least some food for the fighters. Much constant international pressure was required to keep OLS going, of the kind vividly described in the memoirs of America's ambassador in the early 1990s (Petterson, 1999). Though without an ambassador in Khartoum after 1996, the US remained no less aware of the humanitarian problems and if anything even more frustrated with the apparently unending suffering. OLS effectively operated as two parts, in the northern sector – areas mainly under government control – it was run by the UN Coordinator for Emergency Relief Operations (UNCERO); in the SPLA dominated southern sector by UNICEF operating mainly from Kenya. In both sectors OLS was in practice a consortium of over 40 international and national NGOs; with Western NGOs especially regarded with suspicion by an Islamist government, and with the SPLA often wanting to appear just as authoritative in the southern sector. OLS was thus trying to be neutral in a highly political atmosphere; it could do little or nothing about the continuing conflict itself since it had no role in peacemaking; and the division into the northern and southern sectors made organisation and delivery more problematic (OLS, 1996).

However, in confronting the Sudan government the US also needed to look at its main ally, the SPLA, from the standpoint of its relations with civilians in the 'liberated areas' under its control; both for themselves at the time, and in the light of intended greater success for the movement. The picture was not encouraging, especially in comparison with the other liberation movements with which the US had worked. The EPLF and TPLF in particular had paid greater attention to the needs of the civilian populations in areas they controlled, and had certainly won a good press in the West for so doing. In contrast the SPLA had gained for itself a very murky reputation, especially after the split in the movement in 1991 following which the breakaway group had publicised the authoritarianism of the SPLA 'mainstream' and its apparent lack of concern for humanitarian issues; while following the split there was an orgy of inter-ethnic violence in the south, as symbolized by the 'Bor massacre' of 1992 (Johnson, 2003, pp.116-9).

Both USAID and the State Department became involved in a programme first floated in 1997 known as the Sudan Transitional Assistance and Relief programme (STAR). Operating mainly in SPLA held territory in southern Sudan, STAR had to accommodate itself as much to that organisation as OLS had had to do. But OLS was concerned with humanitarian relief: STAR appeared to have greater ambitions for the construction of civil society within the framework of SPLA rule. While STAR officials themselves argued that the programme was putting flesh on the bones of SPLA power, its critics argued that it had been taken over by the SPLA and that some at least of the US staff had 'gone native', just as British administrators in the region had done in earlier years, only in this case going over to the SPLA rather than the 'real' leaders of civil society. The emerging relationship was apparent in the SPLA demand that NGOs operating in the south sign up to a Memorandum of Understanding which in effect made them SPLA compliant – a move that caused a furore in the aid community. While understandable as a move, US support for STAR had limited effect on the liberated areas, and produced yet more controversy about the impact of US policy on the conflict in the south itself. The US persisted in its focus on the SPLA and the NDA with the 1999 Sudan Peace Act. The Act provided for $16 million to develop non-military authority in liberated areas, but was widely seen as a continuing effort to support the opposition to the Sudan government, in spite of the failure of efforts thus far to bring about regime change.

Division in Washington

Towards the end of the Clinton administration it appeared that the US was considering a move from confrontation and possible destabilization, but was still keen to press for regime change by another route. There was still a feeling that some at least of the European states were too forgiving of the government. They were seeking to take the US with them but strong pressure on the Sudan government was still required. The STAR programme should be continued and indeed be expanded to include NDA-controlled areas in eastern Sudan. At the same time the US should help in the preparation and training of potential NDA negotiators; while pushing for NDA inclusion in the IGAD peace talks to ensure a comprehensive peace agreement and not simply a sharing of power between the government and the SPLA. With regard to the Sudan government itself, a critical stance should be continued on terrorism, democracy and human rights. However there were also voices arguing that the administration had got itself into too confrontational a position. Far from the US and its allies having placed Sudan in a box, Sudanese diplomacy had manoeuvred the country out of isolation with both its neighbours and European and Asian states, and it was now the US that was out of step and cut off. Sudan had at least reduced its support for terrorism and might be amenable to peacemaking if carrot could be added to stick. Engagement should now be pursued, and with it the re-opening of the US embassy in Khartoum. A USAID report to Madeliene Albright in 1999 summed up the situation saying that the: 'US government does not speak with one voice on Sudan ... [there were] different camps both within the administration and on Capitol Hill with regard to how to address the long-standing conflict in Sudan.' It continued by saying that there were:

> Different perspectives on whether the US government should continue to minimise contact with the government of Sudan, or constructively engage with the government of Sudan in order to more effectively press for a negotiated settlement, and different opinions as to whether more substantial assistance to rebel movements would engender a balance of power shift and allow a military victory for the south, or simply prolong the war and create more suffering.

It also revealed the kind of agency splits as well as policy differences, commenting that, 'staff engaged in humanitarian issues are not present at key points in our foreign policy decision-making process on Sudan', including the closure of the embassy in Khartoum, the decision to bombard the Shifa factory or to provide non-military assistance to the SPLA.

President Clinton came under pressure to appoint a special envoy to Sudan, and eventually former Congressman Harry Johnson accepted the position. The post itself – to monitor human rights, relief work and peace – appeared to indicate a readiness to engage with the situation rather than seek to undermine the regime, but the appointment was controversial. During his years in Washington Johnson, a former chair of the House sub-committee on Africa, had shown regular concern with the situation in Sudan; but he was also known as highly critical of the government. Voices were raised at the potential confrontational character of the move, with former president Jimmy Carter and a number of aid agencies calling for somebody with a less committed background to America's position in Sudan's conflict. In Sudan itself, the government, still wearing the self-righteousness of the al-Shifa attack, criticised the appointment of Johnson, which it initially refused to accept claiming that it heralded an attempt to justify a planned intervention in the country. Nevertheless Johnston did go to Sudan in July 2000, after which there was something of a thaw. A US counter-terrorism intelligence team then went to Khartoum and began cooperating with its Sudanese counterparts; while later there was even a discrete meeting between Susan Rice and Mustafa Osman Ismail, Sudan's Foreign Minister. Relations were beginning to change.

Conclusion

It appeared that US policy had accepted that the regime in Khartoum was not likely to succumb to military pressure from the opposition. Had the US over-estimated the opposition's capabilities, perhaps due to the exaggeration of the 'Renaissance Leaders'? If the US was backing forcible regime change could it have done more to strengthen the opposition? Had the Eritrean-Ethiopian war in particular weakened support for the opposition and given the Sudan government the opportunity to make diplomatic advances at the expense of both the opposition and the US? Had US hopes for forced regime change led to a lack of interest in the possibility of negotiated peace in Sudan's civil war, the complexity of which had grown steadily and now had an added dimension with the exploitation of oil? Whatever the answers to these questions – which were argued by numerous individuals, agencies and interest groups – it was difficult to disagree with the comment of the report of The Center for Strategic and International Studies (CSIS) in Washington: 'Ultimately ... US policy did not significantly weaken Khartoum, strengthen southern and northern opposition, moderate the conduct of Sudan's war, enhance humanitarian access and deliveries, or promote a process of genuine peace negotiations' (CSIS, 2001).[16]

Notes

1   In France, where they were always suspicious of the Anglo-Saxons in Africa, the new rulers were referred to as the 'Young Princes'.

2   In April 1996 CIA Director John Deutch visited Addis Ababa for secret talks with regional leaders and he was followed in October by Secretary of State Warren Christopher, after which there appeared to be greater unity in following a tough policy towards the Sudan government. I am grateful to J.M. Burr for this point.

3   Mansour Khalid associates the East Africa team in the State Department in 1996 with seeking a 'soft landing' for the Sudan government, apparently due to its calculation that the opposition forces were not strong enough to overthrow it (Khalid, 2003, p.362).

4   Albright had been persuaded to re-open the embassy by State Department officials, but Susan Rice, then at the National Security Council and about to become Assistant Secretary of State for African Affairs persuaded Sandy Berger, National Security Adviser, to overrule her.

5   There were rumours that Occidental Petroleum was also interested in buying in to developments in Sudan and that Vice-President Gore involved to try to ease US restrictions. However any such moves were checked by Turabi's determination to prevent Occidental from gaining a foot in the door (this point is owed to J.M. Burr).

6   The Inter-Governmental Authority on Drought and Development (IGADD) had now dropped 'Drought' from its title becoming IGAD.

7   Susan Rice is quoted as saying, 'They calculated that we didn't have the means to successfully prosecute Bin Laden. That's why I question the sincerity of the offer', *The Village Voice*, 31 October-6 November 2001. This has been disputed especially since bin Laden had already been named a co-conspirator in the case brought by Attorney Mary Jo White in New York City concerning the Trade Towers bombing that was very likely to have led to an indictment by a grand jury. (I owe this point to J.M. Burr.)

8   Albright and other senior officials later denied that they had ignored overtures by Sudan but David Rose stood by his report (*Vanity Fair*, March 2002).

9   Albright and other accused officials vigorously rejected the charges of ignoring Sudan claiming that they did have contacts with the government ('Deperately Seeking Sudan', *Vanity Fair*, March 2002).

10   A similar view of continuing Sudanese involvement in international terrorism is given by Pillar (Pillar, 2003, pp.160-1).

11   A third attack, this time on the US embassy in Kampala, was thwarted by the CIA on 18 September 1998.

12   There were doubts about the intelligence regarding al-Shifa and the alleged links to al-Qaeda in the CIA, the State Department and the National Security Council and a report expressing these went to Madeleine Albright. However

the perceived need for speedy action overcame any reservations (*The Guardian*, London, 6 February 2003).

[13] Prendergast himself had written a book on the humanitarian issues (Prendergast, 1996).

[14] An outstanding account of the impact of war on one of the major communities of southern Sudan is Hutchinson's *Nuer Dilemmas* (Hutchinson, 1996).

[15] USAID also had a programme from 1994 known as the Greater Horn of Africa Initiative a fairly small and mixed programme for humanitarian assistance and development across the region.

[15] International Crisis Group, in which Prendergast was a leading figure, later admitted, 'Bureaucratic in-fighting and a general desire to avoid foreign entanglements meant that Clinton administration actions were more bark than bite and were not aimed at toppling the regime or ending the war'. It was however, 'Effective in using its policy of isolation and containment to develop leverage with Khartoum that the Bush administration can now use in its peace promotion efforts' (ICG, 2002, a, pp.62-3). The claim has not however been acknowledged by the Bush administration.

References

Bodansky, Y. (1999), *Bin Laden: The Man Who Declared War on America*, Roseville California, Prima.

Center for Strategic and International Studies (2002), *US Policy to End Sudan's War*, Washington, CSIS.

Gunaratna, R. (2002), *Inside Al Qaeda: Global Network of Terror*, London, Hurst.

International Crisis Group (2002) (a) *God, Oil and Country: The damaging logic of war in Sudan*, ICG, Brussels.

International Crisis Group (2002) (b), *Sudan's Best Chance for Peace: How not to lose it*, Brussels, ICG.

Hutchinson, S. (1996), *Nuer Dilemmas: Coping with Money, War and the State*, Berkeley, University of California Press.

Khalid, M. (2003), *War and Peace in Sudan*, London, Kegan Paul.

Niblock, T. (2000), 'Sanctions and Pariahhood: the case of Sudan', Paper presented to the Sudan Studies Society of the UK, University of Durham.

Niblock, T. (2001), *'Pariah States' and Sanctions in the Middle East: Iraq, Libya, Sudan*, Boulder, Lynne Rienner.

Osman, M. (2002), *The United Nations and Peace Enforcement: Wars, terrorism and democracy*, Aldershot, Ashgate.

Petterson, D. (1999), *Inside Sudan: Political Islam, Conflict and Catastrophe*, Boulder, Westview.

Prendergast, J. (1996), *Frontline Diplomacy: Humanitarian Aid and Conflict in Africa*, Boulder, Lynne Rienner.

Woodward, P. (2002), 'Religion and Politics in Southern Sudan: the Ugandan Dimension', in Hassan, Y. and Gray, R. (eds) *Religion and Conflict in Sudan*, Nairobi, Pauline Press of Africa.

Chapter 7

Peacemaking in Sudan

The missile attack on the Shifa pharmaceutical plant had shown the frustration of the Clinton administration. The regime in Sudan had not been overthrown in spite of several years of apparent US hopes, and forms of support for the southern Sudan in particular; and the al-Shifa attack had given the Sudan government something of a boost, especially internationally where it added to the sense that it was an inappropriate way to tackle the Sudan problem. A number of European states, that unlike the US had ambassadors in Khartoum, reported a willingness by the government to engage with the international community once more; Middle Eastern governments, amongst which Egypt was predictably prominent, were developing closer relations; as were Sudan's African neighbours. Even in the US critical voices were being raised. Former president Jimmy Carter's interest in Sudan had continued, including an active involvement in health issues in the south, and he had been critical of the Shifa attack. Humanitarian organisations also became more vocal in their criticism with three leading bodies, CARE USA, Oxfam America and Save the Children USA putting out a joint statement in May 1999 calling for a 'Peace First' policy rather than confrontation (Hoile, 2000, p.102). Talk turned instead to the possibility of peacemaking, but the US was hardly in a position to rush forward and policy needed to be re-appraised.

The Bush Administration

The process of re-appraisal was in its early stages when at the end of 2000 the US elections eventually brought forth a new Republican president. At the outset, the election of George W. Bush was not expected to herald an administration with much interest in the world at large. Furthermore it gave every indication of being averse to becoming involved in peace-making or peacekeeping anywhere; and after his father's experience in Somalia certainly not in Africa, in which Sudan had been judged more difficult than Somalia in 1993. Bush's campaign for office had scarcely mentioned the continent, and historically the Republicans were less likely than the Democrats to express concern for the region. Nevertheless it was soon to emerge that President Bush did have time for Africa, and that amongst the items at top of his agenda for the continent was the conflict in Sudan (alongside HIV/AIDS and international terrorism).

The same surprise had occurred when his father was elected in 1988. George Bush senior had a record with regard to Sudan. In the 1970s he had helped American oil companies make contacts with the then Nimeiri government that had led on to Chevron's operations. In 1985 as vice-president he visited the country shortly before Nimeiri's downfall, and some felt that his meetings then prepared the US administration to accept the imminent change. Following his election as president his administration showed a concern for the then famine that had not been seen under Reagan, and led to the pressure on Sudan to accept the establishment of OLS (Scroggins, 2003, p.128).

A similar mixture of motives was to be seen when George W. Bush was elected. As an article in *The Washington Post* on 11 March 2001 put it, 'Suddenly, Sudan'. Bush himself had mentioned southern Sudan in a speech shortly after his election; and Secretary of Sate Colin Powell, who was questioned on Sudan during his confirmation hearing, said that, 'There is perhaps no greater tragedy on the face of the Earth today than the tragedy that is unfolding in the Sudan' (*Washington Post*, 11 March 2001). Probably the greatest influence on Bush himself was that of the religious groups well represented in and around the capital. Senator Bill Frist from Tennessee was a distinguished medical doctor with a missionary spirit that has taken him into the SPLA controlled areas of southern Sudan where he performed surgery in the most primitive conditions, and despite the threat of government bombs. Frist was known as one of Bush's closest ally in the Senate, and as the leader of the Republican majority there the two men were in regular contact. Senator Sam Brownback of Kansas, a member of the Foreign Relations Committee, also campaigned on Sudan calling for greater US efforts to stop the war. In the House of Representatives Frank Wolf from Virginia had for years been campaigning on Sudan in Washington, and Donald Paine, the leader of the Black Caucus, was another prominent figure. It was a cross-party issue. Democrats might be thought of as more concerned with international engagement, but conservative Republicans were also interested: Bush himself had spoken of 'compassionate conservatism' and there seemed few cases more deserving of compassion than the southern Sudanese. The concern of Congressmen themselves was backed by reports from the Congressional Research Service, especially those of Ted Dagne. Another influential voice close to Bush was that of Elliot Abrams who was advisor on human rights in the National Security Council with a particular interest in the Sudan situation (International Crisis Group, 2002, p.63).

Outside government an important voice with Bush was that of Franklin Graham, son of perhaps the world's best-known evangelist, Billy Graham. Both father and son were highly esteemed in the Bush family; and Franklin Graham had been invited to preach at the inauguration of George W. Bush. Franklin Graham also headed a US charity called Samaritan's Purse International that worked in southern Sudan, as well as in the non-government controlled area in the east of the country: it had the highest profile of a number of American evangelical NGOs working in non-government areas of Sudan, sometimes in cooperation with USAID and STAR. These NGOs were generally well endowed and some were vigorously anti-Islam, Franklin Graham himself having said that, 'The Koran provides ample evidence that Islam encourages violence in order to win converts and to reach the ultimate goal of an Islamic world' (Medley, 2003). Even nearer home the President's mother-in-law worshipped at a church in the Midlands Alliance, Texas, which was particulary concerned for the southern Sudan. While encouraging the Bush administration to engage in Sudan, the churches could also be expected to demand a tough stance towards the government with the intention not only of bringing it to the negotiating table, but ultimately of seeking to see its end in one way or another. The evangelicals were also supported by other Christian voices, including the Catholics, for Rome had long had an interest in a region where missionary work had been underway for many years in the tradition of the great nineteenth century missionary, Father Comboni. The issue of slavery had caught on with Catholics in the north-east in particular, as was reflected in the coverage of the *Boston Globe*.

While there is no reason to doubt the spiritual commitment of Bush to the Sudan, there was also a domestic political impetus. White evangelical Christians accounted for approximately 40 per cent of the Republican presidential vote in 2000 and were thus a constituency to be cherished. Presidential advisor Karl Rove in particular saw the value of good relations and shortly after Bush's election a delegation led by Charles Colson and rabbi David Saperstein visited him in the White House to seek US action to end the Sudan conflict (*New York Times* 26 October 2003). They were pushing at an open door: on that and other matters the evangelicals were to enjoy unprecedented access.

Christians were also united with others such as the Congressional Black Caucus in their condemnation of what was described as abduction and slavery in southern Sudan, generally depicted as northern Muslim Arabs raiding, capturing and enslaving southern Sudanese. Horrific in any context, the charges were particularly emotive in the US Much has been written by historians and anthropologists on the appropriateness of the concept of slavery for what has been taking place in Sudan, especially since the mid 1980s. There have also been arguments about the extent of the government's involvement or complicity in the events. Yet these arguments are largely secondary to the barrage of accusations in and around Washington from those convinced of the charge. Indeed the situation had not stopped at protest: organisations had been set up to buy the freedom of slaves by collecting money in the US and bartering with slavers deep in southern Sudan. These activities generated further controversy, especially about the extent to which they redressed the problem or instead encouraged slaving by offering dollar bills to the perpetrators. It also transpired that there were even questions of the authenticity of some of the transactions in which the well-intentioned slave redeemers were engaged; with the possibility that they were dupes for elaborate charades that were staged to enrich all involved.

As well as the Christian and anti-slavery groups there were voices raised concerning human rights abuses in all parts of the country. It was a longstanding concern going back well before the NIF seized power, but one that had grown in the light of Sudan's worsening record. In particular the number and condition of Sudan's political detainees had attracted much adverse attention, especially with the publicity brought by the growing number of asylum seekers in the West. Amongst those concerned influential organizations issuing regular reports were Human Rights Watch and Amnesty International.

The various groups came together in a loose grouping known as the 'Freedom House coalition'. They had their differences, especially over the contentious issues of slave redemption and whether food aid prolonged war, but on the whole formed an effective group. The views of many of the above, if not all, were also reflected in influential reports by 'think tanks' around Washington. Amongst those that were most active were the Center for Strategic and International Studies (CSIS), which had produced an important point recommending a solution along the lines of 'one country two systems'; and the International Crisis Group (ICG).

Whether it was sympathy for the millions of victims of successive regimes, the casualties of war, concern to check the perceived Islamist movement, or engagement with the anti-slavery movement, there were many voices and groups increasingly forming a coalition calling for a halt to the conflict and including several people close to the president. Early in his administration Bush made it clear that he wanted the war stopped: that put the onus on the State Department to deliver. Secretary of State Powell had already shown his concern over Sudan, and in spite of scepticism on the part of National Security Adviser, Condoleeza Rice, Powell believed that peace might be achievable and was certainly worth a try. Below him the baton was passed to the new Assistant Secretary of State for Africa, Walter Kansteiner. Kansteiner had long connections with the continent. Under George Bush senior he had been Director of African Affairs at the NSC and he had also had links with the departments of State and Defense. He also had long business experience in Africa, mainly with the Scowcroft group. He had been a strong believer in commerce and trade as central to Africa's recovery; while recognizing that conflict resolution had to be a key to all aspects of development. Within the State Department, debates had been underway about Sudan policy. The department felt some frustration that it had no permanent representation in Sudan; and that in the later Clinton years there had been drift at the highest level, especially with the Eritrean-Ethiopian war. Furthermore there was consciousness of the critical voices lobbying on Sudan, all of whom wanted a more active policy, and some a more aggressive one. Concern was such that the department organised the Sudan Programmes Group that included representatives of other government departments and agencies, including USAID, Defense and the CIA, though there was criticism of the seniority of the representatives and their consequent limited ability to coordinate activities effectively.[1]

Also maintaining pressure on the State Department, and linking Congressional and lobbying concerns was the US Commission on International Religious Freedom (USCIRF). The Commission was established in 1998 by a Congressional Act, 'To give independent recommendations to the executive branch and the Congress'. Its creation reflected the concern of a number of religious pressure groups and their allies in Congress, against the wishes of the Clinton administration and especially Madeleine Albright who were believed to reflect an unconcern on the part of some State Department officials with religious freedom. (A separate Religious Freedom Ambassador at Large had also been appointed within the State Department.) From its foundation USCIRF singled out the Sudan government as one of the three worst abusers of religious freedom in the world (with Russia and China) and focussed special attention on it. In a testimony statement in 2003 it said, 'For the past three years, the Commission has identified Sudan as the world's most violent abuser of the right to freedom of religion and belief' (House sub-committee on Africa, 13 May 2003). From its establishment USCIRF kept up regular recommendations on Sudan, several of which became incorporated in the evolving US approach to peacemaking, especially in the provisions of the Sudan Peace Act of October 2002. An example of its trenchant views is given in its comment on the State Department's 'Required Report Regarding the Conflict in Sudan' of which USCIRF said that, 'The State Department does not adequately address the concerns of Congress that acts of genocide, and possibly other international crimes, have been committed by the GOS [Government of Sudan]'.

USAID was less overtly critical of Sudan, but generally seen as keener on operating in SPLA-held territory. Indeed its representation in Khartoum was at a very low level and it felt bureaucratically and politically harassed. In contrast, its relations with the SPLA/SPLM allowed it much easier access to southern Sudan. In addition it saw the enormous needs of the south as most deserving of support. Operations had developed since 1998 as a part of USAID's Greater Horn of Africa Initiative (GHAI). As well as putting in its own resources, USAID worked with various local and international NGOs; and it also participated in the Joint Planning Mechanism (JPM) hosted by the World Bank with input from the IMF, the UN, the government of Sudan and the SPLM.

In contrast to this well organized weight of opinion, the Sudan government had few friends in Washington, where it was aware that virtually all actors regarded the southerners as the aggrieved party in the conflict whatever their particular views of the SPLA itself. Not even many of the Arab states were willing to speak up for it. Although it employed lobbyists, they had little on which to work: there were few commercial interests to counter the hostile political barrage apart from occasional voices on the need for gum Arabic from Sudan, and any such voices raised (as well as all government spokespersons) were swiftly targeted by the government's vociferous critics.

All involved in the Sudan situation, on whichever side and for whatever reasons, knew that the events of 9/11 made it more intense. Sudan was still on the US list of states sponsoring international terrorism; it had housed Osama bin Laden and al-Qaeda for several years; and it had its own record of supporting Islamist activities in the Greater Horn of Africa. For the new administration in Washington it was crying out for action.

The State of Play

There appeared to be little in the conflict to encourage hopes of peacemaking in 2001, indeed the reverse appeared to be the case. Memories of a negotiated end to war in 1972 had kept alive flickering hopes for a repeat, but the record of the 1990s had been depressing, not helped by the fact that the 1989 coup had been instigated to pre-empt a possible peace. Following 1989 there had been efforts by the US, former president Jimmy Carter, and Nigeria, but none had achieved a breakthrough and there were doubts about the seriousness of the combatants to achieve peace.

In 1994 the intermittent process of seeking peace had moved to the auspices of the Inter-Governmental Authority on Drought and Development (IGADD). IGADD had been set up in 1986 following the drought and famine in the Horn of the early 1980s, and was inspired by attempts at regional cooperation in West Africa following the western sahel droughts of the previous decade. IGADD eventually was comprised of Djibouti, where its headquarters were established, Eritrea, Ethiopia, Kenya, Somalia, Sudan and Uganda. However, IGADD had little to show in the field of environmental development, not least because of the high levels of conflict across the region. It thus turned its attention to seeking cooperation between member states in conflict resolution. With an ongoing, albeit unsuccessful, series of talks Sudan seemed an obvious candidate; though there was scepticism about the country's commitment from the outset. As a grouping of African states, the SPLA might expect understanding in IGADD, but the government side may have just been trying to push peace pressure away from more powerful international actors at a time when its own individual relations with some IGADD members, especially Eritrea and Uganda, were poor. Nevertheless, in 1994 there were a series of meetings in Kenya. At the time the talks made no progress, but they did produce something of lasting importance known as the Declaration of Principles (DoP), drawn up by the mediators after the second round of talks. The DoP called for a secular state in Sudan, but said that if this could not be agreed, then the southern Sudan should have the opportunity of self-determination in a referendum, and it included the possibility of full separation of the region and its becoming a separate state, as had happened shortly before in Eritrea. At the following meeting the Sudan government struck out the reference to independence, but in any case there was no overall agreement in 1994. However, the idea of self-determination stuck, and in 1997 it surfaced again, and this time with the apparent agreement of the Sudan government. The government had decided to launch its own strategy for peace. Called the Khartoum Peace Agreement it was designed to sidestep both the SPLA and the international community by a peace deal with non-SPLA southern factions. The terms of the agreement included a right of self-determination and potential secession. In subsequent years though the internal agreement had collapsed, while conflict with the SPLA persisted. Indeed the levels of conflict in the south rose by the end of the decade as the prospect of finally exploiting the oilfields in Upper Nile became a reality: oil had fuelled the outset of the conflict in 1983, and it was no surprise that it was doing so once more.

From the point of view of a negotiated settlement the situation thus looked unpromising when the Bush administration came into office, but in time it was to be judged as 'ripe for resolution', due to a conjunction of factors that might have come straight from a conflict resolution textbook.

The starting point was the military situation itself, in which it appeared that neither side was capable of victory. The government had tried and failed in the early 1990s and the SPLA had hopes towards the end of the decade, but few thought a clear victory looked likely by 2001. It was true that the start of oil revenues was helping the government side to acquire new armaments; but there were also reports that the SPLA was stronger, and had friends that would not tolerate its defeat. Thus although there might be the customary ebb and flow of conflict, generally with government advances in the dry season and SPLA counter moves with the onset of rains, the overall picture was one of military deadlock.

The failure to achieve a breakthrough in the military deadlock was matched by a lack of political advance on either side. The government's hope of peace from within enshrined in the Khartoum Peace Agreement of 1997 had come to nought. Its main ally, Riek Machar had become increasingly frustrated at his lack of any real power (partly due to well-placed government mistrust of him); and indeed he defected and later joined up once more with the SPLA. The government side was also weakened by divisions within the NIF resulting from a power struggle between Beshir and Turabi, which the former won in 1999 leading eventually to the latter's detention (after Turabi's faction had even held peace talks with the SPLA). Meanwhile, in the opposition there was also factional and party manoeuvring. A minority of Unionists had left the NDA to return to Sudan and to talks with the government; and later the former prime minister and Umma Party leader, Sadiq al-Mahdi, had also quit the NDA and returned home, but as an internal opposition to pressurise the government.

The military and political deadlocks not only indicated lack of overall success for either side, they were also hurting the leaderships. Oil revenues may have been flowing to the government, but they were less than peace could deliver. There were areas for exploration and exploitation that remained insecure, and the wealth there was denied while war continued. At the same time the oil companies operating were mainly Asian with limited technological capabilities, and the conflict had allowed them to strike unfavourable deals from the government's point of view. The chances of attracting major western companies to invest, especially from the US, were low to non-existent while conflict continued. Sudan's relations with major international organisations, including the IMF, the World Bank and the Paris Club were also constrained while conflict continued. Politically as well any earlier ideological enthusiasm for war had largely dwindled, and conscription, especially of students, was very unpopular for a war that felt increasingly like northern Sudan's Vietnam. As for the SPLA, while some of its leaders had done quite well from the war (including the slave redemption scams), they were aware that the local conflicts in the south as well as the confrontation with the government were causing great suffering and war weariness among the very people they claimed to represent. Church groups and others in what was optimistically called 'civil society' were repeatedly calling for peace.

At the same time, the repeatedly failed talks of the past had produced some overlapping points around which negotiations might take place. Central to this possibility was the DoP of 1994. The issues of religion and secularism were contained there and would need to be addressed again. So too was the question of self-determination for the south, to which the government had apparently signed up in 1997. These may have been the rocks on which past peacemaking efforts had foundered, officially at least, but they also indicated what had to be addressed in the future, including the core of a possible way forward through the self-determination formula in the event of continuing disagreement on religion and the state.

Engagement with Sudan

It was Sudan that was the instigator of contacts over terrorist intelligence in 2000, while Clinton was still in office. Intelligence had been offered at the time of Osama bin Laden's exit from Sudan in 1996, and then again after the US embassy bombings in East Africa two years later, but it was not until May 2000 that US agents made a first visit to Sudan when material was exchanged. The attacks by al-Qaeda on the World Trade Center and the Pentagon on 9/11 brought a new urgency to both the US and the Sudan government. Sudan was motivated largely by the fear that the US might decide to strike out quickly against states such as those on the terrorism list, and was very soon sending signals to Washington that it was ready to cooperate. The US for its part was keen to glean whatever it could: with the intelligence services under mounting criticism for alleged failures that permitted the attack on 9/11 agents were soon dispatched to Khartoum, from where they returned with large quantities of material. Just how much they received and its quality was a matter only for speculation. Some reporters felt that there was a danger to Sudan over the revelation of some materials, and possible charges from Islamists of collaboration with the enemy. On the other hand if material was conspicuously weeded there was a danger that the US would believe that it had been duped with possible worse results than non-cooperation. In fact US intelligence appeared very satisfied with the information that Sudan handed over.

Cooperation over intelligence may have helped ease relations somewhat – though not enough to lift US sanctions on Sudan, or the country's place on the US list of states supporting terrorism – but the central theme was to emerge as a new US engagement in Sudan's stuttering peace process.[2] However there was groundwork on which to build and the administration was soon to start testing its strength. In 1999 the Congressionally-funded United States Institute of Peace (USIP) had produced an influential special report entitled 'A New Approach to Peace in Sudan' (USIP, 1999). It spoke of the problems of the IGAD negotiations and the lead role played by Eritrea, Ethiopia, Kenya and Uganda; and also of the fact that, 'In the past, three of these states have pushed for the ouster of the NIF government in Khartoum government and expected the government to fall soon. But now there is a military stalemate and much less likelihood that the Khartoum government will fall'. And there were also calls for US involvement, 'International assistance, particularly from the United States, needs to be offered to the IGAD negotiating team as a credible and effective mechanism to advance the peace process'. The following year the State Department convened a conference at which similar views were expressed.

Congress was also showing more interest, though the general sentiment was more critical. In June 1999 the House of Representatives passed its first resolution in six years exclusively dealing with Sudan by 416 votes to one. It condemned the Sudan government 'for its genocidal war in southern Sudan', and for its 'continued human rights violations'; and called for more US funding of civil activities in SPLA-held areas. However, at the same time as calling for a strengthening of US sanctions against Sudan, it also sought support for greater mediation efforts to end the conflict through the IGAD process.

· Thus the climate in Washington had been changing even before the arrival of the Bush administration. Once in place a review of policy on Sudan soon took place and concluded that the US should be more involved. On his first trip to Africa after being installed as Assistant Secretary of State, Kansteiner met with SPLA leader John Garang in Nairobi, and announced that Bush would be appointing a special envoy to Sudan. A few weeks later the envoy was named as John Danforth, a former Republican senator for Missouri and an ordained Episcopal minister who was known personally to the Bush family and had undertaken a number of difficult assignments following his retirement. Politically this background made Danforth fireproof with regard to serving Congressmen and the lobbying coalition on Sudan. Danforth himself had been initially reluctant to accept the post, but after the failure of an attempt to bring in Chester Crocker instead he agreed to give it a try. At the same time Danforth was not coloured by a record on Sudan, unlike Clinton's nominee Harry Johnson, nor was he an official, as earlier Melissa Wells had been.

Danforth's appointment as special envoy was announced on 6 September 2001, just five days before the al-Qaeda strikes on the US Those attacks delayed him and added an even greater terrorism dimension to US-Sudan relations, but they did not change the substance of the mission which was to see if there was in his judgement any possibility of peace, in the making of which the US could be involved. He emphasised from the outset that he was looking at the ongoing situation, including the IGAD process, and that there was no US plan that he was about to seek to implement. He may not have had a peace plan, but he did have original tactics to help in the assessment of the situation. He put forward four proposals that could be used to judge the seriousness of the intent of the two main parties to the conflict, the Sudan government and the SPLA, with regard to peace. As he put it, 'If they don't want peace they will tell us by inaction ... if that is what happens and it's clear to me by mid-January, I'm simply going to report to the president that we tried, we did our best and there is no further useful role that the United States can play' (*Associated Press*, 17 November 2001).

The four tests that Danforth proposed were cleverly devised and targeted. The first was for a ceasefire in the Nuba Mountains to be followed by humanitarian and development assistance. The Nuba Mountains are an area of hills in the centre of Sudan between north and south that are culturally and historically distinct from either region. The Nuba peoples had maintained their distinctive way of life, mainly in hilltop villages, and during the war their lands had been fought across repeatedly. Thus in selecting the Nuba, Danforth was not taking sides so much as focusing on a people who had largely been victims, especially of government forces. Moreover in calling for international verification Danforth was testing the willingness of the combatants to allow foreign peace observers into Sudan, something that had never happened before, even in the peace settlement of 1972 or in earlier short-lived ceasefires in the second war. There was also an international dimension to the second test, which was that an international commission be set up to look into the allegations of slavery and abduction and to recommend practical steps to prevent such practices. Third was his call for cessation of fighting in selected areas, described as 'zones of tranquility', so that there could be mass vaccination against polio and rinderpest. This followed up the earlier cessation of fighting in response to Jimmy Carter's call for measures to combat river blindness, and drew attention to the wide range of suffering experienced by the civilian population in the midst of conflict. Finally Danforth called for greater protection for civilians from military attack including bombing. There had been numerous reports of such attacks mainly by the government side, and on targets alleged to include schools and hospitals. With the development of oil, the attacks by government-backed forces on civilians in the areas of the oil fields were intensifying and appeared to include efforts at land clearance, the better to protect the wells and pipelines from the SPLA.

Even as Danforth outlined his tests, there were warnings of other pressures on the Sudan government side. In Congress, where religious right and African-American groups maintained their concern and general sympathy for the southern Sudan, there were moves to block oil companies operating in Sudan from participating in US financial markets, under the title of the Sudan Peace Act. It was carried 422-2 in the House. However the Bush administration eventually moved to block the proposals on access to US capital markets, not from sympathy for Sudan but on the grounds that denial of access to capital markets would set a dangerous precedent for the future. In addition the attacks on the US on 9/11 hardened popular American feeling against Sudan for having once harboured bin Laden. With the attack on Afghanistan also came suggestions that other suspect countries such as Somalia, Yemen and Sudan might be targeted. The Sudan government was not in defiant mode with regard to the Danforth proposals, which put the onus for action on its side more than that of the SPLA.

Danforth returned to Sudan in January 2002 in order to assess the progress, if any, that had taken place with regard to the four points. Only if there had been progress would he be able to report to President Bush that there were grounds for the US becoming actively involved in a bid to bring a negotiated conclusion to Sudan's long-running war. His report, delivered in April, indicated that there had been difficulties but nevertheless some advance had been achieved. The most promising area was that of the Nuba Mountains, especially because the ceasefire established there had been maintained. International monitors were beginning to go into the area, and the Joint Military Committee was beginning to function. The peace had enabled both relief and development aid to begin to get into the areas of conflict. The establishment of wider 'zones of tranquility' to enable inoculation programmes to proceed had proved more difficult, with conflict continuing across much of the region. Nevertheless, the bovine rinderpest programme had been carried out and the one for polio was underway, but the Guinea worm programme had yet to get started. The efforts to halt intentional attacks against civilians were also proving slow to establish, but an international verification programme was being put in place. Finally the requirement to make moves against slavery had led to an international mission of 'eminent persons' with experience of the problem in Sudan that had visited the affected areas shortly before Danforth delivered his report.

Danforth was under no illusions about the difficulty of a US-backed push for peace, but he nevertheless concluded that, 'This is the time for a major push for a compromise settlement. I believe that both the Government of Sudan and the SPLM have given sufficient indications that they want peace to warrant the energetic participation of the United States in a long-term peace process'. Both sides also saw the need for US involvement, as did the other Sudanese groups, and the foreign governments to which Danforth had spoken, 'All expressed the belief that the active engagement of the United States offered the only hope for bringing this conflict to an end' (Danforth, Report to the President, 2002).

The report soon ran into criticism on a number of controversial points, especially those that, as Danforth acknowledged, were his personal recommendations; above all his comments on self-determination and to a lesser extent oil. The IGAD talks since 1994 had interpreted self-determination as including the possibility of secession for the southern Sudan and the establishment of an independent state. Danforth, however, argued against the possibility of separation, on the grounds that it would be very difficult to achieve, and that it would be strongly resisted by the Sudan government side. Instead he said that:

> A more feasible, and, I think preferable view of self-determination would ensure the right of the people of southern Sudan to live under a government that respects their religion and culture. Such a system would require robust internal and external guarantees so that any promises made by the Government in peace negotiations could not be ignored in practice.

On oil, Danforth took the view that it would be a matter of negotiating the sharing of oil revenues; while some supporters of the SPLA believed that since most proven reserves were in the south that was where most of the revenue should go. Of course possible separation would ensure that most oil revenues would be outside the hands of the Sudan government. Nevertheless there was generally support for Danforth's recommendation that there was a possibility of peace and that the US should play an active role. State Department officials in particular were keen to stress that Danforth's overall judgement of a US role in peace, did not mean that his own opinions, especially on self-determination, would become American policy. However shortly before Danforth reported, his view that the US should become engaged was backed by an influential report from the Washington think tank The Center for Strategic and International Studies (CSIS) that came to the catchy formula: 'One Sudan, Two Systems', at least for a transitional period.

Though Danforth had recommended that the US become engaged in Sudan's peace process, there were other international dimensions to be addressed as well. One was America's relationship with IGAD, which had two dimensions: the member states of IGAD itself; and the IGAD Partners' Forum.

Amongst the IGAD members, four states stood out, Eritrea, Ethiopia, Uganda and Kenya. The first three had of course been the neighbours of Sudan most involved with the Sudanese opposition, and indeed that were believed to have encouraged the US to think that regime change by force was possible in Sudan. As far as Eritrea and Ethiopia were concerned the war between them and Sudan's diplomatic advances, especially towards Ethiopia, had put an end to expectations of that kind. They could be expected to encourage negotiations, and would have an influence on the NDA in particular. As for Uganda, its own failure to put an end to the LRA activities in the north, and the knowledge of the importance of southern Sudan for the rebel activities, meant that, however reluctantly, there was a recognition of the need to deal with the Sudan government. Not that Uganda was about to abandon the SPLA, the links were too strong, but it would endeavour to promote peace on terms acceptable to the SPLA. Although the Eritrean-Ethiopian war, and aspects of Uganda's activities in the Democratic Republic of Congo (DRC) were disturbing to the US, it remained on generally friendly terms with all three, and they were unlikely to seek to block it in its extended backing of IGAD's Sudan peace process. With Kenya US relations were different. After spending the early 1990s pouring scorn on the shortcomings of Kenya's political system, relations had improved somewhat. Moreover Kenya was very keen to take the lead on Sudan. It had hosted successive rounds of failed talks, but there still remained the hope for President Moi that there might be some reflected glory for him through hosting successful peace talks. The 1972 Sudan peace was known as the Addis Ababa Agreement, and believed to owe much to the Emperor Haile Selassie: perhaps Moi might be similarly recognized as an enabler of peace in one of Africa's worst conflicts. Clearly Kenya had every reason to cooperate, and improve its standing with the US in the process.

In 1994, in an effort to breath new life into IGADD (as it then was) the main donors – the Netherlands, Norway, Italy, Canada, UK and US – had set up the Friends of IGAD, later to become the IGAD Partners' Forum. It had concerned itself particularly with the peace process, during the course of which the Troika of the US, UK and Norway had emerged. Growing US concern has been seen, but in the other two countries the war also figured large. In Britain there were residual guilt feelings with regard both to British policy in southern Sudan, and also that in granting independence Britain had effectively abandoned the region to its fate. Helping to end the war would at least do something to remove a stain on the imperial record. Prime Minister Blair, decided that like George W. Bush he would appoint a special envoy. His choice was a career diplomat, Alan Goulty, who had been ambassador to Sudan in the mid 1990s and was in close touch with the government at a time when the US had shut down its embassy in Khartoum. After leaving Sudan, Goulty had spent a year in the US studying peacemaking at Harvard, as well as making regular visits to Washington. Norway also had a particular interest in Sudan, especially through the activities of Norwegian Peoples' Aid in southern Sudan, which was a particular *bete noire* of the Sudan government. Since the Oslo Accords, that once seemed promising for Israel and the Palestinians, Norway felt that it had a particular role with regard to peacemaking. Britain and Norway had led the way in developing the Troika, partly to tie the US in to a policy of engagement with Sudan. In addition other European countries were monitoring the developing situation: Italy was less directly involved than

Britain and Norway, but the Vatican had long felt a particular concern for Sudan; while France and Germany were seen as somewhat more sympathetic to the Sudan government.

More challenging for US diplomacy was to be Egypt and Libya, two north African neighbours with both Sudanese and regional interests. Egypt had a long term view of Sudan as a former colony that should, in Egypt's view, have been united with Egypt in 1956. It was indicative that responsibility for Sudanese affairs in the Egyptian government was in the hands of the security services rather than the Foreign Ministry. Egypt had remained a dimension of Sudanese politics throughout the years of the latter's independence, not as a player on the geographical periphery like Eritrea, Ethiopia and Uganda, but as an active participant in central government. President Mubarak himself, then an air force officer, had participated in the Egyptian assistance to Nimeiri in 1970 in crushing the revolt of the *ansar* at Aba Island.[3] Regionally Egypt was concerned about the establishment and development of IGADD. In particular it saw a potential threat to the Nile waters, on which agreement existed only between Egypt and Sudan (last signed in 1959), and a greater use of which was coveted by the upper riparian states, especially Ethiopia. The latter in particular was chronically suspicious of Egypt's intentions in the Horn, and it was largely for that reason that Egypt had been deliberately omitted from involvement in IGADD. Libya's involvement had been more spasmodic and erratic, but nevertheless significant. On Sudan Colonel Qaddafi had proposed a union, with Egypt as well, shortly after he seized power in 1969. Later he became the arch rival of Nimeiri, supporting both his northern and southern opponents; and even once sending a plane to try to bomb the radio and television centre in Omdurman. Regionally, Libya had backed various governments and opposition movements, including both Idi Amin and later Youeri Museveni in Uganda. It was all part of his active Africa policy that increased with time as he sought to play the role of an elder statesman in Africa that he was denied in the Middle East. Egypt and Libya had not always been allies, but the latter was keen to improve relations with the aim of gaining greater international respectability, and the lifting of sanctions that could lead to much fuller development of its oil resources. Although the US had no diplomatic relations with Libya, Britain did and these were used to help bring Libya into line.

Neither Egypt nor Libya was a friend of Sudan for much of the 1990s. As seen, Sudan's Islamism was a threat to Egypt, and also to Libya that had a small underground Islamist opposition to its ideologically maverick ruler. However both came to accept Sudan's apparent change of direction after 1995, but also were concerned at the direction of the IGAD peace process once it appeared that those talks might become serious. The problem for Egypt in particular lay in the DoP of 1994, especially self-determination for southern Sudan. Egypt's main concern was of course the Nile waters: while most of its water came from the Blue Nile and Ethiopia, the great future potential to meet Egypt's growing population lay in better storage management and flow of the White Nile flowing from Uganda through southern Sudan. Egypt and Sudan had even been building the Jonglei Canal in the region to improve the flow of water when civil war had re-opened in 1983 and an attack on it had forced the abandonment of the project. A possible separation of the southern Sudan would, in Egypt's view, only enhance the problems of water development on the White Nile and the very idea had always been anathema to successive Egyptian governments. In addition Egypt was concerned at being left out of IGAD's process that seemed as if it was to be under the ownership of Sudan's African neighbours, when there were implications for the Arab north as well. Though Egypt did become a Friend of IGAD in 1999, it still remained suspicious that it was being held at arm's length by the West and the IGAD member states. Libya did not hold such firm views, but saw strength in standing with Egypt on the issue.

Thus in 2001 the Joint Libyan-Egyptian Initiative for peace in Sudan was launched. The new plan was particularly attractive for the northern Sudanese opposition parties in the NDA, and also the Umma Party, since it called for a conference of all Sudanese parties, and not just the government and the SPLA, in order to establish an all-party transitional government.[4] It also called for an immediate ceasefire that gained general popularity amongst the suffering Sudanese. It deliberately made no mention of secularism and self-determination that were so central to the IGAD process; and this was appreciated by the Sudan government. Cynics saw the new initiative as a deliberate spoiler of IGAD.

The only country in a position to exert effective leverage on the IGAD members and Egypt (to which Libya was effectively tied on the issue) was the US The situation was fully appreciated, and after he was through in Sudan in January 2002, Danforth had gone to Egypt to explain his position. Indeed when his report to President Bush spoke of his belief that separation for the south would be very difficult his critics claimed that he was making a deliberate concession to Egypt. Whatever the reasoning the Libyan-Egyptian initiative was effectively pushed to one side, for a while at least, in order to permit the progress to what was clearly to be the most serious international pressure for peace in Sudan since the ongoing war had started in 1983.

IGAD Peace Process

Once Danforth had reported and the Bush administration had committed itself, there was no delay in pressing ahead with talks. An impetus had been built up not only in Washington but in Sudan itself with the implementation of Danforth's four tests, and it needed to be built on.

Kenya was the obvious place for the talks to be held. IGAD had asked Kenya to lead in its efforts for Sudan peace in 1997, at a time when Sudan was effectively at war with its neighbours, Ethiopia, Eritrea and Uganda. Though the 1997 talks had failed, in the following year an IGAD Sudan Secretariat had been established in Nairobi. However Nairobi was not itself chosen as the location of the talks, but rather the town of Machakos to the east of the capital. It offered greater isolation and privacy, and the international media could be kept at a distance. In fact stories did leak out, but neither side was able to manipulate the media in a way that significantly influenced the talks. The location itself was adequate but deliberately chosen not to be so luxurious that the parties might choose to dwell over long for the sake of the facilities. However probably Kenya's greatest contribution to the talks was the role played by General Lazaro Sumbeiywo who chaired the meetings on behalf of IGAD. Sumbeiywo had past experience of IGAD negotiations on Sudan, and soon won the respect of all those involved.

As for the talks themselves, there were plenary sessions at which each side fielded an eight-man team, but not direct negotiations. Instead the two sides met separately with special envoys going between them as they separately probed each other's positions. The international community was present with representatives of the IGAD members, the Troika and Italy, but their role was as facilitators not mediators. In this role they also brought in various experts, including several from the US, to brief the parties on technical aspects of matters under discussion such as establishing and maintaining a ceasefire, which had not been set in place before the talks began (these were referred to by the parties as 'adult education' sessions). The first two weeks, of what became a five week session, were very slow with both sides very distrustful of one another: one publication described the talks as 'driven largely by the USA and the UK' (*Africa Confidential*, 2002, 43, 15).

From the outset a maximum period of five weeks had been set for the first round of talks in order to maintain pressure for progress. Nevertheless into the middle of the final week there were still doubts as to whether any progress would be made when quite suddenly a breakthrough was announced to considerable surprise in many quarters. As mentioned the DoP had set the agenda for the negotiations, and central to it had been the questions of religion and the state and self-determination for the south. Thus the two thorniest questions in principle, on which successive negotiations hitherto had foundered, became the starting point for negotiations and an agreement had been reached. Some suggested that the late agreement was very much due to international pressure, especially by the US and the UK, but whatever the reasons, the Machakos Protocol was agreed and signed on 20 July 2002.

The Protocol was a compromise between the positions of the two parties. The government had been seeking to create an Islamic state; while the SPLA's position had long been that the state would have to be secular if it was to remain united. The Protocol stated that, 'Nationally enacted legislation having effect only in respect of the states outside southern Sudan shall have as its source of legislation Sharia and the consensus of the people'. The south was to 'have as its source of legislation popular consensus, the values and customs of the people of Sudan including their traditions and religious beliefs, having regard to Sudan's diversity'. The fact that agreement was reached that did not include the whole state becoming secular then triggered the south's right of self-determination, so the Protocol said that after a period of six years and six months from a comprehensive peace agreement there would indeed be an internationally monitored self-determination exercise. The Protocol was met with a varied reception, but the consensus of all the comment was that though it had limitations and ambiguities, it was, in the words of the South Sudan Democratic Forum (a voice of civil society), 'a step in the right direction'. For the US it was an unalloyed step forward that would not have happened without American involvement.

The Machakos Protocol dealt with the principles on which previous talks had repeatedly floundered, there were still many practical matters that had to be negotiated and it was agreed to maintain the momentum beginning with another round of talks at Machakos on 12 August. However developments in the war itself brought delays. It had been earlier decided that there would not be a negotiated ceasefire prior to opening talks. A ceasefire would itself have required a complex negotiation in a war that had flowed back and forth, often with the changing seasons, and there would have been much calculation of advantage. The SPLA in particular was concerned that the government might take advantage of a ceasefire to re-arm using its now unimpeded access to oil and its revenues. As if to demonstrate its continuing capabilities, the SPLA launched a successful attack on the strategically important town of Torit in Eastern Equatoria. The government called foul and mobilised to re-capture in a move that seemed to reflect political calculation on both sides as much as military capacity on the ground. The two sides eventually agreed to a 'cessation of hostilities' (but not a full ceasefire), that enabled talks eventually to be resumed on 17 October and continue until 18 November when there was an adjournment until after the Kenyan elections. On 18 November a Memorandum of Understanding was signed. It did not appear as spectacular as the Protocol, but it did indicate that they were getting down to detailed head-to-head negotiations. The brief Memorandum included the establishment of a government of national unity in the transitional period, during which there would be free and fair elections for a bi-cameral national legislature. Both in the legislature and in other branches of government there would be equitable representation of the 'people of the Southern Sudan'.

Throughout this process the international pressure, led by the US, continued, especially with regard to the 'cessation of hostilities'. But it was a carrot and stick approach as the US was to show in the autumn. At the same time in showing that it had a stick, the Bush administration was also showing the Sudan government's many critics in America that it was not going soft for the sake of making peace. This makes it sound perhaps more coherent than it actually was, with differences and disagreements across Washington; nevertheless, as far as Sudan was concerned carrot and stick was how it played out (*Africa Confidential*, 2002, 43, 22). The Sudan Peace Act had started life in 2001, but its call to prevent access by companies working in Sudan to US capital markets had been opposed by the administration and leading senators on the grounds of being a dangerous precedent. A compromise was reached in order to maintain pressure on Sudan, and on 21 October 2002 the act was finally signed into law by the President. The final act was tied very directly to the peace process and after six months the President would be asked to decide whether the government was negotiating in bad faith, or had 'unreasonably interfered with humanitarian assistance efforts'. In that event a number of sanctions would come into play. The US would oppose any funding to Sudan from the IMF, the World Bank or the African Development Bank. The US would suspend diplomatic relations with Sudan. The US would take, 'all necessary and appropriate steps to deny the GOS [government of Sudan] access to oil revenues' to ensure that it 'neither directly nor indirectly utilizes any oil revenues for the purchase of military equipment'. Finally the US would seek a United

Nations' Security Council arms embargo against the Sudan government. There was also pressure on the SPLA in the bill, for if it was seen to be the cause of failure to attain peace, then the sanctions against the government would not apply. However, while the appearance of pressure on the SPLA was given in the bill, its effect was to make the SPLA feel able to fall back and resist the need to trade in the negotiations. The Act also included $300 million over three years for humanitarian assistance in non-government areas in the south. At virtually the same time the US Treasury Department announced that it was blocking the financial assets of 12 Sudanese organizations. However the US wish to make progress on peace as well was further demonstrated by its hosting of an informal seminar for leaders on both sides about issues of wealth sharing and power sharing that were important parts of the agenda for upcoming formal negotiations.

Though the Sudan government protested at the Peace Act and other US measures still in place, the pressure continued to have effect. A third round of talks was held early in 2003, now moved to the Nairobi suburb of Keren and later to Naivasha. As fighting had flared up, in spite of the official cessation of hostilities, it was agreed that there would be more transparency about troop movements, and free access for the international Verification and Monitoring Team that had been established. Progress was also reported on power-sharing issues, such as how the constitution for the interim period would be drafted, and the holding of a census of Sudan's population, up to four million of whom had been displaced by conflict. However there were still differences concerning the presidency. Wealth sharing was also problematic (and almost simultaneously the government released three more blocks for exploration in northern Sudan). The important issue of the border between north and south, especially the areas of Abyei, Southern Funj, and the Nuba Mountains, was dealt with separately but also proved difficult.

Progress was required if the US was to remain involved. The Sudan Peace Act required the President to report to Congress every six months on whether progress had been made, and in April the decision was due. Special Envoy John Danforth gave his appraisal, which was generally favourable. He recognised that, 'written commitments are periodically broken' and that there had been outbreaks of fighting, 'primarily but not exclusively by the GOS'; however, 'It is my understanding that that, recently, fighting has greatly diminished, and humanitarian access has improved throughout Sudan' (Department of State, 21 April 2003). There had also been face-to-face meetings between President Omer el-Beshir and SPLA leader John Garang. His recommendation was that the US should intensify its efforts with the aim of a final settlement being reached by mid-2003. Danforth was supported by the chairman, Sumbeiywo, who remarked, 'It remains clear ... that the continued involvement of the United States is crucial to the achievement of a just and comprehensive peace' (Department of State, 1 April 2003).

President Bush decided to report to Congress that progress had been made and that the US should remain involved. In doing so the Memorandum of Justification, made it clear that progress had not been easy, and also that it viewed the government side more critically than that of the SPLA, adding that, 'The United States sees the south as the aggrieved party in the civil war'. Nevertheless, there had been progress overall, 'The GOS and SPLM have gradually and grudgingly allowed the concept of a partnership to take hold and, as a result, we have seen a quantifiable increase in compromise and flexibility in recent talks' (The White House, 21 April 2003). He concluded that the process should continue.

The progress did continue, if at times with difficulty, through the remainder of 2003, with important agreements on future military arrangements including separate forces in north and south as well as a combined force and international monitoring. That was followed by agreement on wealth sharing with oil revenues to be divided 50/50 with a supervisory board to oversee the arrangements. In the New Year the final issues were agreed. The national capital, Khartoum, would be under *sharia* law since it is in the northern part of the country, but there will be exemptions for non-Muslims. The three disputed border areas- Abyei, Nuba Mountains and Southern Blue Nile- would have considerable local autonomy and Abyei would have its own self-determination exercise to join north or south at the same time as the south's self-determination exercise after six years. Power sharing was agreed that gave the ruling National Congress Party (NCP) and the SPLM dominance, respectively, in the national government and the government of the south. Thus all the protocols had finally been completed by 26 May 2004, nearly two years after talks had opened at Machakos. There was though still the need to finalise a number of areas before a Comprehensive Peace Agreement could finally be signed but progress was delayed by developments in Darfur in western Sudan.

The situation in Darfur had deep roots and some similarities with the situation of southern Sudan, especially its marginalisation by successive regimes in Khartoum. It also contained resource issues, in this case not oil or the division of the waters of a major river, but rather the division of land between different ethnic groups, with Arab and African racial connotations; as well as between communities that were primarily agricultural and pastoral in nature. These resource issues had been contributing to conflict for over 20 years, magnified by rising population, climate change and environmental degradation. What was different from the southern Sudan however was that this crisis did not involve a Muslim-Christian confrontation but was being carried out in a region that was overwhelmingly made up of Muslims.

While conflict within the region was longstanding, the scale of it grew vastly as a consequence of the success of the peace process between the government and the SPLA. Paradoxical as it may at first sight seem, the logic appeared simple. The peace process seemed to some in Darfur to be very exclusive, and if successful in its existing form might lead to greater control from the central government in the north, at a time when the south had won the right to establish a government of its own through its success on the battlefield: Darfur should follow the south's example. Such thinking appeared to influence a rebel group known as the Sudan Liberation Army (SLA). There was also a second group, the Justice and Equality Movement (JEM), that was believed to have a somewhat different agenda since it included supporters of Hasan al-Turabi who had been forced out of the regime in 1999. Tension had been building for some time before the two groups launched major attacks in Darfur early in 2003.

From the standpoint of the government it was these attacks by what it depicted as new rebel groups rather than land disputes that lay at the core of its response. The regional demands of the SLA would weaken the government in the final talks with the SPLA, and could trigger similar developments in the east of the country, where there had been low level conflict since the late 1990s. Links between the JEM and Turabi's Popular Congress Party (PCP), a splinter movement from the ruling National Congress Party (NCP), could be a direct challenge at the centre, and indeed led to later accusations of a coup plot that led to Turabi's arrest.[5] Force in Darfur had to be met by force. However there were military problems given the scale of Darfur and also possible intra-army issues since many soldiers came from the region. The answer was to arm and support government allies in the region known as the *janjawid*. This tactic had been used by successive regimes in Sudan: it was cheap and was always disclaimed by government as nothing more than 'traditional tribal conflict'. In part the *janjawid* appeared to be lawless bandits and in part it seemed drawn from Arab ethnic groups amongst the pastoralists. With arms and aerial support from the government the *janjawid* would both attack the rebels, and clear the population from areas where they were believed to have support. The estimated death roll rose rapidly to 70,000, while over 100,000 crossed into Chad and around 1,200,000 were estimated as internally displaced.[6] It was while seeking to regain control of Darfur, and crushing a possible challenge from the PCP, that the government appeared to prevaricate on the peace process with the SPLA. Some thought that it was simply trying to strengthen its position before moving to the final agreement: others believed that elements in the government, perhaps in the powerful security apparatus, were trying to derail the whole process, believing that too much had been conceded to the SPLA and that a display of force in Darfur could be the beginning of redressing the ground already lost. Darfur thus posed a dual crisis for the international community. It was both a crisis in itself and a threat to the peace process with the south that had seemed so near to completion.

In the US the developments in Darfur provoked outrage. By the summer of 2004 Secretary of State Colin Powell no less was calling Darfur the greatest humanitarian disaster in the world. And after visiting the region he declared that genocide was taking place: the first time that one government had accused another under the 1948 UN Genocide Convention. If there was a positive point at all, the crisis gave the opportunity for the US to show that its concern in Sudan was not just to sympathise with Christians fighting against Muslims in the south, but also with the conflict in the overwhelmingly Muslim region of Darfur. However alongside outrage was a sense of impotence, militarily over-committed in Afghanistan and Iraq and with diminished international credibility as a result of the latter situation there was no serious question of U.S-led international intervention. That was one reason why in crying genocide Colin Powell did so in a way that placed the responsibility for action firmly on the UN: in itself a notable reversal from Iraq. The UN in turn sub-contracted the job to the African Union (AU). The AU had replaced the discredited OAU with a new determination to take responsibility for conflict resolution in the continent, and this was a situation made to put that resolve to the test. Under heavy international pressure from the West and its neighbours, Sudan eventually agreed to a small AU monitoring team that was intended to build up to some 3,000 monitors and guards drawn from African sources and with expert international assistance. The stick with which the government was threatened was international sanctions, possibly including the halting of the country's oil exports. Such sanctions became themselves an issue in the Security Council, but the government felt obliged to make some concessions to the AU as the situation on the ground in Darfur showed at best limited signs of improvement. At the same time the US and its Troika partners in the peace process with the south were determined to exert maximum pressure on the government and the SPLA to return to Kenya and conclude the process, which was finally achieved at the end of the year. Once that was done, the agreement's terms included the opening up of the political system in ways that could offer opportunities for participation by movements from Darfur in the government system for the north. The final achievement of peace in the south could be linked to peace, rather than as hitherto to conflict, in Darfur as well.

American anger and frustration over Darfur had also be tempered by the cooperation on counter-terrorism and intelligence that it was receiving from the Sudan government, and the 'war on terror' was more important than Darfur, even with genocide. On counter-terrorism, US special forces were allowed access to attack an Islamist group in eastern Sudan; while quantities of intelligence materials were handed over. There were however doubts about the authenticity and quality of much of this cooperation, and the extent to which the Sudan government was stringing the US along (*Africa Confidential*, 6 August and 24 September 2004).

Conclusion

Peacemaking in Sudan had proved slow and protracted, yet it would probably not have happened at all without the weight that the US brought to the process. Elements of the eventual process were in place, IGAD had demonstrated regional concern, the DoP had been worked out years before and a Sudan Secretariat had been established, but there was little momentum at the time Bush entered the White House: it took the new US commitment to make the peace process a reality. The eventual success of the process brought a long and bloody war between successive regimes in Sudan and the SPLA to an end; though in doing so it also contributed to the opening of a new conflict in Darfur. Frustrating though that appeared to be, there were possibilities within the protocols resulting from the peace process to use them as a mechanism through which to turn to peacemaking in Darfur as well.

Notes

[1]   USAID also had its own Sudan Task Force that gave particular attention to the areas of the south outside government control. Its Director, Roger Winter, had

long been a thorn in the side of the Sudan government and had thus won the approval of its many critics in the US

[2] The US abstained in the Security Council vote of 2001 that lifted UN sanctions on Sudan.

[3] Following President Nimeiri's coup in 1970 a wing of the Umma Party led by al-Hadi al-Mahdi had attempted to mount an armed revolt. The *ansar*, the traditional followers of the Umma Party were the footsoldiers of the uprising which was vigorously crushed.

[4] It is widely believed that the call for an all-party conference was first put to Libya and Egypt by the Umma leader and former Prime Minister Sadiq al-Mahdi.

[5] The government claimed to have uncovered an arms cache to be used by Turabi's supporters in the capital: in fact it had itself established a number of caches in the early 1990s for its NIF supporters to use in the event of a military challenge from the army or outside.

[6] Even before the Darfur crisis Sudan had the highest number of internally displaced peoples (IDPs) in the world. Dr Francis Deng, a distinguished Sudanese diplomat and academic, was appointed Representative of the UN Secretary-General on IDPs.

References

Hoile, D. (2000), *Farce Majeure: The Clinton administration's Sudan Policy, 1993-2000*, London, European-Sudanese Public Affairs Council.

International Crisis Group (2002), *God, Oil and Country: Changing the Logic of War in Sudan*, Brussels, ICG.

Medley, M. (2003), 'Feeding Hameshkoreb', *Sudan Studies*, 30.

Scroggins, D. (2003), *Emma's War: Love, Betrayal and Death in the Sudan*, London, Harper Collins.

United States Institute of Peace (1999), *A New Approach to Peace in Sudan*, Washington, USIP.

Chapter 8

Somalia's Long Shadow

While US policy on Sudan was moving from confrontation to engagement, Somalia was largely out of American minds. This was mainly because of the perception of an apparently easy operation having turned into a nightmare, and that the best thing to be done was to move on. During the years after the withdrawal of US troops in 1994 Somalia largely continued along the same lines as those existing at the time of the pull out, though the fighting was generally less intense than it had been when the factions were sucked into the vacuum left by Barre's rapid exit in 1991. At that time in addition to the intensified conflict in the south, there was already the autonomous area of Somaliland in the northeast; and by the later 1990s a similar development was emerging in neighbouring Puntland in the northwest.

Somaliland was the older and larger of the two territories that appeared to demonstrate that largely from their own devices Somalis in parts of the country at least were capable of creating political order and a degree of statehood. The area of former British Somaliland had long been strongly opposed to the rule of President Siad Barre. In the early 1990s elements of the mainly Isaaq clan who inhabited the area had conducted opposition activities under the banner of the Somali National Movement (SNM) from across the border in Ethiopia. The agreement between Barre and Ethiopia's President Mengistu in 1988 to rein in their respective opponents led to the SNM's decision to make a pre-emptive strike that came close to capturing the major town of Hargeisa. However that in turn triggered a bloody reprisal by Barre's forces that left wanton death and destruction in its wake and in turn ensured the alienation of the north from the central government in Mogadishu in the south.

With the collapse of Barre's regime in 1991, the SNM, declared the independence of the new state of Somaliland headed by President Abdel Rahman Ali Tour. The claim for independence was based in part on the argument that since Somaliland had been a separate territory until Somalia's independence in 1960, and had subsequently been treated badly by central government, it should have the right to secede. Its leaders pointed to the international recognition of Eritrea's right of self determination in 1991 nearly 40 years after it had joined with Ethiopia: an argument that was all the stronger when Eritrea did indeed vote overwhelmingly for independence two years later. As will be seen Somaliland was denied international recognition, but in spite of some difficulties was able to develop and maintain a government, in contrast to the south of the country (Bradbury, Abokor and Yusuf, 2003).

Initially the new government appeared very weak and prone to intra-clan tensions that led in 1993 to the replacement of President Ali 'Tour' by an old political figure and former prime minister of Somalia in the 1960s, Mohammed Ibrahim Egal. However stability was restored, not least because of the resuscitation of traditional forms of dispute settlement involving elders, religious leaders, popular poets and women, who could utilise their marriage networks. These had all contributed to the four-month national council or *guurti* of 1993 that had appointed Egal, and agreed new guidelines for authority combining local voices with those of the leaders in the capital Hargeisa. As well as improved security and a new leader the council also produced a bi-cameral constitution, with appointed elders in the upper house and representatives in the lower. Under Egal the state took on more of the expected characteristics with an improved police force, efforts to de-militarise the sub-clan militias, a central bank and national currency, and a functioning bureaucracy that could engage with foreign NGOs. Egal was re-elected in 1997, and his death in 2002 and replacement by the Vice-President Dahir Riyah Kahin did not lead to any significant change in the maintenance of Somaliland's political system, or its lack of success in achieving international recognition. At the same time Somaliland had shown itself capable of economic survival. It was long an area of trade to Arabia and beyond, especially through the port of Berbera which became a booming entrepot, while opportunities overseas and the sending of remittances by Somalis in the diaspora also supported the economy.

To the immediate east of Somaliland another claimant for recognition also arose by 1998, in the form of the territory calling itself Puntland. With the overthrow of Barre in 1991, and the claimed independence of Somaliland, there was the opportunity for the peoples of this extreme tip of the Horn to assert their own autonomy, initially under the impetus of the Somali Salvation Democratic Front (SSDF). However, unlike Somaliland, the leaders of Puntland did not present a claim for international recognition of full independence. This resulted largely from the links that they had with the south, especially the strong ties to the southern port of Kismayo (Lewis, 2002, p.289). Within this area it was apparent that an indigenous form of order had been growing in the 1990s, partly around the council that existed in the Bari region. By 1995 a series of congresses was held and a regional sense of political autonomy was being expressed. There were rivalries of major faction leaders, but they did not prove destructive of the new entity; while once again clan elders and other respected 'traditional' figures played their parts in arriving at a consensus that permitted an administration to be established. And while the Majerteen clan was the major group in the new authority, it also endeavoured to incorporate representatives of a number of other clans and sub-clans. Like Somaliland, the peoples of Puntland also demonstrated their entrepreneurial and trading skills, and their port of Bossaso boomed, in contrast to the often conflict-ridden docks at Mogadishu to the south.

In contrast to these two northern regions, the south remained with many areas of of localized violence, especially in and around Mogadishu itself, and in the river valleys, notably the Juba and Shabelle. Here clan and sub-clan rivalries continued and with them the persistence of the activities of the warlords who had first come to prominence after Barre's downfall in 1991. Following the withdrawal of the last UN forces in 1995, three leaders were at the forefront. At different times both Ali Mahdi, backed mainly by the Abgal, and Mohammad Farah Aideed, supported by the Habar Gidir, had claimed to be leaders of a national government but in neither case could a broad enough base of support be established to make it faintly credible. The third major figure was Osman Otto, who had been financier to Aideed but broke away to try to seek his own political as well as financial fortune. In 1996 Mohammad Aideed was wounded in an escalation of fighting and died shortly thereafter. His place was taken by his son Hussein, but the pattern was largely unbroken with the three each holding sections of the former capital. Beyond the city were a variety of local groups and militias as political life became ever more centrifugal throwing up a bewildering and ever changing array of factions. In some areas the prospects of another autonomous area developed, notably among the Rahanweyne around Baidoa, but such development did not go as far as the new reconstructed political organizations of the north that might become the building blocks of a new Somalia, once contemplated by Mohammad Sahnoun and later taken up by the European Union (EU). The general picture, however was that the levels of local order were better north of Mogadishu, than in the area south of it stretching down to the Kenyan border. In this latter area the influx of outside clans during the course of the civil war contributed much to the higher levels of conflict.

While there remained a lack of any state-like facilities or functions, there was an array of economic activities. The UN intervention itself gave a considerable boost to the local economy, not only through the dollars poured in while its staff and troops were in the country, but also after they had left. Lewis sub-titles a section of his *Modern History* following the UN's departure as, 'The scrap merchants of Mogadishu' (Lewis, 2002, p.275; Little, 2003). There were all kinds of scavenging to be done, and the Somalis made sure that everything the UN had left was thoroughly dismantled and re-cycled to sell or to patch up their much damaged properties. Urban properties were both a source of wealth and of contention contributing to the political economy of factional conflict. Another contributing factor was that of agricultural and pastoral land. Agriculture had been at its strongest in the river valleys of the far south, and here the Barre years, as well as those following his downfall, had seen repeated land grabs, especially for the irrigated lands on which bananas, the major export crop, could be cultivated. It was in these contested urban and agricultural areas that violence was most commonplace, including militia rivalry to control the production and exports of bananas. While traditional patterns of pastoralism were associated with subsistence, the Barre and post-Barre years saw the growth of livestock trade, much of it to neighbouring countries. This trade was another source of wealth and rivalry. Other areas of activity included telecoms and the banking sector. It all contributed to a picture of a complex evolving political economy in which the successful learned how to grow rich in a stateless society. They had also somewhat weakened the power of warlords by creating their own militias rather than simply paying protection money to the existing faction leaders. There were many informal mechanisms to help them in establishing their positions, and it became a matter of argument whether or not the new 'big men' really would favour a political settlement that restored a degree of statehood in the south, or whether the beneficiaries of the continuing violent conditions – mafia-style merchants, clever financiers, militia leaders and the young men who fought for them, and even sub clans that had taken territory – effectively kept the system functioning (Menkhaus, 2002, 2003)?

However, while the big men prospered, the majority continued to suffer. Local order remained precarious with little more than localised arrangements of a neighbourhood watch or vigilante character in the towns, and some more traditional forms of dispute settlement in rural areas. The education system from the Barre era was largely destroyed, though there were some localised pockets of Muslim elementary education. Health care was almost non-existent for the majority.

It was partly the realization of the suffering of the Somali people that maintained the international concern for Somalia. The continuing levels of conflict greatly restricted the work of international aid and development organizations, both governmental and non-governmental, and to many it appeared that only efforts to help secure a more peaceful environment would make assistance to the population at large feasible. However with the US wanting as little as possible to do with the country, and other major outside powers adopting a similar attitude, it was largely left to regional powers to try to patch up the collapsed state; though, they in turn had their own agendas that included rivalry with each other in regard to the future of Somalia.

The country most directly concerned with developments in Somalia was Ethiopia. Ethiopia had long had reason to know of the threat posed by its eastern neighbour. In the 1960s Somalia's irredentist claim had led to guerrilla actions in the Haud and Ogaden regions, while in 1977-1978 the two countries had fought the largest conventional war in Africa since World War II. While Ethiopia was hardly likely to regret the passing of Siad Barre, whose downfall coincided, not entirely accidentally, with that of Mengistu Haile Mariam, the new situation brought particular concerns. One of these was the fact that the independence of Eritrea in 1993 had left Ethiopia landlocked, and in its search to diversify the ports on which it was forced to rely Berbera in Somaliland had attractive potential. Thus Ethiopia tended to be sympathetic to the Somaliland cause. Another major concern was with the activities of Islamists across the region. The movement continued to seek to build its strength in Ethiopia, especially among Muslim communities such as those in the Ogaden and Oromo areas. These activities were believed to lie behind a number of terrorist incidents, some in Addis Ababa itself especially between 1994 and 1996. The main group believed to be involved was al-Ittihad al-Islamiyya which also had bases on Somali territory. Ethiopia thus sent its troops across the border when it considered it necessary, such as in 1996 when it attacked al-Ittihad units surviving in its surviving stronghold in the town of Lugh in Gedo region in the southwest of Somalia. Following these raids Ethiopian troops remained on the ground, sometimes for several months at a time, and also distributed arms to local allies, although elements of al-Ittihad were still believed to be operating.

In an effort to go beyond 'policing' Somalia in this way, Ethiopia also sponsored efforts to restore some form of national authority. Its major effort came at the Sodere conference of 1997, backed by the OAU. Numerous factions were prevailed upon to attend and eventually agreed upon the formation of a National Salvation Council. However there were notable absentees without whom no real progress could be made. The deliberate absence of certain factions was related to the perceived agenda of Ethiopia that was seen as favouring particular groups, such as Ali Mahdi in Mogadishu, and the Rahenwayne. Ethiopia had also sought to include Somaliland in the agreement, but the authorities there stayed away; as also did Hussein Aideed's Somali National Alliance. Ethiopia's initiative therefore came to little.

Meanwhile, Egypt was seen as a rival to Ethiopia. Egypt had long had an interest in the coastal strip, as Boutros-Ghali's involvement had indicated. In part that reflected a long running rivalry with Ethiopia that went all the way back to their rival imperial ambitions in the Horn in the nineteenth century. In the twentieth century that rivalry had moved on to particular concern for the Nile waters that had long been vital to Egypt, and was of growing significance to Ethiopia itself. Egypt's concern for Somalia was thus seen in Ethiopia as closely associated with the wish for a re-constituted independent state that would contain and thereby weaken Ethiopia. Egypt thus sought to sponsor its own peace process in Somalia. In particular in 1997 Egypt convened a conference of a number of factions in Cairo, where some initial agreement was reached that would be followed up by a further meeting in Baidoa in 1998. However this plan was also prey to Somalia's chronic factionalism, and thus Egypt was no more successful than Ethiopia had been. (It should also be added that both countries had used their best efforts to frustrate the work of the other.)

For most of the 1990s Kenya was less active than Ethiopia or Egypt, but it still wished to avoid seeing either power extend its hegemonic ambitions to the north of Kenyan territory. Kenya was influential for much movement to and fro of the Somali inhabitants was across the common border, while the international monitoring of the situation was largely conducted from Nairobi. Thus while Kenya and Ethiopia had generally seen eye to eye with regard to the Barre regime before 1991, after his downfall there was generally mutual suspicion with regard to the Somali situation.

Minor parts in the Somali situation were also played by Italy, the EU and the UN. As the former colonial power, Italy still felt a particular concern, and indeed affinity for Somalis, especially in the south. For that reason it strongly opposed international recognition of Somaliland or Puntland, and instead backed the re-unification of the country. The EU had spoken of its wish to see Somalia restored by the establishment of local 'building blocks', leading to an eventual decentralised state, and regarded developments in the north in this light. Compatible with this was development assistance to the new northern entities. The UN for its part made similar noises from time to time since it wished to continue to maintain some semblance of concern for a collapsed member state that it (the UN) had intervened to assist in 1992.

These rivalries generally created something of a dilemma for the US Two of the states involved, Ethiopia and Egypt, remained significant American allies even after the Cold War was over. Egypt was clearly of continuing importance with regard to the Middle East (and had contributed a substantial number of troops to the Gulf War of 1990-1991); while Ethiopia was seen as an ally with regard to US efforts to use African regional powers to promote America's view of peace in the continent. Thus while sympathising with Ethiopian attacks on al-Ittihad, the US had no wish to take sides with regard to Somalia, which was in any case a place from which it preferred to stay clear of engagement. This uncertainty and reluctance to act was indicated in 1999 when President Egal was invited to Washington but not offered US recognition of Somaliland's independence, although some in the administration were apparently sympathetic (*Indian Ocean Newsletter*, 9 October 1999). US relations with Kenya declined after the Cold War, largely because the Moi regime was thought to embody many of Africa's ills, in contrast with the new brooms in neighbouring Uganda and Ethiopia. However this did not really affect the US view of Somalia, but meant simply that it took little account of Kenyan concerns, beyond issues such as the activities of Islamists that could spread into East Africa, and the mafia-type trading that often involved Kenya as well (sometimes with links to prominent members of the Kenyan elite).

The year 1998 proved a difficult year for the US with regard to its general wish to stay out of Somalia, and its regard for Ethiopia as an ally. The first problem was the unexpected eruption of war between Ethiopia and Eritrea. Two 'renaissance' leaders were at one another's throats, and it was inevitable that Somalia would play a part in calculations. Eritrea saw an opportunity to assist factions opposed to Ethiopia particularly that of Hussein Aideed, as well as being accused of sending arms through Somalia to the Oromo Liberation Front (OLF) in Ethiopia. It was also alleged that Arab backers including Libya and Qatar were giving aid (*Africa Confidential*, 24 September 1999). As seen, the US could do little more than regret the Ethiopia-Eritrea war that its own diplomatic efforts had failed to halt. The other cause for concern for the US in that year was the bombing of its embassies in Kenya and Tanzania, almost followed by a third embassy in Uganda.

The attacks on 7 August, the anniversary of the arrival of US troops in Saudi Arabia, killed 13 Americans and over 200 Africans. They were organised and carried out by al-Qaeda and linked to Somalia. In al-Qaeda's announcement justifying the attacks it said that, 'The attack was justified because the Government of Kenya admitted the Americans to have used their land [sic] to fight Muslim neighbours especially Somalia' (Gunaratna, 2002, p.162). From the US point of view, although the direct responses to the attacks were against Afghanistan and Sudan, there was a strong suspicion that the situation in Somalia, including the continued activities of elements of al-Ittihad, had been linked to the preparations that had begun as early as 1994, and been postponed in 1996 following Sudan's involvement in the attempted assassination of Mubarak. Specifically the US belief was that al-Ittihad activists had routed money and materiel from their surviving bases in Somalia to local al-Qaeda members in East Africa who had organised the actual attacks, with planning input from bin Laden himself.

9/11

Whatever may have been the understanding in the US of Islamist involvement in Somalia in 1992-1993, by the end of the decade there was no doubting that the Horn had become a centre of activity with the attacks on US interests in East Africa and Yemen. A policy of cooperating with governments in the region against terrorism had already been put in place, even including Sudan which in earlier years had done so much to incubate the Islamist movement. But the particular problem created by Somalia was that there was no government with which to cooperate, and instead it appeared that the country's very statelessness provided an opportunity for al-Qaeda to exploit. Thinking about policy for such an environment had already begun both in general terms and in relation specifically to Somalia, but it was given greater impetus by the attacks on American soil on 9/11. In fact there was no direct connection between Somalia and 9/11 but the attacks brought a fresh focus on the whole of the Horn as a strategically significant area of President Bush's new 'war on terror'. The rapid expansion of US activity with regard to Sudan has been seen, but Somalia also demanded intensified attention. A major question was appreciating the threat that might be posed by Islamist groups in Somalia? While it was obviously the case that the Somali population was overwhelmingly Muslim this did not of itself indicate an interest in Islamism as a contemporary ideology. And even it was possible to ascertain the existence of such Islamist groups that did not necessarily mean an actual or potential interest in acts of terrorism, whether or not linked to al-Qaeda.

Various Islamic groups were known to be in existence, but attention focused mainly on al-Ittihad. Although it had been comparatively unsuccessful in the early 1990s, it was believed still to have activists in all parts of the country, as well as across the border in Ethiopia. Indeed following the attacks by Ethiopia in 1996 al-Ittihad and sympathisers were thought to have changed to a longer term strategy. It involved a range of activities, many of which were appealing to local communities, but taking no chance the US branded al-Ittihad as a terrorist organisation with an Islamist agenda. In view of the collapse of state institutions some schools and local medical centres were run by Islamic organisations, often funded by Muslim charities based in Saudi Arabia and the smaller Gulf states. They were also involved in a variety of business ventures, financial transactions and banking.[1] One of the main sources of money for local people was remittances from relatives in the Somali diaspora that had been much swelled by the years of conflict; while the businesses that did continue locally could find finance from similar sources. Indeed the largest employer in Somalia following the collapse of the state was the Barakat Bank and it was closed down by the US causing remittance problems for many Somali families. In turn the Somali financial system was linked to the Gulf, especially Dubai where a leading Somali financier, Ahmed Nur Ali Jimale, was based (*Africa Confidential*, 23 November 2001). In an effort to cut such ties the US severed internet links with Somalia and closely monitored flights in and out of the country. Al-Ittihad was also thought to have significant links with some of the factions that continued to compete for power. A part of Mogadishu was controlled by the Transitional National Government (TNG) that was believed to be sympathetic to al-Ittihad; and al-Ittihad was also believed to have a finger in the pie of the newly self-proclaimed territory of Puntland. On this front the US worked closely with Ethiopia in supporting rival factions such as the Somali Restoration and Reconciliation Council (SRRC) led by Hussein Aideed, son of America's old enemy.

Concern with al-Ittihad was easily linked to questions about possible al-Qaeda connections. As seen earlier there had been links between the assorted Islamists in Sudan in the early 1990s and developments in Somalia. However with the retreat of the UN intervention in Somalia and bin Laden's expulsion from Khartoum there appeared to be few or at least less conspicuous links. That did not mean though that members of al-Ittihad had lost sympathy for an international network whose members held a similar ideological orientation. Individuals or local groups belonging to al-Ittihad could still be active and the threat needed to be monitored and assessed. But that had been a problem ever since the regional activities had developed in the late 1990s, and especially the attacks on the US embassies in 1998. There was also a possible new al-Qaeda dimension with the US-led intervention in Afghanistan to overthrow the Taliban and seek to crush al-Qaeda at source. While bin Laden and his immediate entourage appeared to disappear into the mountainous borderlands of Afghanistan and Pakistan, there were fears that some might escape into the urban sprawls of Pakistan. And if those became too hot, some at least might head west towards Yemen where there was also a significant Islamist movement and infrastructure. In both Pakistan and Yemen there were however governments that could be pressured into at least a degree of cooperation with the US, even though constrained by their own state weakness and political constraints in Muslim populations. For pure statelessness there appeared nowhere as attractive as Somalia as a possible bolt hole, together with local sympathisers and at least some past experience and contacts from ten years previously. Once there it was anticipated that any al-Qaeda cells would not simply hide, but continue the activities in the region. (There were also fears that a similar scenario could develop again in the vast spaces of Sudan in spite of the government's apparent enthusiastic support for the 'war on terror'.) In addition to its statelessness, Somalia's other assets included a long coast line on one side and long borders with potential target states (Ethiopia and Kenya) on the other; as well as numerous small dirt airstrips widely used for activities such as the ubiqitous *qat* trade. It would thus be comparatively easy to move men and materiel in and out of Somali bases, whether hidden in towns or in remote rural areas.[2]

However a common problem in assessing both al-Ittihad and al-Qaeda was a lack of intelligence. From 1993 until 2001 there had been little attempt to collect and analyse intelligence, and while the efforts were much greater after 9/11 there were fears that the US agencies were relying heavily on collaboration with Ethiopian counterparts who had a vested interest in demonising al-Ittihad and playing up the possible involvement of al-Qaeda in Somalia. In response to any possibility of US attack Somali factions declared their innocence of any connection at all with al-Qaeda and loudly offered to collaborate with US intelligence.

Containing the Threat

Speaking to a Senate committee shortly after his appointment as Assistant Secretary of State for Africa Walter Kansteiner described Somalia as a 'failed state' and went on to say, 'Where there should be a nation-state, there is a vacuum filled by warlords. What better place for the seeds of international terrorism and lawlessness to take root?' (*Public Diplomacy Query*, 7 February 2002) He went on to outline three goals for US policy: the removal of the existing terrorist threat and prevention against Somalia's use as a terrorist base; the prevention of developments in Somalia that could threaten the region; and the overcoming of the lack of governmental authority that made Somalia a possible base for terrorism.

One part of the strategy to implement the policy was the monitoring of the region through the establishment of a Joint Task Force, Horn of Africa (JTF-HOA), the military concern of which was indicated by its being answerable to the Department of Defense (Bollee, 2003). JTF-HOA based about 1,800 military and civilian personnel, including 400 special forces, at Camp Lemonier in Djibouti, as well as establishing a CIA presence. It was America's only base on the African continent. The US also had offshore capability centred around the command ship USS Mount Whitney: this created a combat force of 800 US marines by ship-borne attack helicopters and jump-jets. Exercises were carried out with Djibouti and Kenya; and in November 2002 a strike using unmanned aircraft was made against reported al-Qaeda leaders in Yemen.

JTF-HOA also worked closely with other non-regional forces in the region. France had long had a force of 3,200 men in Djibouti, and a new Task Force 150 was also established there. Under it, Spain commanded a naval and air force to patrol the Bab el Mandab straits and to intercept possible al-Qaeda members moving from Yemen to Somalia (though with the numerous small craft around it was difficult to conduct). Task Force 150 was also supported by German ship and air patrols, and 1,000 German personnel were stationed in Djibouti.

While trying to isolate Somalia from contact with terrorist groups beyond its frontiers, the US was also involved in some direct actions pertaining to alleged terrorist groups and centres within the country. One action was the freezing of the assets of al-Barakat on the grounds that it was transmitting money for both al-Ittihad and al-Qaeda. In conjunction with Saudi Arabia the US moved against the supposedly charitable al-Haramain Islamic Foundation. It was alleged that al-Haramain used its support for Islamic educational projects and the construction of mosques to the same two organizations.

The US was also involved in more direct intervention, both on its own and in conjunction with Ethiopia. Whatever American feelings about the futility of the Ethiopia-Eritrea war, or Ethiopian domestic politics, the latter was an obvious and enthusiastic ally in the 'war on terror' in the Horn, especially with regard to Somalia. Ethiopia had of course its own agenda there. A united Somalia was regarded as the source of conflict in the guerrilla fighting in the 1960s and a major war a decade later. In the 1990s Ethiopia, now a landlocked country, was seen as a supporter of the coastal regions of Somaliland and Puntland, though not going as far as seeking international recognition for either. At the same time it was regarded as suspicious of the TNG in Mogadishu and its alleged sympathy for al-Ittihad and the cause of Islamists generally. This was even more apparent in the war with Eritrea and indications that the latter was supporting opposition in Ethiopia via Somali territory and making overtures to the TNG. In response Ethiopia was thought at one time to be developing links with Hussein Aideed's faction. With or without the agreement of the US it was clear that Ethiopia would intervene in Somalia: after 9/11 it was clear that there would be at least occasions to work together.

Ethiopia was already a recipient of US funds to African forces, particularly through Foreign Military Financing (FMF) and International Military Education and Training (IMET). These funds had focused on equipment procurement and professional and technical training. They had been suspended in the Ethiopia-Eritrea war but after 9/11 were restored to both countries. The State Department also had an Anti-Terrorism Assistance (ATA) programme. In the wake of 9/11 all these funds support for US friends in the region were enhanced; and in 2002 the US also resumed arms supplies to Ethiopia, albeit on a modest scale.

It was also reported that the US was directly engaged in operations. In 2002 there was a small group of American military instructors in Gode in south-east Ethiopia training pro-Ethiopian Somalis and US agents also went across the border to western Mogadishu and Baidoa (*Indian Ocean Newsletter*, 16 February 2002). In Mogadishu they were said to be involved in snatch operations against suspected organisers of arms shipments into and through Somalia (*The Spectator*, 15 November 2003); a tactic recommended by the experienced Ted Dagne in his Congressional Research Service report ('Africa and the War on Terrorism', CRS for Congress, 17 January 2002). Actions of this kind were comparatively easy to execute, but a much more challenging response to the apparent threat caused by statelessness was also being considered: that of seeking the reconstitution of some kind of viable authority. It would improve the lot of the majority of the population by carrying out tasks for which there was no substitute for a state, and would also be able to cooperate in the international 'war on terror'. It was the third, and most difficult, of Kansteiner's three 'policy goals' for Somalia. At a meeting of the Africa sub-committee of the Senate Foreign Relations Committee in February 2002 Kansteiner said that the US had 'begun the idea of marshalling ideas and resources', but he cautioned, 'if the United States and the international community want good governance for Somalia more than the Somalis do themselves, the effort is doomed to fail'. Chairman Feingold added that the US had to find ways, 'To strengthen the law enforcement capacity of weak states and avoid the mistake of the Cold War, when, in the name of resisting and containing communism, this country assisted some truly appalling regimes in Africa – governments that pursued policies antithetical to our national values – leading to disastrous results that ultimately did not serve our national interest' (Public Diplomacy Query 8 February, 2002).

There had been no lack of efforts and conferences to solve the problems of Somalia's statelessness, fourteen in total, but all had come to nought. They had however produced some new thinking. By 1996 it was becoming common to speak of the necessity to work with Somali 'building blocks' rather than thinking that a new national system could be delivered from on high. In part this went back to thoughts of grass roots building from the bottom up of the kind associated with Mohammed Sahnoun in 1992. But it also reflected the reality that in Somaliland a political authority had been established, that it might be followed in neighbouring Puntland, and that there was a possibility that another potential block might be taking shape in the area under the control of the Rahanweyn Resistance Army (RRA) in the south-west. However the building block approach remained anathema to the factions wrestling for control of Mogadishu with their more nationalistic dreams. In 2000 IGAD took a fresh initiative with Djibouti hosting meetings that became known as the Arta process. It led to the formation of a Transitional National Government (TNG) in Mogadishu, but although it received some recognition, many significant groups remained outside the process and the TNG was unable to develop significant power. Thus by the time Kansteiner was calling for new ideas, there had been little progress towards an overall solution based on either building blocks or a more centralist approach. Instead, the successive attempts to solve the problems of Somalia generally collapsed in a fresh wave of violence.

In spite of this there were still some grounds for hope. The post 9/11 concern for Somalia meant that there was much more international input from outside the region. In this the US was only one player, though an important one. Another major actor was the EU. Several European powers had past or current involvement that contributed to their concern for Somalia. Italy and Britain were former colonial powers with a continuing sense of involvement including numbers of Somali refugees in both countries. France still retained its military presence in Djibouti, while Germany was involved in patrolling the region. The EU was also a major aid donor, and there were to be substantial aid carrots to try to induce the Somalis to eventual agreement. There were also sticks in the form of conditions that had to be met, including cooperative arrangements with such regional authorities as had already been established in the country, and the threat of sanctions against leaders such as major warlords or businessmen who sought to obstruct the process. The Arab League was also involved in backing the initiative. Saudi Arabia had long connections with Somalia, especially in the form of economic and financial ties and the movement of Somalis across the intervening seas. Politically it was thought to favour the TNG. Egypt was also believed to have its own agenda, often seen as one of seeking to contain Ethiopia, while Yemen and Libya were also Arab League members with past interest in Somalia.

While much of the drive came from the wider international community, the immediate regional players were directly involved through the fact that another new conference was to be held under the auspices of IGAD. This, it was hoped, would give it regional ownership, and also strengthen the organization itself. While the conference was hosted by Kenya, a Technical Committee was established with Djibouti and Ethiopia as well. All three had particular concerns. Kenya linked the rise of terrorism on its soil to the lawless Somali situation; Djibouti had hosted the previous round of talks known as Arta, and was generally thought to be pro-TNG; while Ethiopia's concern has been seen and was usually regarded as anti-TNG.

The conference began in October 2002 with meetings first in Eldoret and later in the Nairobi suburbs. In the light of previous experience, it was decided that a blueprint for government needed to be drawn up before any sharing out of power. That would ensure that those eventually acquiring power would do so on an agreed basis to which all participants were publicly committed, rather than seeking to distribute power at the outset and then leave it to the newly appointed authorities to work out a central government. The latter approach, it was feared, could simply lead to a return to the repressive and predatory ways of the past. It would also mean that when new rulers did take up their posts they would be able to move directly to govern, rather than embarking on making power-sharing arrangements. Finally it was hoped that the process of arriving at a blueprint would itself build confidence in the outcome. Thus it was that figures from numerous factions and civil society organizations converged on the talks claiming to be representatives and thereby entitled to a place at the various tables established.

The first phase of the talks had as its main purpose the question of representation, and it was soon clear that this in itself gave rise to major problems. It had been expected that about 300 delegates would participate in the talks, but in the event over 1,000 arrived in Eldoret. To try to sort it out a Leaders' Committee was established. There were three rough 'constituencies' to be considered: faction leaders; clan representatives; and leaders from 'civil society'. In fact the representative character and legitimacy of all of them were open to question. The faction leaders or warlords were seen as inevitable because of the armed groups they were thought to have at their disposal. But in actual fact their strength was often queried with intra-faction fragmentation having appeared to take place in several of them. Clan leaders were seen as necessary since Somalia had traditionally been seen in clan terms, but there were doubts about the strength of the clan system, especially in the south, in the light of the pragmatic social mobility widely displayed by the people over the previous two decades in particular. As for 'civil society', that was a novel concept fashionable in the international community that might or might not have much bearing on reality. As the International Crisis Group (ICG) put it pithily, 'Some to whom it [civil society] is applied are respected figures who have the demonstrated community leadership either at home or abroad, while others have no greater claim than a custom-made business card or the funds to buy a return ticket to Eldoret' (ICG, 2003, p.16). Relations between the different categories were also difficult, as ICG went on to say, 'Faction leaders perceive civil society delegates as opportunistic rivals for posts in a future government and complain they are little more than proxies for foreign donors and NGOs'. In the end it was agreed by the Leaders' Committee that seats would be mainly allocated by clan, but that the faction leaders would have the major say in who the clan leaders filling the seats would be; perhaps a crude Somali version of checks and balances. In practice decisions on participation were to be largely academic since the representatives came and went from the talks apparently for a bewildering variety of personal and group reasons that complicated the whole process.

In theory the issues of representation had been addressed after the first weeks, and the conference could then move on to phase two where a series of

Reconciliation Committees were intended to address key problems regarded as central to the establishment of a lasting peace.

One crucial issue was that of the constitution and form of government. On this committee two views soon emerged, those favouring federalism, and those wanting a centralized state. Past events seemed to favour the former since the centralised system under Siad Barre was seen as the cause of the disaster that had made Somalia the one fully collapsed state in the world, and in parts of the country there had been the emergence of regional authorities. However, the most stable of these, Somaliland, was not participating in the conference, and instead continued to seek international recognition as a fully independent country. Other possible claimants, such as Puntland and the Rahanwayne claimed area of 'Southwest Somalia' looked more dubious. Other federal units would be at least as difficult to delineate, and even if achieved might lead to minority claims for further recognition of the kind that developed in Nigeria. Such developments could lead to future fragmentation of a Somali state reconstructed on the federal principle. However centralist claims not only had history to contend with, but also the widely held fear that its implication was likely to be the domination of a particular clan and/or faction, and that that in turn would be equally threatening to the reconstituted state. While there were attempts to draft some form of compromise, an agreed solution proved very elusive.

In comparison with the centrality of the governance issue, other committees appeared less urgent, but were nevertheless rightly seen as necessary. Land and property was an important issue, especially since it had been a major problem, especially in the south, since the days of Siad Barre. There had been armed incursions on land, notably in the river valley areas, that had contributed to the fighting after 1991. The relevant committee sought to take the long view on land disputes, and to call for the withdrawal of militias in the affected areas. Economic recovery was the subject for another committee, but that too had an uphill task. Without knowing the structure of government it was hard to know from where resources would be found, or how they should be distributed. The apparent assumption of foreign aid was highly optimistic given Somalia's history with regard to aid, and the general reluctance to be generous after the Cold War. There was also the problem that in reality the most successful businessmen in the country were those exploiting the opportunities provided by the unstable conditions and they might have little interest in seeking to resolve existing situations. There was also a Committee for Demobilisation, Disarmament and Reintegration and it too faced formidable questions. It estimated that approximately 100,000 militiamen would need to be demobilised, but who was to do it? In Somaliland community leaders had played a significant role, but it was not thought that such figures had comparable powers in many parts of the south. The committee had hopes of international support, but that brought up fears of a possible repeat of the UN intervention ten years previously and international reluctance to be involved. Local and Regional Conflict Resolution was the concern of another committee. Here much of the problem lay in defining its role given the numerous conflicts and the uncertainty of the constitutional framework in which they might be addressed.

As if there were not enough problems in having these parallel committees at work, there were further complications as well. The Technical Committee had its own contribution to make. There were difficulties with the chair, held by the host country, Kenya, and clearly crucial to maintaining the momentum of such a complex process. The first incumbent, Elijah Mwangale, soon proved out of his depth and was replaced by the more experienced Bethwel Kiplagat. At the same time the other two governments were regarded as having their own interests. As seen, Djibouti was perceived as using its position to favour the 'centralists' and Ethiopia was accused of encouraging the 'federalists'; while the influence of other regional actors was also a problem, as too was the absence of Somaliland. The conference organisers hoped for its presence, and were prepared to offer it proportional representation. However the leaders of the would-be independent state were hardly likely to accept such a position, and instead kept their powder dry, pending the emergence of a government in Mogadishu to which they might then talk.

By June 2003 the conference was in theory moving on to its third phase, that of constructing a power-sharing government with a proposed 351 member parliament and over 80 ministers. But in practice many of the issues from the second phase were still unresolved, and the talks appeared to be drifting towards deadlock. It was also questionable by that stage whether anybody cared? Many of the Somali representatives had drifted away from the conference leaving its committees manned only by a rump. Meanwhile back in Somalia awareness of the conference's work appeared to be diminishing so that even had more progress been made in Kenya it might have counted for little on the ground. With fears of possible collapse, President Museveni of Uganda, as Chair of IGAD, stepped in to rescue the conference and by October 2004 a president had been agreed. The man chosen, Abdullah Yousuf, President of Puntland, looked as likely a prospect to rebuild Somalia as anyone, but it still looked a huge task and there were even questions of if and when he would be able to take up his task on the ground rather than remaining in Kenya. By the end of 2004 he and his new government were still in Kenya, though the latter's patience with their continuing presence was beginning to run out.

In all this the US seemed mute, especially in comparison with its role in the Sudan peace process taking place at the same time in the same country. Perhaps it was memories of past intervention in Somalia, or perhaps it was pessimism about the likely outcome; whatever the reason the contrast was very apparent. When Colin Powell visited Kenya in October 2003 Sudan was high on his agenda, whilst Somalia hardly received a mention. At the same time there were signs of a more sympathetic approach to Somaliland. The contrast between Somaliland's post-Barre development and the rest of the country was made more apparent by the quagmire into which the conference in Kenya appeared to have fallen. It was also apparent that Somaliland was increasingly involved in contacts with a number of regional governments, especially those of neighbouring Djibouti and Ethiopia, as well as international donors including the World Bank and UN agencies. While there were clear divisions in the international community over Somaliland, some voices in the US were expressing the need to address the question and not simply to regard the future of Somalia as necessarily meaning the restoration of Somaliland's status as a part of the country.[3] Meanwhile for the US government the obvious priority remained that of seeking to act against any possible terrorist threat based in the failed state and preventing any threat to the region. Regional management seemed more 'doable' than re-constructing Somalia, and involved building up all aspects of security in what were now known as anchor states. In relation to Somalia and the Horn the anchor states chosen were Kenya and Ethiopia.

Kenya had long been regarded as a regional friend. After the Cold War President Moi's reluctance to reform the political system caused something of a rift, but ten years later a combination of the attacks on the US in East Africa and America and the democratic election of a new government in Kenya brought closer cooperation once more. From the time of the attack on the US embassy in Nairobi in 1998 US and Kenyan security authorities were combining in a number of areas. Existing border and airport security was inadequate to keep out possible terrorists, and it was also feared that there were sleeper cells in the country, especially among the Muslim community, mainly located on the coast. Money and training for the Kenyan authorities was stepped up; and there were also agreements under which the US could use Kenya as a base for counter-terrorist operations across the region. These included US security personnel operating in the Muslim areas on the coast; and military exercises involving the US, Britain and Germany that led to speculation about a possible strike into Somalia (Kikaya, 2003).

As seen, Ethiopia was more than willing to be an ally in the war on terrorism. The problem for the US was that Ethiopia might be almost too enthusiastic. Ethiopian intelligence might be intended as much to solicit US support as to accurately reflect developments on the ground. In addition Ethiopia's open hostility to the TNG in Somalia in the past had provoked criticism, not only among the many Muslims in Somalia who were not involved in terrorism in any shape or form, but also among states friendly to the US such as Egypt, widely seen as a long time rival to Ethiopia in the Horn. The US thus had to try both to support and curb Ethiopia, a tricky diplomatic tightrope to walk.

Also keen to present itself as a friend to the US in the war on terror was Eritrea. It too was concerned to contain Islamic terrorism and thought that it could offer port facilities not available in Ethiopia. Eritrea did receive some security-related aid, but the US was not rushing to regard it as an anchor state. Its aggressive style in foreign policy was perceived as having caused it a degree of isolation and suspicion in the region, while its domestic political and economic performance was viewed critically. In spite of these shortcomings the US was prepared to tolerate Afwerki's regime seeing it as preferable to any possibility of an Islamist alternative. To the annoyance of the Ethiopian government, the US also saw Eritrea as a route to the OLF with a view to combating Islamists in the Oromo areas of Ethiopia. However it was not the Eritrean ports of Masawa or Asad that appealed to the US, instead it was Djibouti that was preferred as the strategic port for the region, not only by America but the other Western powers involved in the war on terror.

On the other side of the sea, Yemen's growing cooperation was also welcomed. While the country itself was seen as an area of al-Qaeda operations, the government was willing to cooperate in the war on terror, and received encouragement from Washington. Moreover when the US did strike against al-Qaeda figures on Yemeni territory, there was no complaint of breached sovereignty from the authorities in Sanaa.

Conclusion

The contrast between the US policy in Somalia and Sudan could hardly have been greater. In contrast to the involvement in the latter, Somalia was not a problem with which Washington wished to become engaged and seek to resolve. In part this was the result of continuing memories in the executive branch especially of the failure there in the early 1990s; in part it reflected the lack of a positive belief in the government as a whole that Somalia was 'doable'; and in part it was the lack of a domestic constituency in America of the kind that urged action in Sudan. In addition, the concerns of America's allies in the region were more consensual on Sudan: for a variety of reasons states from Egypt to Kenya and Chad to Djibouti were supportive of peace efforts there; whereas there were differing outlooks, and even mutual suspicions with regard to state reconstruction in Somalia. It all added up to encouraging a US policy of 'wait and see', while containing any terrorist threat that might develop in the collapsed state.

Notes

[1]   One author entitled his book, *Al-Ittihad: Political Islam and Black Economy in Somalia* (Tadesse, 2002).
[2]   One expert on Somalia however has queried the desirability of a stateless environment and suggested that the urban outskirts of a weak state might be more amenable to terrorists since such locations offer more facilities and greater anonymity (Menkhaus, 2004).
[3]   This view was expressed by David Shinn, former ambassador to Ethiopia and Head of the East Africa Section of the State Department (Public Diplomacy Query, 13 March 2003).

References

Bollee, A. (2003), 'Djibouti: From French outpost to US base', *Review of African Political Economy*, No.97.
Bradbury, M., Abokor, A. and Yusuf, H. (2003), 'Somaliland: Choosing politics over violence', *Review of African Political Economy*, No.97.
Gunaratna, R. (2002), *Inside al-Qaeda: Global Network of Terror*, London, Hurst.

International Crisis Group (2003), *Negotiating a Blueprint for Peace in Somalia*, Brussels, ICG.

Kikaya, D. (2003), 'A vulnerable continent: Africa', in Buckley, M. and Fawn, R. *Global Responses to Terrorism: 9/11, Afghanistan and beyond*, London, Routledge.

Lewis, I. (2002), *A Modern History of Somalia*, Oxford, James Currey, 4th ed.

Little, P. (2003), *Somalia: Economy without state*, Oxford, James Currey.

Medhane, Tadesse (2002), *Al-Ittihad: Political Islam and Black Economy in Somalia*, Addis Ababa, Meag.

Menkhaus, K. (2002), 'Somalia: next up in the war on terrorism?', *Africa Notes*, January, 2002, no.6.

Menkhaus, K. (2003), 'State Collapse in Somalia: Second Thoughts', *Review of African Political Economy*, No.97.

Menkhaus, K. (2004), *Somalia: state collapse and the threat of terrorism*, Oxford OUP, for International Institute for Strategic Studies (IISS), Adelphi Paper No.364.

Conclusion

Following the end of the Cold War the directions of US foreign policy were far from clear and in the subsequent years there was an outpouring of reviews of possible directions that it could and should take. There was also much reflection on the US role historically and the approaches of the past with possible relevance for the future.[1] There were also differences of approach in the post-Cold War presidencies of George Bush, Bill Clinton and George W. Bush at a time when policy choices seemed less constrained than they had when the USSR threatened. Presidential choice, as in Bush senior's New World Order or Clinton's limited international interest, left more flexibility of possibilities for departments and agencies as well to push their various agendas. At the same time the stocktaking that such a situation permitted could extend to greater opportunities for Congress and interest groups.   But in all such varied reflections Africa remained comparatively low on the overall agenda: writing in 2004 two experienced Americans referred to, 'The past habit of treating Africa as an humanitarian afterthought' (Kansteiner and Morrison, CSIS, 2004, p.2). From that perspective Somalia after 1993-1994 was about as low as one could go in the eyes of many Americans, especially when television pictures had shown the body of a dead US soldier being dragged through the streets of Mogadishu by a cheering crowd.

Yet if international relations were changing for the US they were doing so for the states in Africa as well. The Cold War had contributed significantly to the domestic and international relations of the Horn. Domestically both superpowers had sought to back up their client regimes and provided them with the weapons: the arms may have been intended for protection from hostile neighbours, but they were used far more to prosecute civil wars. As such the superpowers had helped to forge repressive autocratic regimes that across the Horn at least were met with armed resistance and long and bloody cycles of violence ensued (Woodward, 1996; Clapham, 1998). The alignment of regimes with rival superpowers and the need for resistance movements to seek cross-border support made tension and rivalry rather than cooperation the norm in regional relations. It was a peculiarity of the Horn that the regimes all changed superpowers from time to time, but the pattern remained the same. Towards the end of the Cold War as superpower tension receded it was no coincidence that the clients fell from power, though what they left were varied situations reflecting the differences within the states involved: in Ethiopia and then newly independent Eritrea the resistance movements took power largely ending domestic conflict; in Sudan an Islamist movement seized control in yet another of the country's coups and reinvigorated civil war; while Somalia imploded to destroy the old regime and with it the Somali state as it had developed from independence in 1960. The resulting changes produced new problems for the states' relations, but they were now largely regional relations rather than being shaped by major international powers let alone the sole surviving superpower.

For the US the 'Somalia syndrome', as it was often known, reflected a low point encouraging American disengagement from Africa, but the continent could not be ignored. The humanitarian challenges continued to arise and some form of action was required, as the response to international inaction in the Rwanda genocide in 1994 indicated. At the same time humanitarian crises were viewed less as the result of natural disasters, as they had been in the famines in Ethiopia and Sudan in the 1980s, and more as the product of conflict. And conflict was understood largely in terms of weak and failing states rather than great struggles of ideological rivals (Reno, 1998). The US was involved in efforts at peacemaking in Sudan and state-building in Ethiopia, but it was fairly low key and with limited results at best. At the same time the humanitarian involvement mainly took the form of being the largest supplier of food aid, and where that was being delivered to areas of continuing conflict, as in Sudan, it might feed fighters as well as victims thus perpetuating the cycle. The situation might have continued indefinitely had not Africa risen on the US agenda after 9/11. The rise was less for reasons of grand strategy and global thinking than pragmatic reasons, several of which were particularly relevant to the Horn. The most conspicuous reason was the 'war on terror'. The al-Qaeda network had been largely created in Sudan and Sudan might still have a role to play in regard to terrorism. Somalia was both a Muslim country with traces of Islamism and a failed state where terrorist organisations might find sanctuary and new operating bases. It raised the questions of when and how to act.

In reviewing the experience of the US in the Horn a number of different approaches had been tried since the end of the Cold War. The most obvious approach had been full scale military intervention. In Somalia that intervention had been in connection with a humanitarian crisis, and while it is claimed that overall lives were saved by the action, nevertheless it was a poorly planned operation with uncertain tactics, poor coordination with international partners, and with an undesirable aftermath for both US policy in Africa, and the situation on the ground in much of Somalia. Nevertheless discussions about the possible importance of military intervention in humanitarian crises continued, even though the Somali experience had made it less likely that it would involve the deployment of substantial regular US forces (Haas, 1999; Clarke and Herbst, 2001). The US was to use force again in the Horn, but this time for security reasons in the wake of the al-Qaeda attacks on the US embassies in East Africa in 1998. However, although the missile attack on an alleged chemical weapons factory in Sudan in 1998 caused concern to the country's rulers it was not followed up militarily. It led instead to a perception of limited US action against an innocent pharmaceutical factory that created some international sympathy for Sudan, in the Arab world at least, as the wronged 'little guy'. Clearly America has the capability to act militarily in Africa and elsewhere but, since 'war is politics by other means', the politics have to be well thought out if military intervention is to be a successful instrument. Direct US military action in the Horn in the 1990s had been less successful than policy makers in Washington had expected.

An alternative possibility involving force was destabilization with the help of indigenous opposition movements and neighboring states. Such a combination had unseated anti-American regimes in the past, including the Mengistu regime in Ethiopia once it had been deprived of the backing of the Soviet Union. The US may only have admitted to supplying food aid to the areas controlled by the guerrilla movements, though there were suspicions of more involvement, but it did nothing to discourage its allies in the Arabian peninsular from supporting Mengistu's opponents. From the mid-1990s, when Sudan's Islamist threat was more fully appreciated in Washington, the US was ready and willing to encourage its friends in Eritrea, Ethiopia and Uganda to back the Sudanese opposition. The friends not only represented a new future for Africa in American eyes, they were also all experienced guerrilla fighters who had achieved in their own countries what they were seeking for Sudan. The idea was attractive and though not immediately successful might have worked; it was to fail in the light of the unexpected conflict between Ethiopia and Eritrea. The risk of working with proxies is of course that they have their own agendas and may not always have the same priorities as patrons. There was no simple way to achieve military solutions, whether direct or indirect.

Sanctions appeared to be another option. They had been regarded as significant in the past, especially against the apartheid regime in South Africa, in whose demise Chester Crocker and the US State Department had been actively involved; and were seen as containing if not actually weakening the regime in Iraq, in the 1990s at least; as well as being used against Libya. The US was active in support of international sanctions against Sudan from the early 1990s, but ran into problems. The international community took different positions on sanctions and in consequence it proved difficult to achieve support for measures that were as strong as the US wished. In the 1990s it was Sudan's Arab neighbors led by Egypt that were reluctant to see sanctions that would be seriously destabilizing; not from any liking for the regime in Sudan, but calculating that moves that would hurt the population (as sanctions against Iraq were doing) might produce a backlash more threatening to their interests in Sudan. When possible international sanctions were raised again in 2004 in response to the situation in Darfur, it was two permanent members of the Security Council, China and Russia, that saw their private interests best served by blocking punitive sanctions against Sudan. Frustration with weak UN sanctions led the US to adopt its own, and later to threaten further sanctions in the light of the crisis in Darfur. Yet here too there were frustrations in that while the sanctions had partial success with regard to denying Sudan US assistance and investment and discouraging major international institutions from involvement in the country, they also could be at least partially circumvented. In particular Sudan was able to cultivate support in Asia to develop its oil potential, possibly to the longer term frustration of US oil interests as long as its unilateral sanctions remain in place.

A further possibility was support for negotiation to address the perceived problems. While there had been US backing for successive Sudan peace processes in the 1990s, the efforts had often been half-hearted. It took a much stronger commitment from the George W. Bush administration, led by the president himself and with strong support from his political heartland in and out of Congress, to transform the peace process. The war in the south had long been condemned in America with a growing chorus of critics, especially from the groups involved in the Freedom House coalition. In addition there was an agenda for peace under the auspices of IGAD which Britain and Norway in particular were pursuing but with only limited impact: a new US willingness to explore the potential of the peace process and then to commit to it proved vital to driving it forward. With US involvement progress was made that had not previously seemed likely. There were criticisms of some of the detail of US involvement, especially the frequent changes of personnel and the distraction when leading American figures dropped in on the talks, but as much as the direct involvement of the US in the actual negotiations it was America's weight that counted. With America's push, success was achieved on the south, but only for that success to be one factor triggering a new conflict in Darfur. From a US perspective the outstanding feature that the situations in the two regions had in common was the role of the Sudan government, which was perceived as deserving of condemnation for its conduct of war in both, but was simultaneously also perceived as a significant partner in the 'war on terror'. In both cases the pressure from the US on the government was to be exerted by a combination of sticks and carrots.

US sanctions remained in place, for they still had an impact though not decisive, and there were inducements in the form of waiting aid packages from the US and elsewhere, as well as debt relief and the likelihood of new international investment in Sudan's significant mineral and agricultural potential. On the face of it the carrots looked good even if the sticks were not that bad, but for the parties to peacemaking in Sudan there was also the question of the terms of the agreement they were being pressured to sign. This led to discussion of the extent to which the parties had constructed a peace that would be of benefit to the country as a whole and was not just to their own advantage: in short a 'good' peace or a 'bad' peace. One concern was whether the strength of American commitment to the peace process meant that it was in effect an international imposition with which the parties to the conflict would feel no sense of ownership, and on which they might then seek to renege if US attention turned away. The possibility of US interest diminishing with time also raised the importance of continuing international support for the post-peace situation, for peace making appeared comparatively simple compared with the enormous tasks of post peace reconstruction in such a devastated country (Esposito and Crocker, 2004). Another major concern was the apparent exclusivity of the Sudanese parties to the conflict since neither party could demonstrate wide popular support. It contributed to the opening of a new revolt and conflict in Darfur, and might be followed by further violence in the east of the country.

There are always risks in peacemaking, and even if the US hopes are met only in part is that a better outcome than standing aside from such a process as America chose to do in Somalia? The option being chosen in this case was one of containment. A combination of sour memories of America's experience in Somalia ten years previously and doubts about the possibility of re-constructing a viable state led the US to take a back seat to the Europeans in the Somali peace talks. But America was busy addressing the need to contain Somalia to prevent it becoming a haven for Islamists in the future. In this its involvement was both direct with forces deployed to Djibouti and offshore, and indirect through cooperation with Somalia's immediate neighbors. The question then was whether containment of this kind could continue indefinitely, or should a more constructive approach be taken at some time in the future? The lesson, especially with 1992-1993 in mind, is that any such move should not be for the US alone but would need the cooperation of regional states with an interest in the country to have a chance of success.

The major policy options available are not of course exclusive to each other. It is possible for a number of elements to be involved, but does require a degree of policy coordination and effective cooperation among the departments and agencies involved. It also requires thinking not only of short term policy objectives, but longer term developmental activities as means to combat the likes of humanitarian crises and terrorist threats.

These have all been policy issues for the US involving various 'hard' and 'soft' options, but there are still the underlying analytic questions concerning the regions to which policy is being applied, in this case Muslim societies in the Horn. The most obvious question has been that of al-Qaeda and how the organization that had mounted an unprecedented challenge to the US on 9/11 had got off the ground apparently unappreciated until it was well established; and its leader, Osama bin Laden, had apparently escaped falling into American hands in 1996? In the accusations and counter-accusations that have raged since 9/11 it has become apparent that there was information about bin Laden and his group from the early 1990s, but it is hard to disagree with the conclusion of Dick Clarke that, 'There were failures in the organizations that we trusted to protect us, failures to get information to the right place at the right time, earlier failures to act boldly to reduce or eliminate the threat' (Clarke, 2004, p.238). Better intelligence better used was clearly the message.

Yet, as important as learning to pick up on such groups is the need to appreciate and evaluate particular Muslim societies that might provide the context for Islamist groups. This was especially relevant in Sudan's case with its long history of the politicization of the religion at least from the late nineteenth century. The Mahdist state from 1885-1898 was the direct forebear of the later Mahdist movement and its political party al-Umma that was to be central to party formation and the periods of liberal-democratic government in the country. Mahdism in turn contributed to the character of its rival Democratic Unionist Party that operated around the patronage of another major spiritual movement the Khatmiyya and its Mirghani family leaders. Their rivalry and central roles in Sudanese politics in turn helped to set the scene for the emergence of the Muslim Brotherhood that displayed unusual capabilities in preparing to seize power and govern. It was in the specific context of the seizure of power by the NIF, a success unique in the *suni* Muslim world, and its revolutionary foreign as well as domestic policy that the opportunity for al-Qaeda to grow came about.

In contrast to Sudan, neither Somalia nor Ethiopia offered comparable opportunities. Islam was an issue in Somali politics for years, but it was not the basis of organized movements of national significance. Instead in such a segmented society it was clan and sub-clan mobilization that took precedence, on occasions to the detriment of those who were seeking to establish new Islamist groups. That does not mean that US surveillance can be relaxed and when necessary action taken, but it does mean that stateless Somalia may not be as propitious for an Islamist group as Sudan of the early 1990s had been. In addition foreign terrorist groups, it has been argued, are in practice quite conspicuous in stateless environments, whether Muslim or non-Muslim, and may fair better in the more anonymous environs of the urban areas of weak states, where they can benefit from available infrastructure and perhaps strike covert deals with existing rulers (Menkhaus, 2004).

In Ethiopia there may be even less of a challenge, but that does not mean that there is not still a need to monitor the situation, especially of the young men attending the mosques in the urban centres where radical messages can so easily be disseminated (Shinn, 2002). In the immediate future however it is nationalism rather than Islamism that appears to hold the major challenge in Ethiopia and Eritrea. It is a regional tragedy that two of the most successful and idealistic guerrilla forces in Africa, the EPLF and the TPLF, should in government have been transformed into nationalistic rivals that have already fought two bloody rounds of war between Eritrea and Ethiopia with the dispute not yet effectively resolved. It will probably need the international community to do more than judge the border issue in their dispute and seek instead to contribute to more underlying issues. Continuing conflict is only likely to worsen conditions in both countries, and then new ideological challenges, including Islamism, may emerge. In the case of Ethiopia the US has a strong ally to help it contain Islamism, both within the country and in Somalia as well; but that should not make it too one sided with regard to Eritrea lest the latter should then seek to foment Islamism in the region in its struggle with Ethiopia. Rather continuing international support for diplomatic efforts to solve the Eritrea-Ethiopia situation without resort once more to conflict appeared to be making progress by the end of 2004.

When the question of relations between Ethiopia and Eritrea are added to the peace processes in Sudan and Somalia, it is clear that by the end of 2004 the Horn was balanced between war and peace. The processes were in origin separate: peace between Ethiopia and Eritrea, and in Somalia and Sudan were not directly linked, nevertheless they were connected and failure in one or more was likely to impact on the others, for such have been the relations of the region for decades. The US has been involved in these processes in varying degrees, marginally in Somalia, unsuccessfully in Ethiopia-Eritrea and centrally in Sudan's peace talks in Kenya.

The situation across the Horn underlines the point that it is insufficient to rely on US unilateral capabilities for security to the neglect of international cooperation at all levels. After Afghanistan and Iraq Djibouti became the third centre for US military deployment after 9/11, but it has been essentially 'smart' deployment and with the cooperation not only of Djibouti but the neighbouring 'anchor states' of Ethiopia and Kenya in addition to Yemen and somewhat ambiguously Sudan as well. These represent essentially a series of bi-lateral deals between the US and these strategic countries. At a regional level IGAD has also been involved in both Sudan and Somalia peace efforts and can only be strengthened as an organisation by any progress that comes from one or both processes. Its role has been as much to do with the legitimacy of the processes in regional and African eyes and it has required international backing to play its part. While IGAD has limited capacity of its own and has required international support, it nonetheless serves to bring a number of countries together and could become something of a counterpart to the regional organisations of West Africa and Southern Africa. The Darfur crisis has in turn brought in the African Union (AU) and with it a fresh need for international cooperation. The AU's mandate includes tackling problems within Africa's sovereign states in ways that its forebear the Organisation of African Unity (OAU) never could; and Darfur has become the first major test of the new body. However, like IGAD it too lacks resources and thus requires broader international support if it is to be successful. The wider international community has thus become involved from Somalia in the east to Darfur in the west.

The role of the US has been vital, but it could not have acted to the extent that it has without the cooperation of national governments and regional and international organizations. The regional dimension is especially important given the character of so many African states. Most are at best comparatively weak states and with their marginalized interiors and porous international borders a regional dimension, whether through bi-lateral relations or regional organizations, is bound to be crucial. However with weak states as members it is not likely that regional organizations on their own will be strong and they thus need wider international support. In the Horn this received its most dramatic recognition when in November 2004 the UN Security Council made one of its very rare excursions outside New York to Nairobi to discuss Darfur, 'the world's worst humanitarian disaster' as it was called at the time. Though there was disappointment in some American circles in particular at the weakness of the resolution finally adopted, the session endorsed the completion of the work of IGAD with regard to the Sudan peace process between the government and the SPLA/M seeing it also as a step to addressing the Darfur conflict, and also endorsed the role of the AU in the region.

Such multi-layered international relations are highly relevant to a weak state situation since all levels are significant in any search for a solution. Most states in Africa are after all the product of international politics stretching back at least to the nineteenth century, rather than indigenous processes of 'nation-building' within current borders. It is therefore at least in part an international responsibility if they are to be re-built, and the international community will also have to share the various consequences, including possible increases in terrorism, of a failure to address the situations. There may of course be criticism of the functioning of one or more of the international agencies, but that should be a cause for their reform and improvement rather than ignoring them altogether. If the alternative is to be a US willingness to act unilaterally whenever and wherever, the burden will be enormous and with the risk of intervention proving counterproductive creating more not less threats. This is not to say that direct intervention will never be appropriate: the lack of US intervention in Liberia contrasted poorly with Britain's involvement in Sierra Leone, but it is not the only form of involvement. In contrast, if the US is successful with its important contribution to stabilizing the Horn through its backing of coordinated international responses at all levels, it will be a major fillip for US foreign policy in both the Muslim world and one of the most conflict-torn areas of Africa. And it will show what can be achieved without resort to armed intervention.

There will also be new interests and benefits for the US showing that Africa is not just a 'humanitarian afterthought' at a time when there is much new talk about African oil in an administration under George W. Bush from 2001 that has been closely linked to the oil business. Two reasons are particularly important: the insecurity of the Middle East and the possible effect of supplies from there; and the longer term problem of diminishing capacity in existing fields. In looking to Africa for new resources it has been West Africa that has stood out for both security and reserves, but the Horn is not irrelevant, especially the possibilities in Sudan. Yet Sudan and to a lesser extent Ethiopia as well have shown another challenge to American interests looking forward. In so far as there is a potential rival to the world's single superpower it appears to be China and Asia more generally; and in both oil and trade China, India and Malaysia have been moving significantly into the Horn and elsewhere in Africa. It appears then that there are pragmatic as well as moral imperatives to take Africa more seriously, but the question is not only what should be done, but what can be done? The ends have to be matched by the means, and it is here that the experiences of the Horn since the end of the Cold War have contained if not that overblown phrase 'the lessons of history' then certainly food for thought.

Note

[1]   One such characterises past foreign policy perspectives as Jeffersonian, Jacksonian, Hamiltonian, Wilsonian and Continental Realists and speculates about such application in the future (Mead, 2002).

References

Clapham, C. (1998), *African Guerrillas*, Oxford, James Currey.
Clarke, R. (2004), *Against all enemies: Inside America's war on terror*, New York, Free Press.
Clarke, W. and Herbst, J. (2001), 'Somalia and and the Future of Humanitarian Intervention', in Council of Foreign Affairs (2001), *Intervention and American Foreign Policy*, New York, Foreign Affairs Editions Choice Series.

Esposito, D. and Crocker, B. (2004), *To Guarantee the Peace: An action strategy for a post-conflict Sudan*, Washington, Center for Strategic and International Studies.

Haas, R. (1999), *Intervention: The use of American military force in the post Cold War world*, Washington, Brookings.

Kansteiner, W. and Morrison, S. (2004), *Rising US stakes in Africa: Seven Proposals to Strengthen US-Africa Policy*, Washington, Center for Strategic and International Studies.

Mead, W. (2002), *Special Providence: American foreign policy and how it changed the world*, New York, Knopf.

Menkhaus, K. (2004), *Somalia: State collapse and the threat of terrorism*, Oxford, Adelphi Papers No.364.

Reno, W. (1998), *Warlord Politics and African States*, Boulder, Lynne Rienner.

Shinn, D. (2002), *Ethiopia: Coping with Islamic fundamentalism after September 11*, Washington, Africa Notes No. 8, Center for Strategic and International Studies.

Woodward, P. (1996), *The Horn of Africa: politics and international relations*, London, Tauris.

Bibliography

Abrams, Elliot (2001), *The Influence of Faith: Religious Groups and US Foreign Policy*, Lanham MD, Rowman and Littlefield.

Aideed, Mohammed and Ruhela,Satya (1993), *The preferred development in Somalia*, New Delhi, Vikas.

Alagiah, George (2001), *A Passage to Africa*, London, Little and Brown.

Albright, Madeleine (2003), *Madam Secretary: A Memoir*, Basingstoke, Macmillan.

Anderson, Norman (1999), *Sudan in Crisis: The failure of Democracy*, Gainesville, University of Florida Press.

Armstrong, David (1993), *Revolution and World Order: the revolutionary state in international society*, Oxford, Clarendon Press.

Benjamin, David, and Simon, Steven (2003), *The Age of Sacred Terror*, New York, Random House.

Berman, Bruce, Eyoh, Dickson and Kymlicka, Will (2004) (eds), *Ethnicity and Democracy in Africa*, Oxford, James Currey.

Bodansky, Yousef (1999), *Bin Laden: The Man Who Declared War on America*, Roseville CA, Prima.

Bowden, Mark (1999), *Black Hawk Down*, London, Corgi.

Blumenthal, Simon (2003), *The Clinton Wars*, New York, Farra, Strauss and Giroux.

Buckley, Mary, and Fawn, Rick (2003), *Global Responses to Terrorism: 9/11, Afghanistan and Beyond*, London, Routledge.

Burke, Jason (2003), *Al Qaeda: casting a shadow of terror*, London, Tauris.

Burr, Millard, and Collins, Robert (1995), *Requiem for Sudan: War, Drought and Disaster Relief on the Nile*, Boulder, West View.

Burr, Millard, and Collins, Robert (1999), *Africa's Thirty Years' War: Chad, Libya and the Sudan, 1963-1993*, Boulder, West View.

Burr, Millard, and Collins, Robert (2003), *Revolutionary Sudan: Hassan al-Turabi and the Islamist state, 1989-2000*, Leiden, Brill.

Clapham, Christopher (1998) (ed), *African Guerrillas*, Oxford, James Currey.

Clarke, Richard (2004), *Against all enemies: Inside America's war on terror*, New York, Free Press.

Clarke, Walter, and Herbst, Jeffrey (1997), *Learning from Somalia: The lessons of armed humanitarian intervention*, Boulder, West View.

Clinton, Bill (2004), *My Life*, London, Hutchinson.

Cohen, Herman (2000), *Intervening in Africa: Superpower Peacemaking in a Troubled Continent*, Basingstoke, Palgrave.

Council of Foreign Affairs (2001), *Intervention and American Foreign Affairs*, New York, Foreign Affairs Edition Choice Series.

Cox, Michael (1995), *United States' Foreign Policy after the Cold War: Superpower without a mission?*, London, Pinter for RIIA.

Crockatt, Richard (2003), *America Embattled: September 11, anti-Americanism and the global order*, London, Routledge.

Deng, Francis and Zartman, William (2002), *A strategic vision for Africa: the Kampala Movement*, Washington, Brookings.

De Waal, Alex (2004), *Islamism and its enemies in the Horn of Africa*, London, Hurst.

El-Affendi, Abdelwahab (1991), *Turabi's Revolution: Islam and Power in Sudan*, London, Grey Seal.

Esposito, Dina, and Crocker, Bathsheba (2003), *To Guarantee the Peace: An action strategy for a post-conflict Sudan*, Washington, Center for Strategic and International Studies.

Fukayama, Francis (1992), *The end of history and the last man*, London, Hamish Hamilton.

Gerges, Fawaz (1999), *America and Political Islam*, Cambridge, Cambridge University Press.

Haas, Richard (1999), *Intervention: The use of American military force in the post-Cold War world*, Washington, Brookings.

Halberstam, David (2002), *War in a Time of Peace: Bush, Clinton and the Generals*, London, Bloomsbury.

Halperin, Morton (1974), *Bureaucratic Politics and Foreign Policy*, Washington, Brookings.

Hassan, Yusuf, and Gray, Richard (2002), *Religion and Conflict in Sudan*, Nairobi, Pauline Press.

Hendrickson, Ryan (2002), *The Clinton Wars*, Nashville, Vanderbilt University Press.

Hersman, Rebecca (2002), *How Congress and the President Really Make Foreign Policy*, Washington, Brookings.

Hoile, David (2000), *Farce Majeure: The Clinton Administration's Sudan Policy, 1993-2000*, London, European-Sudanese Public Affairs Council.

Huntington, Samuel (1996), *The clash of civilizations and the remaking of world order*, New York, Simon and Schuster.

Hutchinson, Sharon (1996), *Nuer Dilemmas: Coping with Money, War and the State*, Berkeley, University of California Press.

Gunaratna, Rohan (2002), *Inside Al-Qaeda: Global Network of Terror*, London, Hurst.

Gurdon, Charles (1994), *The Horn of Africa*, London, University College London Press.

Halberstam, David (2002), *War in a Time of Peace*, London, Bloomsbury.

Hempstone, Smith (1997), *Rogue Ambassador: an African Memoir*, Sewanee Tennessee, University of the South Press.

Hirsch, John, and Oakley, Robert (1995), *Somalia and Operation Restore Hope*, Washington, US Institute of Peace.

Hurst, Stephen (1999), *The Foreign Policy of the Bush Administration: in search of a new world order*, London, Cassell.

International Crisis Group (2000), *God, Oil and Country: The Changing Logic of War in Sudan*, Brussels, ICG.

International Crisis Groups (2003), *Negotiating a Blueprint for Peace in Somalia*, Brussels, ICG.

Johnson, Douglas (2003), *The Root Causes of Sudan's Civil Wars*, Oxford, James Currey.

Kansteiner, Walter and Morrison, Stephen (2004), *Rising US stakes in Africa: Seven Proposals to Strengthen US-Africa Policy*, Washington, CSIS.

Karim, Ataul, *et al* (1996), *Operation Lifeline Sudan: A Review*, UN Department of Humanitarian Affairs.

Kepel, Gilles (2002), *Jihad: The Trail of Political Islam*, Cambridge Massachusetts, Belknap.

Khalid, Mansour (2003), *War and Peace in Sudan*, London, Kegan Paul.

Korn, David (1986), *Ethiopia, the United States and the Soviet Union*, London, Croom Helm.

Laitin, David and Samatar, Said (1987), *Somalia: Nation in Search of a State*, Boulder, West View.

Lewis, Ioan (1998), *Saints and Somalis: popular Islam in a clan-based society*, London, Haan.

Lewis, Ioan (2002), *A Modern History of the Somali*, Oxford, James Currey, 4th ed.

Lipsett, Seymour (1064), *The First New Nation*, London, Heinemann.

Mead, Walter (2002), *Special Providence: American foreign policy and how it changed the world*, New York, Knopf.

Medhane Tedasse (2002), *Al-Ittihad: Political Islam and the Black Economy in Somalia*, Addis Ababa, Meag Printing.

Menkhaus, Kenneth (2004), *Somalia: state collapse and the threat of terrorism*, Oxford, Oxford University Press, IISS, Adelphi Paper No.364.

National Committee on Terrorist Attacks upon the USA. (2004), *The 9/11Commission Report*, New York, Norton.

Negash, Tekeste and Tronvoll, Kjetil (2002), *Brothers at War: Making sense of the Eritrean-Ethiopian War*, Oxford, James Currey.

Niblock, Tim (2001),*'Pariah States' and Sanctions in the Middle East: Iraq, Libya, Sudan*, Boulder, Lynne Rienner.

Nyaba, Peter (1997), *The Politics of Liberation in South Sudan: an insider's view*, Kampala, Fountain.

Osman, Mohamed (2002), *The United Nations and Peace Enforcement: Wars, terrorism and democracy*, Aldershot, Ashgate.

Peters, Joel (1992), *Israel and Africa*, London, Tauris.

Peterson, Scott (2000), *Me Against My Brother: At war in Somalia, Sudan and Rwanda*, London, Routledge.

Petterson, Donald (1999), *Inside Sudan: Political Islam, Conflict and Catastrophe*, Boulder, West View.

Prendergast, John (1996), *Frontline Diplomacy: Humanitarian Aid and Conflict in Africa*, Boulder, Lynne Rienner.

Rolandsen, Oystein (2005), *Guerrilla Government: Political Changes in the Southern Sudan during the 1990s*, Uppsala, Nordiska Afrikainstitutet.

Reno, William (1998), *Warlord Politics and African States*, Boulder, Lynne Rienner.

Ruhela, Satya (1994), *Mohamed Farah Aideed and his vision of Somalia*, New Delhi, Vikas.

Sahnoun, Mohamed (1994), *Somalia: The missed opportunities*, Washington, US Institute of Peace Press.

Samatar, Said (1991), *Somalia: A Nation in Turmoil*, London, Minority Rights Group.

Sardar, Ziauddin and Davies, Merryl (2002), *Why do people hate America?* Cambridge, Iconbooks.

Schraeder, Peter (1992), *Intervention in the 1980s: US Foreign Policy in the Third World*, Boulder, Rienner.

Schraeder, Peter (1994), *US Foreign Policy Towards Africa: Incrementalism, Crisis and Change*, Cambridge, Cambridge University Press.

Scroggins, Deborah (2003), *Emma's War: Love, betrayal and death in the Sudan*, London, Harper Collins.

Simone, Abdou (1994), *In Whose Image?: Political Islam and Urban Practices in Sudan*, Chicago, Chicago University Press.

United States Institute of Peace (1999), *A New Approach to Peace in Sudan*, Washington, USIP.

Vaughan, Sarah and Tronvoll, Kjetil (2003), *Structures and Relations of Power in Ethiopia*, Stockholm, SAREC/SIPA.

Waterbury, John (2002), *The Nile Basin: National determinants of collective action*, New Haven, Yale University Press.

Wondu, Stephen and Lesch, Ann (2000), *The Battle for Peace in Sudan: An analysis of the Abuja Conference, 1992-1993*, Maryland, University Press of America.

Woodward, Bob (2002), *Bush at War*, New York, Simon and Schuster.

Woodward, Peter (1979), *Condominum and Sudanese Nationalism*, London, Rex Collings.

Woodward, Peter (1996), *The Horn of Africa: politics and international relations*, London, Tauris.

Index

Abboud, Ibrahim 30, 33
Abd al-Rahman, Umar 51–2
Abdullahi, Khalifa 28
Abrams, Elliot 114
ACRI *see* Africa Crisis Response
    Initiative
al-Afghani, Jamal al-Din 46
Afghanistan 13, 48, 49, 102
    Soviet Union in 26, 37, 47
    US attack on 104, 122, 142
Africa Crisis Response Initiative
    (ACRI) 12, 98
African Union (AU) 131–2, 159
African-Americans 7, 10, 122
Afwerki, Issayas 49, 83, 95, 96,
    97, 149
agriculture 137
Aideed, Hussein 69, 70, 137, 139,
    140, 142, 144
Aideed, Mohammed Farah 61, 62,
    63, 66–70, 71, 72–3, 137
al-Ittihad 60, 68, 83, 138, 140,
    141–4
al-Qaeda xii, 3, 7, 9, 13, 154, 157
    African embassy attacks 104,
        140, 154
    Somalia 73, 140, 141, 142
    Sudan 48, 51, 52, 110n12, 117
    training camps 102
    Yemen 143, 150
Alagiah, George 66
Albright, Madeleine 3, 54, 67–8,
    94, 108, 110n4
    concern over Sudan 98–9
    religious freedom 116

Sudanese intelligence
    controversy 102, 110n8, n9,
    110n12

Algeria 38, 51, 88
Ali Mahdi Mohammed 61, 62,
    66–7, 71, 137, 139
Ali, Mohammed 28, 29
Amin, Idi 95, 125
Amnesty International 8, 39, 81,
    96, 115
Andom, Aman 21
Angola 11, 44
anti-Americanism 13
anti-globalization movement 12
Aptidon, Hassan Gouled 89
Arab League 145
Arab-Israeli conflict 2, 30
Arabization 40, 41
Arabs 27, 28, 31, 115
    Darfour 130
    nationalism 19, 21, 30, 33, 34
Arafat, Yasir 56n9
Arta process 145
Aspin, Lesley 74n8
Ato, Osman 71
AU *see* African Union

Baker, James 3
Balkans 6
al-Banna, Hasan 38
Barre, Mohammed Siad 15n1,
    24–5, 59–60, 61, 68, 72, 139
    agriculture 137
    centralized government 147
    collapse of regime 27, 60, 135,
        136, 138

    Egypt backing of 73, 74n9
    invasion of Ethiopia 22
    Mengistu pact with 26
    Somaliland opposition to 135
Berger, Sandy 105, 110n4
al-Beshir, Omer 39, 42, 44–5,

99–100, 104, 119, 129
'big men' 137–8
bin Laden, Osama 68, 74n11,
    110n7, 142, 157
    African embassy attacks 140
    intelligence on 120
    Sudan 48, 51, 53, 100, 101–3,
        104–5, 117, 122
Biro, Gaspar 55
Bishop, James 61
Blair, Tony 124
Blumenthal, Sidney 74n8
Bodansky, Yossef 103, 104
Boutros-Ghali, Boutros 62, 63–4,
    66, 67, 70, 71–2, 139
Brownback, Sam 114
bureaucratic rivalries 6, 7
Bush, George 3, 153
    Djibouti 89
    New World Order 2, 11, 12, 62,
        64
    NGO/media influence on 8
    Somalia 62–3, 64, 65–6, 72
    Sudan 32, 38, 113–14
Bush, George W. 2, 3, 153
    'axis of evil' 14
    military power 5
    NGO/media influence on 8
    oil interests 160
    Rice appointment 12
    Sudan 111n15, 113–17, 121,
        122, 126, 128, 129–30, 132,
        156
    'war on terror' 13, 141

Canada 124
capitalism 14
Carney, Tim 94, 97, 98, 101–102,
    104

Carter, Jimmy
    Carter Doctrine 26
    Ethiopia 21, 77, 84
    Iranian revolution 37
    Somalia 25
    Sudan 44, 45, 109, 113, 118,

122
    sustained involvement in Africa
        8
Castro, Fidel 22
Center for Strategic and
    International Studies (CSIS)
    109–10, 116, 123
Central Intelligence Agency (CIA)
    4–5, 143
    mujahadin trained by 47
    Sudan 53, 57n12, 97, 98,
        102–103, 105, 111n12, 116
Chad 31, 150
Christian groups xii, 7–8, 99,
    114–15
Christianity 18, 47
    Ethiopia 49
    Sudan 27–8, 41
Christopher, Warren 3, 74n8, 94,
    110n2
CIA *see* Central Intelligence
    Agency
Clarke, Dick 157
Clarke, Walter 63, 74n5
Clash of Civilizations thesis xii, 14,
    37–8
Clinton, Bill 2, 3, 64, 116, 153
    Congress relationship 7
    Ethiopia 84, 85
    National Security Adviser 6
    NGO/media influence on 8
    Somalia 65, 67, 69, 73
    Sudan 94–5, 98, 102, 103,
        105–106, 108–109, 111n15
Clinton, Hilary 98
Cohen, Herman 'Hank' 4
    Ethiopia 77, 84
    Somalia 61, 62–3, 65
    Sudan 42, 44, 45, 54, 55

Cold War xii, 1, 10–11, 17–35, 89,
    153
    CIA role 4
    end of the 7, 8, 13, 77, 78
    strategic location of the Horn 2
    US assistance to African

regimes 144
colonialism 11, 23
Colson, Charles 115
conflict prevention 96–7
conflict resolution xii, xiii, 12, 45
   African Union 131
   IGADD 118
   Somalia 147
Congress 7, 153
   Somalia 26, 62, 69
   Sudan 43, 44, 54–5, 99, 114,
      122, 129, 156
Crocker, Chester 4, 44, 121, 155
CSIS *see* Center for Strategic and
   International Studies
Cuba 11, 13, 22, 53

Dagne, Ted 114, 144
Danforth, John 121–3, 126, 129
Darfur 130–132, 155, 156, 159
Defense Department 5, 6, 97, 116
democracy
   democratization 12, 13
   Eritrea 83
   Ethiopia 78, 79, 80, 84, 85
   Somalia 70
   Sudan 30, 39, 43
   US policy concerns 38, 96
Deng, Francis 133n6
Dergue 20–21
Deutch, John 110n2
Djerejian, Edward 56n1
Djibouti 1, 88–9, 158–9
   border problems with Eritrea 85
   French control over 17, 22
   IGADD 118
   JTF-HOA 143
   non-recognition of Somaliland
      71–2
   Somalia 145, 148, 150
   US troops in 2
   war on terror 149
Dulles, John Foster 19

economic issues 9, 10
   Eritrea 83–4

Ethiopia 81
Somalia 137, 147
Sudan 40
education
   Ethiopia 82
   Somalia 138
   Sudan 39, 40
Egal, Mohamed Ibrahim 24, 71,
   136, 140
Egypt 9, 10, 12, 19, 38, 139–40
   Copts 18
   Ethiopia rivalry with 139, 149
   Islamism 34
   sanctions against Sudan 93, 94,
      155
   Somalia 139, 145, 150
   Sudan relationship 28–31, 42,
      51–2, 55, 100, 106, 113,
      125–6
EHRC *see* Ethiopian Human Rights
   Council
Eisenhower, Dwight 30
El-Affendi, Abdelwahab 39
ELF *see* Eritrean Liberation Front
environmental protection 97
EPLF *see* Eritrean Peoples
   Liberation Front
EPRDF *see* Ethiopian Peoples
   Revolutionary Democratic Front
Eritrea 1, 9, 22, 44, 77–88, 153
   Albright's role 3
   British control 17, 18–19
   IGAD 118, 120, 123–4
   political system 12
   recognition of independence 72,
      135
   Somalia relationship 144
   Sudan relationship 49, 55, 95,
      103
   US military aid to 97–8
   war with Ethiopia 6, 20, 21,
      85–8, 99, 101, 140, 158
   war on terror 149
Eritrean Liberation Front (ELF) 19,
   21, 83
Eritrean Peoples Liberation Front

(EPLF) 21, 49, 77–9, 83, 85,
    107, 158
Ethiopia xi, xiii, 1, 77–88, 139–40,
    153, 160
    Albright's role 3
    British role in 10, 17
    Cold War period 17–22, 34
    destabilization policy against
        155
    downfall of Mengistu regime 45,
        60, 77
    ethnic federalism 44, 79–81
    Falasha 22, 31, 77, 78
    humanitarian intervention 154
    IGAD 118, 120, 123–4
    Islam xii, 158
    Israel relationship 9
    non-recognition of Somaliland
        71–2
    OAU summit 52
    political system 12
    relief aid 12
    Sodere conference 138–9
    Somalia conflict with 18, 19–20,
        21, 22, 24, 25–6, 59, 138
    Somalia relationship 139, 145,
        148, 149, 150
    Soviet influence on 11
    Sudan conflict with 18, 21, 28,
        49
    Sudan relationship 55, 95, 96,
        103
    US bi-lateral strategic deals with
        159
    US military aid to 97–8
    war with Eritrea 6, 20, 85–8, 99,
        101, 140, 158
    'war on terror' 143–4
Ethiopian Human Rights Council
    (EHRC) 81–2
Ethiopian Peoples Revolutionary
    Democratic Front (EPRDF) 77,
    79–82, 84–5, 86, 90
ethnic cleansing 41
ethnic federalism 44, 79–81, 83, 84
Europe 10, 55, 101, 108, 139, 145

Faisal Islamic Bank 33
Falasha 22, 31, 77, 78
famine 1, 8, 10, 154
    Somalia 2, 61
    Sudan 31, 106, 114
Farrekhan, Louis 7
Federal Bureau of Investigation
    (FBI) 5, 102
federalism
    ethnic 44, 79–81, 83, 84
    Somalia 147
finance 33, 48, 141
FIS *see* Islamic Salvation Front
France 2, 19, 110n1
    Djibouti 17, 22, 88–9, 143, 145
    Fashoda crisis 29
    Somalia 70
    Sudan 125
free trade 12, 97
Frist, Bill 114
Fukuyama, Francis 12

Garang, John 32, 44, 45, 49, 52, 95,
    98–9, 121, 129
genocide xii, 117, 120, 131, 132
Gerges, F. 37, 48
Germany 101, 125, 143, 145, 149
Ghannouchi, Rashid 56n9
Gingrich, Newt 7
globalization 11
Gorbachev, Mikhail 22, 32
Gordon, Charles 28
Gore, Al 3, 110n5
Goulty, Alan 124
Graham, Franklin 114
Great Britain
    decline of empire 10
    Ethiopia 17, 18–19
    Sierra Leone 160
    Somalia 22, 23, 24, 145, 149
    Sudan 28–9, 101, 124, 156
Guelleh, Ismail Omar 89
Gulf War (1990-1991) 2, 12
    Djibouti 89
    Sudan position on 44, 46–7, 48,
        50, 51, 53, 55

Haile Selassie 2, 17–20, 22, 24, 78, 79, 90n2, 124
Halberstam, David 2–3, 68
Haley, Alex 7
Hamas 47–8, 56n9, 103
al-Haramain Islamic Foundation 143
Hehir, B. 7
Hempstone, Smith 65
Herbst, Jeffrey 63, 74n5
Hicks, Irving 85
Hizbollah 47, 50, 103
Houdek, Robert 97
Howe, Jonathon 67, 68, 73
human rights 7, 8
    Eritrea 83
    Ethiopia 21, 78, 81, 82
    Somalia 26
    Sudan 39, 43, 54, 55, 106, 115, 121
    US policy concerns 96
Human Rights Watch 8, 81, 115
humanitarian issues xii, 2, 5, 7, 10, 154
    Cold War period 34
    Ethiopia 81
    interest groups 8
    international bodies 12
    Iraq 65
    long term developmental activities 157
    Somalia 63, 65, 66, 70
    Sudan 42–3, 45, 106–108
    see also famine
Huntingdon, Samuel 14, 37–8

ICG *see* International Crisis Group
Idris, Salah 105
IGAD *see* Inter-Governmental Authority on Development
IGADD *see* Inter-Governmental Authority for Drought and Development
Ijaz, Mansoor 102, 103
IMF *see* International Monetary Fund

intelligence 4–5, 157
    al-Qaeda 102, 110n12
    bureaucratic rivalries 7
    Somalia 69
    Sudan 57n13, 98, 102–104, 120, 132
    see also Central Intelligence Agency
Inter-Governmental Authority on Development (IGAD)
    Egypt 52
    Partners' Forum 101, 123, 124–5
    Somalia 145
    Sudan 45, 100, 101, 108, 120, 123–7, 132, 156, 159
Inter-Governmental Authority for Drought and Development (IGADD) 45, 97, 118, 124, 125
interest groups 7–8, 153
International Crisis Group (ICG) 111n15, 116, 146
International Monetary Fund (IMF) 26, 40, 54, 85, 117, 119, 128
Iran 13, 14, 26, 34, 37
    Somalia relationship 68
    Sudan relationship 50–51
    terrorism 53
Iraq 13, 14, 47
    chemical weapons claims 105
    humanitarian aid 65
    sanctions against 94, 95, 155
    Sudan relationship 50, 53
    terrorism 53
Islam xii–xiii, 2, 8
    Clash of Civilizations thesis 14, 37–8
    Eritrea 83
    Ethiopia 18, 21, 80, 82–3
    interest groups 7
    Somalia 23, 27, 68, 69, 158
    Sudan 28, 31, 33, 127
    US Christian group opposition to 114
    see also Islamism
Islamic Jihad 47, 51, 52, 103

Islamic Salvation Front (FIS) 48
Islamism xii, xiii, 2, 34
    Ethiopia 80, 82–3, 85, 138, 158
    international dimensions of
        45–52
    rise of 3
    Somalia 27, 60–61, 68, 73, 138,
        140–41, 144, 154, 157, 158
    Sudan 9, 13, 33, 37–58, 93, 95,
        103, 117, 125
    terrorism 13, 90
    see also Islam
Ismail, Mustafa Osman 99, 104,
    109
isolationism xi, 10, 11, 14
Israel 9, 11, 19, 47
    Arab-Israeli conflict 2, 30
    Falasha 22, 31, 77, 78
    support for Sudanese opposition
        100
Italy
    Eritrea 78
    Ethiopia 17, 18, 19
    IGAD Partners' Forum 101, 124
    Somalia 22, 23, 59, 70, 139, 145
al-Ittihad 60, 68, 83, 138, 140,
    141–4

janjawid 131
JEM *see* Justice and Equality
    Movement
jihad 41
Jihad Islamiya Eritrea 83
Jimale, Ahmed Nur Ali 141
Johnson, Harry 85, 109, 121
Joint Task Force, Horn of Africa
    (JTF-HOA) 143
Jonah, James 61
JTF-HOA *see* Joint Task Force,
    Horn of Africa
Justice and Equality Movement
    (JEM) 130, 131

Kagame, Paul 96
Kahin, Dahir Riyah 136
Kansteiner, Walter 62, 116, 121,

143, 144, 145, 153
Kennedy, John F. 2
Kenya
    IGAD 118, 120, 123–4, 126–7
    JTF-HOA 143
    Somalia 139, 140, 145, 148,
        149, 150
    Sudan relationship 49–50
    US bi-lateral strategic deals with
        159
    US embassy attack 104
Khalid, Mansour 110n3
Khartoum 3, 6, 27, 30, 48, 57n12,
    98, 104
Khartoum Peace Agreement (1997)
    100, 118, 119
Kiplagat, Bethwel 148
Kittani, Ahmed 63, 66, 67
Kony, Joseph 96
Kuwait 11, 47, 50

Laitin, David 24
Lake, Anthony 6, 54, 88
Lakwena, Alice 95–6
Lesch, Ann M. 48
Lewinsky, Monica 105
Lewis, Ioan 23, 74n1, 137
liberal democracy 11, 14, 39, 43,
    59
Liberia 160
Libya 12, 31, 32, 140, 145
    Aden Treaty 22
    Eritrea relationship 88
    sanctions against 94, 95, 155
    Sudan relationship 51, 55, 125,
        126
    terrorism 13, 53
Live Aid 8
Lord's Resistance Army (LRA) 50,
    96, 101, 124

McElligott, Janet 102
McGovern, George 45
Machakos Protocol 127–8
Machar, Riek 44–5, 100, 119
al-Mahdi, al-Hahdi 133n3

al-Mahdi, Mohammed Ahmed 28, 29, 46
Mahjoub, Mohamed Ahmed 55
Marxism-Leninism 11, 20–21, 38, 82
al-Mawdudi, Abu 38
media 8, 26–7
Menelik, Emperor 17, 18, 20, 22
Mengistu Haile Mariam 20, 21, 22, 31
   assimilationism 90n2
   Barre agreement with 26, 135
   destabilization policy against 155
   downfall of regime 45, 49, 60, 77, 78, 79, 138
   education 82
   ethnic federalism 79
Middle East 2, 3, 106
   Cold War 11, 29
   democratization 12
   Islamism 13, 34, 38
   oil supplies 6, 9, 26, 160
   Sudan relationship 50, 113
military intervention 5, 8–9, 154–5
Mogadishu 3, 23, 26, 93, 135
   clan rivalries 136, 137
   Transitional National Government 141–2, 144, 145
   UNITAF 65, 73
   UNOSOM 60, 61, 62, 63
   UNOSOM II 68, 69, 70, 73
Moi, Daniel Arap 124, 140, 149
Moose, George 43–4, 96
Morocco 4
Morrison, Stephen 153
Mozambique 11, 44

Mubarak, Hosny 52, 54, 85, 93–4, 100, 104, 125, 140
multilateralism 14
Museveni, Yoweri 95, 96, 97, 98, 125, 148
Muslim Brotherhood 31, 33–4, 38, 46, 50, 99, 157
   see also National Islamic Front

Mwangale, Elijah 148

al-Nahda 48, 56n9
Nasser, Gamal Abdel 19, 21, 29, 30, 55
Nation of Islam 7
National Islamic Front (NIF) 33–4, 39–42, 44, 48–51, 100, 103–104, 119, 133n5, 157
   see also Muslim Brotherhood
National Salvation Revolution 34, 39, 56
National Security Council (NSC) 6–7, 62, 63, 98, 105, 110n12
nationalism 10, 46, 106
   Arab 19, 21, 30, 33, 34
   Ethiopia/Eritrea conflict 86, 88, 99, 158
   Iran 37
   Somalia 23–4
Natsios, Andrew 61
Negash, Tekeste 87
Netherlands 101, 124
New World Order 2, 11, 12, 62, 64, 153
NGOs *see* non-governmental organizations
Niblock, Tim 94
Nidal, Abu 48
NIF *see* National Islamic Front
Nile 27–8
Nimeiri, Jaafar 30–33, 41, 55, 56n11, 99, 113–14, 125
non-governmental organizations (NGOs) 5, 8
   evangelical 114
   Somalia 65, 66, 71, 72

   Sudan 31–2, 40, 45, 107, 108, 117
North Korea 11, 13, 14, 53
Norway 124, 156
NSC *see* National Security Council

Oakley, Robert 66, 69
OAU *see* Organization of African

Unity
Obote, Milton 95
OIC *see* Organization of the
    Islamic Conference
oil 3, 6, 9, 12, 14, 34
    Bush administration 160
    Carter Doctrine 26
    Ethiopia 101
    Sudan 31, 113–14, 118–19, 122,
        123, 128, 155
OLF *see* Oromo Liberation Front
Operation Lifeline Sudan (OLS)
    32, 43, 106, 107, 114
Organization of African Unity
    (OAU) 2, 24, 52, 78, 87–8, 131,
    139, 159
Organization of the Islamic
    Conference (OIC) 46, 47
Oromo Liberation Front (OLF) 78,
    80, 140, 149
Oromo people 49, 78, 80, 82–3
Osman, Abdel Aziz Khalid 95
Otto, Osman 137
Ottoman Empire 46
Oxfam 8

PAIC *see* Popular Arab and Islamic
    Conference
Paine, Donald 114
Pakistan 37, 142
Palestine Liberation Organization
    (PLO) 48, 56n9
Palestinians 31
pan-Islamism 46, 47, 60
pastoralism 22–3, 24, 137
PDF *see* Popular Defense Force
peacekeeping 6, 63, 64, 66

People's Front for Democracy and
    Justice (PFDJ) 83, 84, 89
Petterson, Donald 53, 54–5, 56, 95,
    104
PFDJ *see* People's Front for
    Democracy and Justice
PFLP *see* Popular Front for the
    Liberation of Palestine

PLO *see* Palestine Liberation
    Organization
policy makers 1–9
Popular Arab and Islamic
    Conference (PAIC) 46–7, 49,
    50, 51
Popular Defense Force (PDF) 39,
    41, 47
Popular Front for the Liberation of
    Palestine (PFLP) 47–8
poverty 81
Powell, Colin 5, 64–5, 114, 116,
    131, 148
pre-emptive action 5
Prendergast, John 98, 106
press freedom 82
Puntland 136, 139, 142, 143, 145,
    147

Qaddafi, Muammar 51, 125
al-Qaeda xii, 3, 7, 9, 13, 154, 157
    African embassy attacks 104,
        140, 154
    Somalia 73, 140, 141, 142
    Sudan 48, 51, 52, 110n12, 117
    training camps 102
    Yemen 143, 150
Qatar 140

Ras Tefari *see* Haile Selassie
Reagan, Ronald 5, 26, 32, 37
Red Sea 2, 9, 19, 22, 29, 34, 88,
    100
refugees 59–60, 61
Rice, Condoleeza 12, 116
Rice, Susan 86–7, 98, 101, 102,
    109, 110n4, n7
Rove, Karl 115
Rumsveld, Donald 5
Rwanda 87, 96, 100, 154

Sadat, Anwar 31
Saddam Hussein 50
Sadiq al-Mahdi 31, 32–4, 42, 55,
    119, 133n4

SAF *see* Sudan Alliance Forces
Sahnoun, Mohamed 62, 63, 65, 71,
    72, 73, 137, 145
Samatar, Said 23, 24
Sanchez, Ilich Ramirez ('Carlos the
    Jackal') 48, 56n10, 102
sanctions 54, 93–5, 101, 120–121,
    128–9, 132, 155, 156
Saperstein, David 115
Saudi Arabia 25, 27
    bin Laden 48, 102
    Somalia relationship 145
    Sudan relationship 51, 55, 100
    US relationship 9, 34, 37, 38
Save the Children Fund 8
Sayed Mohammed Abdille Hasan
    23
Scowcroft, Brent 62, 116
self-determination
    Eritrea 78, 79, 135
    Sudan 45, 118, 119–20, 123,
        126, 127, 130
September 11th 2001 terrorist
    attacks xii, 3, 9, 13, 117, 120,
        121, 154, 157
    bureaucratic rivalries since 6, 7
    Somalia 141–2, 144
    Sudan 120, 121, 122
    US troops to Djibouti 2
sharia 31, 32, 33, 34, 39, 41
    Khartoum 130
    Machakos Protocol 127
    Ottoman Empire 46
    Somalia 23
Shermarke, Abdirashid 24
shia Muslims 37, 47, 50
Sierra Leone 160
Six Day War (1967) 9, 30, 55
SLA *see* Sudan Liberation Army
slavery 115, 122
Smith, Gayle 98, 106
SNA *see* Somali National Alliance
SNM *see* Somali National
    Movement
socialism 24, 27, 30, 33
Solarz, Steven 45

Somali National Alliance (SNA)
    67, 68, 69, 70, 71, 139
Somali National Movement (SNM)
    26, 71, 135
Somali Salvation Democratic Front
    (SSDF) 71, 136
Somalia xi, xiii, 1, 59–75, 135–51,
    153–4, 158
    Cold War period 22–7, 34
    Congress concerns about 7
    containment policy 156–7
    Eritrea relationship 88
    Ethiopia conflict with 18,
        19–20, 21, 22, 24, 25–6, 59
    famine 2
    IGAD 118, 159
    Islam xii, 49, 158
    Italian control over 17
    Kenya conferences (2002-2003)
        145–8
    lack of US representation in 3
    peacekeeping 6, 113
    post-9/11 response to 122
    Soviet influence on 11
    State Department operations 4
    terrorism 14, 50
    US military leadership 5
Somaliland 1, 22, 26, 88, 145,
    148–9
    British control over 17
    claim for independence 71–2,
        135–6, 147
    Ethiopian sympathy for 138,
        139, 143
    US relationship 140
South Africa 4, 155
Soviet Union (USSR), former
    Afghanistan conflict 37, 47
    Cold War xii, 10–11, 19, 29–30,
        34, 89
    collapse of xi, 11, 84
    democracy 12
    Ethiopia relationship 20, 21–2,
        31, 77
    Somalia relationship 21, 24, 25
    Sudan relationship 32

Spain 143
SPLA *see* Sudan Peoples
    Liberation Army
SSDF *see* Somali Salvation
    Democratic Front
STAR *see* Sudan Transitional
    Assistance and Relief
    programme
State Department 3–4, 6, 17, 155
    Angola 44
    Anti-Terrorism Assistance
        programme 144
    Somalia 61–2, 63
    STAR programme 107
    Sudan 42, 54, 95, 97–9,
        102–103, 105, 110n3,
        110n12, 116–17, 123
strategic interests 2, 9
Sudan xi, 1, 93–112, 113–33, 153,
    157
    British role in 10, 17
    Christian groups 8
    Cold War period 27–34
    Congress concerns about 7
    destabilization of 3, 95–9, 155
    economic interests 9, 10
    engagement with 120–26
    Eritrea relationship 85–6
    Ethiopia conflict with 18, 21,
        28, 49
    foreign policy 45–52, 55
    humanitarian intervention 154
    Islamism xii–xiii, 9, 13, 37–58
    lack of US representation in 3
    military coup (1989) 34, 37,
        38–9, 41, 42–3
    oil supplies 12, 160

    peace process 126–32, 155–6,
        158, 159
    relief aid 12
    Rice on 87–8
    sanctions against 93–5, 155
    Somalia relationship 68, 69
    Soviet influence on 11
    State Department operations 4

    terrorism 9, 13, 14, 90, 141, 142
    US bi-lateral strategic deals with
        159
    US missile attack 104–106, 113,
        154
    USAID 6, 31, 43, 111n15,
        132n1
Sudan Alliance Forces (SAF) 95,
    96, 98, 99, 100–101
Sudan Liberation Army (SLA)
    130–131
Sudan Peace Act (1999) 108
Sudan Peace Act (2002) 117, 122,
    128, 129
Sudan Peoples Liberation Army
    (SPLA) 32, 44–5, 49–54,
    98–101, 109, 132
    humanitarian aid programmes 6,
        107–108
    peace talks 106, 127, 128,
        129–30, 131
    sharia 33
    Ugandan support for 95–6
    US engagement with Sudan 117,
        118–19, 121, 122, 123, 124
Sudan Transitional Assistance and
    Relief (STAR) programme
    107–108
Suez Canal 9, 19, 28, 29
Sufism 23, 28, 40
Sumbeiywo, Lazaro 127, 129
suni Muslims 37, 47, 50
sustainable development 97
Syria 13, 53

Taha, Ali Osman Mohammed 39,
    40, 99

Taliban 47, 102, 142
Tanzania 104, 140
terrorism 3, 5, 9, 13–14, 154, 159
    African embassy attacks 104,
        140, 149, 154
    Djibouti 89
    Ethiopia 138
    Kenya 145, 149

long term developmental
  activities 157
Somalia 140, 141–2, 143–4,
  149, 150
stateless environments 158
Sudan 49–50, 53–6, 90,
  93–4, 102–103, 104, 117,
  120, 132
Uganda 50
see also al-Qaeda; September
  11th 2001 terrorist attacks
Tigrean People's Liberation Front
  (TPLF) 22, 49, 77, 78, 79, 83,
  85, 107, 158
Tour, Abdel Rahman Ali 71, 135,
  136
TPLF *see* Tigrean People's
  Liberation Front
Tronvoll, Kjetil 87
Tunisia 51
al-Turabi, Hasan 31, 33, 38–40, 42,
  52, 55
  Beshir rivalry with 100, 104,
    119
  bin Laden 48, 102, 103
  Islamism 46–7, 50
  Justice and Equality Movement
    130, 131

Uganda
  Albright's role 3
  attempted embassy attack 140
  IGAD 118, 120, 123–4
  Libya support for 125
  Sudan relationship 49–50, 55,
    95–6, 100, 101
  US military aid to 97–8

Umma Party 29, 30, 31, 40, 119,
  126, 133n3, 157
UN *see* United Nations
Unified Task Force (UNITAF)
  65–7, 68, 69, 70, 72–3
unilateralism 14, 159
Unionist Party (Sudan) 29, 30, 40,
  119, 157

UNITAF *see* Unified Task Force
United Nations (UN) xii, 12
  Darfur 131, 159
  Ethiopia/Eritrea conflict 88
  Joint Planning Mechanism 117
  Operation Lifeline Sudan 32, 43,
    106, 107, 114
  sanctions against Sudan 93–4,
    95
  Somalia 59–73, 137, 139
  Somaliland 71, 148
  Sudanese human rights
    violations 39
  terrorist attacks against 53
United Nations Operation in
  Somalia (UNOSOM) 60–63, 72
United Nations Operation in
  Somalia II (UNOSOM II) 66,
  67–71, 73
US Agency for International
  Development (USAID) 5–6, 26,
  43, 45, 107–108, 116, 117
US Commission on International
  Religious Freedom (USCIRF) 4,
  116–17
USAID *see* US Agency for
  International Development
USCIRF *see* US Commission on
  International Religious Freedom
USSR *see* Soviet Union, former

Vietnam War 2, 5, 20

Wassen, Asfer 20
water issues 9
Weapons of Mass Destruction
  (WMD) 14, 104, 105

Wells, Melissa 45, 121
Winter, Roger 132n1
Wisner, Frank 54
WMD *see* Weapons of Mass
  Destruction
Wolf, Frank 114
Wolfowitz, Paul 65
women 40

World Bank 9, 26, 54, 117, 119,
128, 148
World Trade Center attack (1993)
51–2, 53, 110n7
see also September 11th 2001
terrorist attacks
Yemen 122, 145, 159
Aden Treaty 22

border problems with Eritrea 85
Egypt's involvement in 19
terrorism 51, 141, 142, 143, 150
Yousuf, Abdullah 148

Zaire 4, 100
al-Zawahiri, Ayman 104
Zenawi, Meles 84, 96, 97